AMERICAN HIROSHIMA

THE REASONS WHY AND A CALL TO
STRENGTHEN AMERICA'S DEMOCRACY

Guy and Akemi, Best wishes!
Your friend, Dave

DAVID J. DIONISI

TRAFFORD

USA ▪ Canada ▪ UK ▪ Ireland

Cover photography and graphic design assistance by Melissa Cannata. The Hiroshima Peace Park image is licensed from iStockphoto.
A very special thank you to my wonderful wife Stephanie and my incredible friends for their comments and suggestions to strengthen this book. Experts in several highly technical fields have helped validate and improve this book. One amazing expert, Jimmy L. Spearow, Ph.D, who volunteers as a speaker with the Physicians for Social Responsibility, has shared key ideas to help save lives both in the United States and around the world.
Foreword by David Krieger.
Edited by Jeannette Cézanne (Customline Wordware, Inc.) and Joan Barrett.

Note for Librarians: A cataloguing record for this book is available from Library and Archives Canada at www.collectionscanada.ca/amicus/index-e.html
ISBN 1-4120-4421-9

Printed in Victoria, BC, Canada. Printed on paper with minimum 30% recycled fibre. Trafford's print shop runs on "green energy" from solar, wind and other environmentally-friendly power sources.

TRAFFORD
PUBLISHING

Offices in Canada, USA, Ireland and UK

Book sales for North America and international:
Trafford Publishing, 6E–2333 Government St.,
Victoria, BC v8t 4p4 CANADA
phone 250 383 6864 (toll-free 1 888 232 4444)
fax 250 383 6804; email to orders@trafford.com
Book sales in Europe:
Trafford Publishing (uk) Limited, 9 Park End Street, 2nd Floor
Oxford, UK oxi ihh UNITED KINGDOM
phone 44 (0)1865 722 113 (local rate 0845 230 9601)
facsimile 44 (0)1865 722 868; info.uk@trafford.com
Order online at:
trafford.com/04-2229

20 19 18

FRONT COVER

THE DESIGN OF THE FRONT cover is intended to communicate key themes of the book. A key message of this book is that the United States is on the path toward experiencing an American Hiroshima. The location for the picture is the Hiroshima Peace Park in Japan because the atomic explosion in Hiroshima on August 6, 1945 inspires people around the world to abhor nuclear weapons and work for peace. This book seeks to do the same.

In the center portion of the picture is the former Hiroshima Prefecture Industry Promotion Hall. The building is now known around the world as the Atomic Bomb Dome. This Atomic Bomb Dome, very close to where the atomic bomb exploded, reminds the world of the destruction and death that are the sole function of nuclear weapons.

The view of the Atomic Bomb Dome is from the Cenotaph for the Atomic Bomb Victims. A cenotaph is a monument erected in honor of the dead without the remains of the dead included in the monument. Looking through the Cenotaph you can also see the Peace Flame. The Peace Flame will be maintained until all nuclear weapons are destroyed. The Cenotaph includes books with the names of the people who died in the days, weeks, months, and years after the bomb was dropped. The shape of this monument is a stone coffin in the form of an ancient house to keep the souls of those who perished out of the rain.

The United States can help bring about a more peaceful world or help make the world a more dangerous one. This book explains what must be done and how Americans can wake up in time to prevent something similar happening here. Will Americans wake up before, or only become informed and engaged after, an American or global Hiroshima?

FOREWORD

BY DAVID KRIEGER

WHILE PEACE HAS ALWAYS BEEN a desired yet seemingly utopian goal, in the Nuclear Age it has become an imperative. Peace, along with environmental protection, upholding human rights and the alleviation of poverty, stands as one of the foremost imperatives of the 21ˢᵗ century.

The creation and use of nuclear weapons was a watershed moment in human history. We obtained weapons which, for the first time, had the capacity to destroy the human species and most other life on the planet. With this power came new responsibility, the responsibility of people everywhere to wage peace. One of the most insightful men of the 20ᵗʰ century, Albert Camus, noted this almost immediately after the bombing of Hiroshima. "Before the terrifying prospects now available to humanity," Camus wrote, "we see even more clearly that peace is the only battle worth waging."

During the Cold War, powerful nations relied heavily on nuclear deterrence for security. This was a strategy fraught with danger since nuclear deterrence always had grave problems. The success of deterrence was dependent upon avoiding miscommunications, miscalculations, accidents and human irrationality in times of crisis – a nearly impossible task. Deterrence always demanded greater perfection of humans and our systems than we are capable of assuring, particularly in situations where there is zero tolerance for error.

If nuclear deterrence had problems during the Cold War standoff, its problems dramatically increased in the post-Cold War period. Deterrence simply has no value when applied to non-state extremist groups. It is impossible to deter those who cannot be located or who do not care about the consequences of their acts. The most powerful nuclear arsenals in the world cannot provide an ounce of security against a terrorist group armed with a single nuclear weapon. A truth that has been difficult for the leaders of nuclear weapons states to grasp is that nuclear weapons have far greater utility in the hands of the weak than in those of the strong.

If the most powerful weapons in the world cannot provide security to the most powerful countries in the world, what are we to do? We must chart a new course toward the creation of a peaceful and nuclear weapons-free world.

How to obtain such a world is the subject of the book you are holding in your hands. The book seeks to turn the United States into an "instrument for peace." From where we stand today that would be a big change, but it is one that is absolutely essential if we are to create a secure and peaceful future for our planet and the life it harbors. Because of its history and its economic and military power, the United States must be a leader on the path to peace if we are to achieve peace.

Preventing an American Hiroshima requires a new way of viewing the world. There is no longer room for policies of U.S. exceptionalism. All nations must adhere to international law, and no nation can stand above the law, including the United States. If peace is an imperative of the Nuclear Age, the way to peace is through the strengthening and enforcement of international law, applied equally and fairly to all.

The United Nations Charter was created to "save succeeding generations from the scourge of war" by leaders who had lived through the two devastating world wars of the 20th century. The Charter prohibits war except in self-defense or upon authorization of the U.N. Security Council. It is neither lawful nor wise to engage in preventive war, attacking another nation on the assumption that nation may be considering an attack on you. Such actions by powerful nations not only lead to the tragedy and misery of war, but set a precedent that could result in international chaos.

The United States takes pride in its long-standing ethic of abiding by the law and of upholding the principle that no person stands above the law. The law of the land, according to Article VI, Section 2 of the U.S. Constitution, includes treaties duly signed and ratified by the United States, including therefore the United Nations Charter. We share an obligation to uphold the U.N. Charter and to help maintain its provisions limiting the use of force.

Governments do not always do the right thing, nor what is lawful. It is the responsibility of citizens to hold their governments in check and to hold their leaders accountable when they violate the law. The great lesson of Nuremberg after World War II was that no leader, no matter how high his or her position, stands above international law, and if leaders violate that law, they shall be brought to account. Today, the Principles of Nuremberg have been brought into the Nuclear Age by the creation of an International Criminal Court. Although some 100 countries, including nearly all U.S. allies, are parties to the treaty establishing the Court, the United States withdrew its signature from the treaty and has actively opposed the Court. This represents a great failure of U.S. leadership in the world.

To make the United States an "instrument for peace" in the 21st century will require a great effort by U.S. citizens. It will require us to step forward and demand of our government an end to international lawlessness and the active promotion of peace and human rights throughout the world. Peace cannot stand without justice, and justice cannot stand without an active citizenry promoting it. There must be one standard for all, and that standard must be justice for all, as called for by the Universal Declaration of Human Rights.

Peace is an ongoing process. It begins with the first step and it does not end. We, all of us alive today, are the gatekeepers of the future. The world we bequeath to our children and grandchildren will depend upon our success in building a more peaceful and decent world. Some 50 years ago, Bertrand Russell and Albert Einstein issued an appeal in which they concluded, "Remember your humanity and forget the rest. If you can do so, the way lies open to a new Paradise; if you cannot, there lies before you the risk of universal death."

Let us remember our humanity, choose hope and peace, and accept our own share of responsibility for waging peace now and throughout our lives. Each of us by our daily acts of peace and our commitment to building a better world can inspire others and help create a groundswell for peace too powerful to be turned aside. This book provides a guiding light on the path to peace.[1]

A NOTE TO READERS

*A*MERICAN HIROSHIMA DELIVERS CONCRETE IDEAS for individuals and policymakers to strengthen America's democracy, prevent wars, reduce weapons of mass destruction and establish the United States as a 21st century instrument for peace. This book is intended to promote peace and prosperity not only in America, but around the world.

American Hiroshima is written by a person who started the book as a conservative Republican and, in the process of completing this book, is no longer a Republican.[2] My core values did not change, only my understanding of what was really going on. As a result, I feel I am more empathetic to people who disagree with me. As you start this book, it may be helpful to know that my military, business and international volunteer experiences are the basis for my observations and conclusions. Additional information on these experiences and my process of discovery are shared in Appendix A.

I also write as a person who feels that citizens of the United States have a special opportunity, because of the resources Americans possess, to make the world a better place. A necessary condition to achieving this better world is a willingness to improve America's democracy. By improving America's democracy, Americans will be better able to see and respond to injustice in our world. Free speech, fair elections, the right to assemble, freedom of religion, impartial justice, peace, prosperity and love of family are values widely cherished around the world and worthy of America's support.

We seem to so badly want what we believe reinforced that we quickly change the subject if we sense that the direction is heading toward an outcome in conflict with our beliefs. I observe this happening in many situations and it is, to me, strikingly limiting to talk only to people who already agree with me. My confidence that I am on the right track in my pursuit of truth comes from the fact that I've had to acknowledge that some of my beliefs were wrong. No doubt the pursuit of ideas that promote a more peaceful world will shed light on things I still cannot see.

Understanding that America's foreign policy, blinded by oil, was designed to defeat democracy in the Middle East from 1953 to the present, will help you understand why even now America is making the world a more danger-ous place. With an open mind and a willingness to learn from the past, past mistakes need not be repeated. New insights and wisdom come from a will-ingness to acknowledge that some of what you believe can be changed. If you continue reading this book, you might just modify your thinking about previous, current and future wars.

The Introduction or Chapter One sets the stage for the remaining chapters by defining "American Hiroshima." You may be shocked in this chapter to learn about two separate and collaborating American Hiroshima forces. This chapter calls for a new way of thinking to solve our problems and stresses cur-rent policies are certain to result in an American Hiroshima.

Chapter Two covers the media and why citizens in America's democracy are uninformed. This chapter begins with a review of what democracy is and why justice is essential. This chapter also helps explain why the information in this book will at times be hard to believe. On a related note, prior to September 11, 2001, it would have been hard to believe warnings about a terrorist attack that would kill thousands of Americans. Imagine what you would have said to someone who told you in 2002 or 2003 that Iraq was not a weapons of mass destruction threat to the United States. If you find something in this book is hard to believe, be sure to take a moment to check the Notes at the back to learn more, and to visit the American Hiroshima site at www.americanhiro-shima.info.

Chapter Three stresses the dangers of being dependent on a fuel for the economy that results in injustice. A key point of this chapter is that Ameri-cans have supported injustice in the past. When slavery fueled the American economy, many Americans stuck their heads in the sand and ignored this injustice. This chapter provides insights on mistakes made in the past so that injustices today can be better seen and understood.

Chapter Four reminds the reader of key military interventions and acts of terror since World War II. The terrorist acts noted help highlight a key Septem-ber 11, 2001 lesson: billions of dollars spent on the military and intelligence services did not stop nineteen people with box cutters. Americans have a false sense of security when they think that increasing defense spending, starting wars, and reforming intelligence services will make America safe from terror-ists. Unless the root causes of terror are addressed, acts of terror will continue. Nuclear weapons, especially highlight this point, as these weapons do more to empower the weak than they do to protect the strong.

Chapter Five reveals how evil alliances have created problems that are now undermining America's democracy. The information in this chapter puts the spotlight on corrupt foreign policies leading up to the current Bush administration. President George W. Bush's foreign polices have made and continue to make the world a more dangerous place. The information in this chapter also explains why the invasion of Iraq has helped al Qaeda more than it has hurt it.

Interdependent international relationships are presented in Chapter Six. Without interdependent safeguards the question is no longer if, but when, a weapon of mass destruction will be used against the United States. Americans must realize that the second superpower in the world to help protect against weapons of mass destruction is no longer another nation, but a worldwide network of nations whose willingness to assist the United States can be measured by world public opinion.[3] Understanding this point sheds light on one of the key levers to defeat terrorists.

Chapter Seven explains how war profits hurt America's democracy. This is accomplished with a discussion of the current insane level of nuclear weapons arsenals and the U.S. role in international arms sales. The Bush family's war profiteering is presented going back to the First World War. This chapter illustrates a key driver of wars. Conflicts of interest are common; with the Bush family, they are downright criminal.

Chapter Eight warns of the threat to the world from the ongoing U.S. effort to dominate outer space and integrate space power throughout military operations. Many Americans are completely unaware that in addition to the land, sea, and air, space is now the fourth medium of warfare. This chapter explains why National Missile Defense is really a cover program for a much more offensive effort for the United States to be the global masters of space. A historic opportunity to keep space free of weapons of mass destruction exists at this moment. Historians may look back at this time and determine that the weaponization of space by the United States was one of humanity's greatest missed opportunities to reduce the dangers of weapons of mass destruction.

Chapter Nine challenges key historical conclusions so that the correct learning points for today are clear. The victor writes the history books. Learning from the past requires that the truth of the vanquished not be conveniently forgotten.

Chapter Ten dispels the myth that individuals are powerless to do anything about the global issues of our time. There are specific actions that each and every person can perform to make the world more peaceful and at the same time strengthen America's democracy. This chapter highlights several key forces for peace along with a recommendation for a Department of Peace to balance the Department of War. This chapter concludes with thoughts about allegiance to a specific country.

The final chapter, Chapter Eleven, is a proposal to defeat terrorists and offer a brighter future for the world. I believe that the war on terrorism, leading to an American Hiroshima, would end in a blink of an eye if President Bush had the courage to pursue the alternative solution proposed in this chapter. This is not to say that some form of violence would not happen at any point in the future. The point is that current wars, a future war with Iran, and the path of endless subsequent wars would not be needed. The forces interested in executing an American Hiroshima would face internal struggles in the event they went forward with their plans. The United States would be more likely to receive defectors from groups continuing to promote violence. The worldwide network of nations, a superpower in its own right, would be far more motivated to help protect America as all interests would be aligned to defeat terrorists.

Throughout this book you will find information that is Top Secret and illegal for government insiders to disclose; but this same information is common knowledge among al Qaeda leaders and foreign intelligence services. The classified piece of a puzzle is often the critical piece to understanding what is really going on. Intelligence officers are quick to realize that much of the information they protect is only classified because it would hurt the current or a previous U.S. administration. Foreign intelligence services and international terrorists are naturally more circumspect than U.S. citizens and are quick to connect the dots. A specific example is provided to illustrate this point. I wish to note that the following example used is known by many people outside the United States. The information disclosed in this book does not violate any agreements that I have with the U.S. government and in no way would help a terrorist but will help strengthen America's democracy.

Consider the popular support of the Patriot Act following 9/11. You may know that there is a U.S. law on cryptographic exports. Software products used in the United States, like Microsoft's encryption, must be compliant since they are also available for purchase in other countries.[4] The U.S. law requires computer code that makes documents and files protected from unauthorized viewers to be reviewed by the National Security Agency, or NSA.[5] The NSA technical evaluation means the U.S. will only allow for export security systems that can be defeated by the U.S. government. When you realize that computer security systems can be defeated and the Patriot Act authorizes the U.S. government to access citizens' computers, Americans have unknowingly yielded rights that they cherish. The NSA can look inside any Microsoft Windows computer that is connected to the Internet. This means every American is subject to having Uncle Sam access and view everything they do on their computer, as all files on their computer are easily accessible. Would Americans have supported the Patriot Act if they understood that their computers, even with encryption, are easily accessible?

Spying on Americans, in violation of the US law, is a routine NSA activity. Someday US citizens will realize the full extent of the government's surveillance activity and will be shocked. Few Americans realize that carrying a cell phone means your location can be tracked at all times the phone is turned on. In addition the NSA can produce a report of people you meet with who are also carrying a cell phone. The cell phone data can be supplemented with locations where you used a credit card or passed a toll booth in your vehicle. While this is often unknown by Americans, potential al Qaeda recruits and others wishing to harm Americans can access tips on how to avoid NSA monitoring and maintain COMSEC (communication security) by visiting their local Internet cafe. The real danger in illegal spying on Americans, as legal spying is easily obtained when requested by the government, is to our democracy. When groups with opposing opinions are targeted for surveillance, they may be just a step away from being targeted for elimination.

In addition, many Americans are unaware that the Central Intelligence Agency is funding books and studies to influence U.S. policy. This practice is a violation of the CIA's charter. Rare views into this and related practices are only now surfacing, as secret books and covert propaganda are part of a well-guarded CIA program.[6] The Church Committee of the Senate revealed that the CIA has published thousands of books to help define history and suppress the truth.[7] Americans should be concerned when the CIA is also approving and assisting the publication of anonymously written books like Imperial Hubris. We now know that Imperial Hubris was written by a CIA employee named Michael Scheuer. Why is a person with secrecy agreements extending beyond the year 2028 allowed to publish a book that reveals detailed information on al Qaeda? Is the answer that Scheuer makes the case that America must "get used to and good at killing?"[8]

Furthermore, the CIA's Counterterrorist Center has spent millions of dollars funding studies, reports and conferences to influence American opinions.[9] In Chapter Two, the subject of government propaganda is discussed, raising the red flag that too much secrecy is a threat to America's democracy. Even selecting the right people to lead the government is obstructed as information that could influence a voting decision is often suppressed in classified documents that may never be disclosed, or if disclosed, will only become known after the election.

A book with a hidden agenda can mean that the information in the book may not be the author's sincere understanding of the situation. While this is obvious, I mention it because American Hiroshima is not sponsored or supported by any other entity. American Hiroshima does not promote a Republican, Democratic or other specific political party perspective, but rather pursues free thinking focused on providing actionable ideas for all of us to achieve a just and prosperous world. You may be thinking that I am certainly benefiting in some way by writing this book. This is true only insofar as my favorite non-profits benefit from your purchase of this book. Profits from this book help orphans in Africa, as well as help humanity eliminate nuclear weapons.[10] Anyone who wishes to join me on a trip to Africa to help some of the 11 million orphans is welcome – and is subject to also becoming transformed in how he or she sees the world. To learn more about an upcoming trip to Africa, you can find my contact information at www.americanhiroshima.info.

You may find that this book presents ideas that challenge what you have previously learned. I realize that when beliefs are challenged, anger is a natural outcome. If you feel angry, I encourage you to take a few moments to reflect on why that is so. There was a time in my life when I served in the military; and, at that time, anyone who criticized the United States would have put me on the defensive. My mind would have been closed to hearing a critical perspective. I likely would have thought that a person questioning the government did not appreciate the brave people, living and dead, who made tremendous sacrifices for America's freedom. The saying, "America: love it or leave it," might have come to mind. My intent is to put the spotlight on injustice and not create anger that feeds hatred. I believe that it is possible to love someone who is the agent of injustice and simultaneously not approve of their unjust act. For example, you will find that I am very critical of President George W. Bush. At the same time I do not hate him; I do hold him accountable for his actions.

History is a wonderful teacher. The historian David Alan Rosenberg once said, "There are five ways you can use history in public policy. You can use it to impress, you can use it to inform, you can use it to inspire, you can use it to admonish, and you can use history to empower."[11] The truth often requires all five; and American Hiroshima is a sincere effort to present the truth so that nuclear disaster can be prevented. I have exercised care to present the truth from hundreds of sources and from my own life experience. All authors lack some objectivity. I recognize this and my view of current and historical events is very much from the perspective of the poor and suffering.

No discussion of America's foreign policy is complete without an understanding of the Palestinian and Israeli dispute. One could argue that terrorism as a strategy for effective change in the Middle East was born when Israel succeeded in removing the British in 1947. Certainly the support of the United States has been a constant source of anger and perceived injustice by Arabs since the creation of the state of Israel in 1948.[12] In Chapter Four on Terrorism, the direct connection between U.S. support for Israel and terrorist attacks against U.S. citizens may be eye-opening for many Americans.

Some Americans believe that criticizing American foreign policy or military policy, such as the invasion of Iraq, is anti-American and disrespectful of the sacrifices made by the U.S. military. A brief story will help me challenge this notion. Imagine that you have three children. One stays at home and is very well-behaved. Another works for justice at home and sometimes travels abroad to help the poor. The third child is overseas all the time and you know little about his/her life or actions. One day, you become aware that your third child is hurting people and wasting the family resources. You would not be anti-family if you called attention to the wrong actions of your third child. America at home does great things. America abroad does some great things.[13] America abroad also promotes injustice. Criticism of these injustices does not take away from the good at home or overseas. This simple story illustrates why I believe a person who criticizes the U.S. is not anti-American. As a matter of fact, the failure to speak up about injustice is itself inconsistent with the courage to speak the truth that Americans hold dear.

The following chapters will illustrate why the evolution of America's current democracy from narrow nationalist policies to multilateral interdependencies is the clear path for peace. As the title of this book indicates, the time has come where wars will no longer be conveniently fought between military forces in far-away places. The cycle of increasing waves of violence and suffering around the world must be stopped. Unless Americans demand a new set of solutions to our most pressing foreign policy problems, an American Hiroshima will at a minimum kill many Americans and create economic problems that will last for decades. Appendix E helps explain the world that post-American Hiroshima survivors will confront. For now, I encourage you to read the book and focus your energy on what we can do to prevent an act of nuclear terror from happening anywhere in the world.

A final motivation for writing this book is the polarization of the United States. While extreme kindness or extreme generosity are good things, other forms of extremism are sometimes used to deny the value of another life. If the ideas in this book are judged to be extreme, I hope time proves they are extremely good.

Teachers wishing to use American Hiroshima in the classroom will find additional resources and free lesson plans at www.americanhiroshima.info. The following maps may be helpful for sections of the book that discuss the Middle East and the Korean Peninsula.[14]

MAP 1 – THE MIDDLE EAST

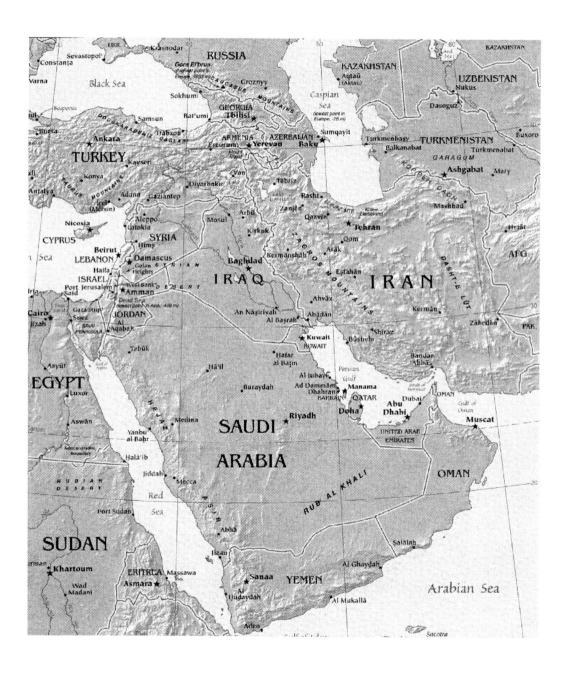

MAP 2 – THE KOREAN PENINSULA

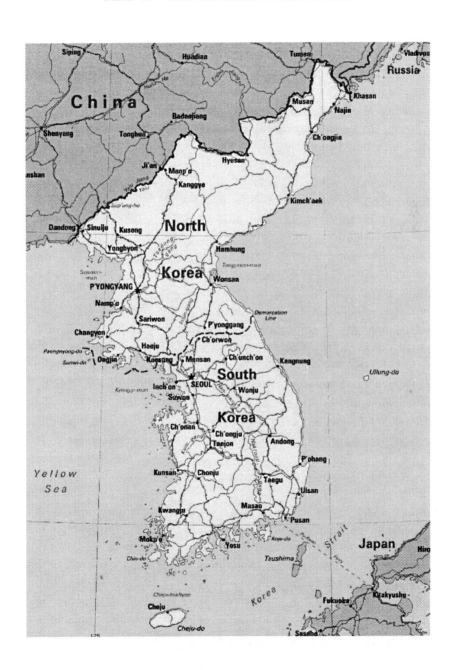

CONTENTS

1

INTRODUCTION

"We have too many men of science, too few men of God. We have grasped the mystery of the atom and rejected the Sermon on the Mount... The world has achieved brilliance without wisdom, power without conscience. Ours is a world of nuclear giants and ethical infants. We know more about war than we know about peace, more about killing than we know about living."

(General Omar N. Bradley, Chief of Staff, United States Army)[15]

AN AMERICAN HIROSHIMA IS THE guaranteed outcome, unless we adopt a new way of thinking about fighting terrorism and the use of force. We face an unassailable fact: nuclear weapons have proliferated across the globe and do more to empower the weak than protect the strong. When chemical or biological weapons are considered, we are well beyond unilateral efforts to contain the proliferation of weapons of mass destruction.[16]

The answer to defeating terrorists is not war in Iraq, followed by war in Iran.[17] Nuclear weapons are in at least 14 countries and many more countries have the potential to make them.[18] More than 3,700 metric tons of highly enriched uranium and plutonium are dispersed in at least 60 countries.[19] No matter how much military spending is increased, or how many preemptive wars are initiated, unless the root causes of terror are addressed, the 21st century will be the bloodiest in history, with an estimated 225 million civilians killed by acts of terror.[20]

Albert Einstein understood this new reality when he observed that "through the release of atomic energy, our generation has brought into the world the most revolutionary force since prehistoric man's discovery of fire. This basic force of the universe cannot be fitted into the outmoded concept of narrow nationalisms. For there is no secret and there is no defense; there is no possibility of control except through the aroused understanding and insistence of the peoples of the world."[21]

AMERICAN HIROSHIMA DEFINED

The United States has learned of at least two American Hiroshima plans.[22]

American Hiroshima is the name of a plan to detonate nuclear weapons in the United States. Many U.S. government insiders, like General Habiger, a retired four-star general, have already concluded that a nuclear attack is inevitable.[23] The founding dean at Harvard's Kennedy School of Government, Graham Allison, is a little more optimistic with a 51-49 projection that an American Hiroshima will happen.[24] The following information explains why a mushroom cloud in the United States is on the horizon and what can be done to stop the escalating cycle of violence.

AL QAEDA'S AMERICAN HIROSHIMA PLAN

The first American Hiroshima plan to come to the attention of U.S. intelligence officials is the effort underway by al Qaeda. Al Qaeda's American Hiroshima plan is understood to be a very real and serious threat. Illustrating this point is the fact that in October of 2001 the United States government went on high alert. Vice President Dick Cheney left Washington with several hundred federal employees for a secret site to begin "continuity of government" operations. Why did this happen? The Presidential Daily Intelligence Briefing by George Tenet on October 11, 2001, informed President Bush that al Qaeda had acquired a ten-kiloton nuclear bomb. The CIA director revealed that an agent, code name Dragonfire, reported that the stolen Russian weapon was already in New York City.[25] Fortunately, the Dragonfire intelligence report was wrong. Unfortunately, reports that Osama bin Laden has an active al Qaeda Manhattan Project that he calls "American Hiroshima" are accurate.

The packaging of al Qaeda's first nuclear act of terror is important to Osama bin Laden, because he is fully aware that killing millions of people, especially children, can hurt the long-term growth of his movement and religion. Osama bin Laden is very conscious of how history will view his "American Hiroshima" and he places tremendous value on a plan that will be seen far into the future as innovative and symbolic. An analysis of Osama bin Laden's past reveals a basic formula. He achieves his innovative and symbolic objectives by using a relatively small weapon compared to the actual destruction achieved. The small weapon is used to change the purpose of an existing commercial resource and thereby maximize the destruction. On 9/11 this was a boxcutter used to change an airplane into a guided missile and destroy large buildings filled with people.

Osama bin Laden's October 2004 statement of responsibility for the 9/11 highjackings is sometimes confused with acceptance of all the events that happened on 9/11. While there is a clear record of attempts by al Qaeda to attack the U.S. going back to 1993, it should be noted that Osama bin Laden was surprised by some of the events on that tragic day. If you open your mind even 10% to the possibility that the 9/11 Commission Report is not the full story, you may conclude that some of the events were magnified by the U.S. government to promote an already established agenda to invade both Afghanistan and Iraq. David Ray Griffin's book, The New Pearl Harbor, is one resource to help you explore the questions that remain unanswered.[26] To see a list of warnings and intelligence that the U.S. had prior to 9/11 visit www.american-hiroshima.info/911warnings.htm.

Long before 9/11, Osama bin Laden has been thinking about how to inflict an innovative and symbolic American Hiroshima attack. Osama bin Laden wanted the Muslim world to attack the "Far Enemy" as the priority target. His "Near Enemy" is Israel and in Osama bin Laden's mind targets like the Twin Towers or the Pentagon are Jewish targets. By attacking the U.S., he wanted to topple authoritarian regimes in the Muslim world. Why? The U.S. is the source of their protection.[27] Attacking the United States on 9/11 was first and foremost a means to unite fragmented movements in the Muslim world so that they would change their primary target to the "Far Enemy."

Uniting fragmented Muslim movements is one reason why Osama bin Laden did not allow the 9/11 highjackers originating from Logan airport in Boston to crash into the Indian Point nuclear power station 40 miles north of Manhattan.[28] A second key reason is Osama bin Laden wanted U.S. nuclear power facilities to remain as easy targets. Khalid Sheikh Mohammed, the chief planner of 9/11, has provided information on why the nuclear power plants were spared.[29] He is in U.S. custody and has revealed to the CIA that senior al Qaeda leaders wanted to include nuclear power plants in the 9/11 attacks. Khalid Sheikh Mohammed said Osama bin Laden was unyielding in his opposition to crashing airplanes into nuclear power plants. Osama bin Laden wanted nuclear facilities to be left alone "for now."[30] His "for now" is significant because if al Qaeda did not crash airplanes into nuclear facilities, he calculated that the U.S. government would not harden these targets.[31]

Osama bin Laden understands that a weakness of his enemy is that the U.S. is influenced by businesses not wanting to lose profits. The influence of the airline industry prior to 9/11 prevented needed security improvements to airline cockpit doors. Only after 9/11 was the U.S. government quick to require that action. Osama bin Laden, not having a nuclear weapon in 2001, feared that the U.S. would harden nuclear facilities in advance of al Qaeda's acquisition of a few nuclear bombs. His calculations have thus far proved to be correct as a panel in April 2005 concluded that U.S. nuclear facilities remain exposed because the Bush administration does not want to create additional costs for businesses.[32] The additional costs for the nuclear energy industry and concerns of an educated public about this danger could effectively shut down nuclear power projects for decades.

Congressman Curt Weldon has disclosed that an al Qaeda cell was captured in Canada in 2003 as it plotted to fly a plane into the Seabrook nuclear power plant in New Hampshire. The Seabrook nuclear power plant is approximately 40 miles from Boston and would have exposed millions of people to radiation poisoning. Another serious attempt, indicating that the American Hiroshima threat is a global one, was defeated in November of 2005. On November 8, 2005, the BBC reported the arrest of terrorists seeking to attack the Lucas Heights nuclear facility. The Lucas Heights nuclear facility is Australia's only nuclear reactor and is located approximately 25 miles southwest of Sydney.

Al Qaeda's American Hiroshima target list requires a population density where a few nuclear weapons could kill four million Americans.[33] To provide an example of the destructive power of a ten-kiloton weapon, the Hiroshima Little Boy bomb had a yield of approximately thirteen kilotons.[34] U.S. and the International Atomic Energy Agency experts see a ten-kiloton nuclear bomb as the most likely weapon configuration, because the blueprints for this weapon have been aggressively sold by Pakistan. For example, a blueprint for a ten-kiloton nuclear bomb was found in the files of the Libyan weapons program in 2004.[35] Intelligence experts wonder whether Col. Muammar Abu Minyar al-Qadhafi, Libya's ruler since September 1, 1969, made his full disclosure to the Bush administration because he had concluded that al Qaeda's American Hiroshima plan would be successful and he wanted Libya off the U.S. retaliation target list.

A ten-kiloton weapon could be as small as a suitcase and far easier to get into the United States than a large shipment of illegal drugs. To kill four million Americans with conventional weapons or airplanes, al Qaeda could need over one thousand 9/11-like attacks. Even with ten-kiloton nuclear bombs that can kill a few hundred thousand people, al Qaeda would need many attacks. The optimal and most likely way to achieve the American Hiroshima four million killed goal, with the exception of obtaining a far more powerful nuclear weapon, is to detonate nuclear bombs at a few nuclear power plants. A ten-kiloton weapon, detonated in this manner, can become a weapon that can kill millions of Americans.[36] The reason for the magnification is the explosion of a football sized amount of plutonium or highly enriched uranium at a nuclear power plant would disperse in the atmosphere highly radioactive nuclear power plant fuel and waste. The initial explosion would certainly kill many people. The subsequent downwind radioactive fallout, traveling from the nuclear power plant for hundreds of miles downwind, could kill millions of Americans and make it unsafe to live in large regions of the country. Illustrative examples of how far highly radioactive material could travel downwind are available at www.americanhiroshima.info.

The al Qaeda target list prioritizes urban areas that have large Jewish-American concentrations. At the top of the list is New York City, and specifically

Manhattan.[37] Other American Hiroshima cities on the target list are Washington, Miami, Los Angeles, Philadelphia, Chicago, San Francisco, Las Vegas and Boston.[38] The actual locations that are impacted are much greater than the few high priority al Qaeda targets. The subsequent downwind radioactive fallout, because of the force multiplier effect of blowing up a nuclear power station, would likely require listing thousands of downwind cities and towns.

How real is the al Qaeda threat? CIA Director Porter Goss was asked in 2005 by Congress if al Qaeda could have the essential ingredient for a nuclear bomb. Goss's response confirmed that enough Russian nuclear material is missing that "those with know-how" could construct a nuclear weapon if they were to obtain it.[39] The CIA has debriefed Sultan Bashiruddin Mahmood, a former official from Pakistan's nuclear weapons program. Mahmood met with Osama bin Laden and confirmed that al Qaeda had succeeded in acquiring nuclear material for a nuclear bomb from the Islamic Movement of Uzbekistan.[40] Osama bin Laden has also said "I wish to declare that if America used chemical or nuclear weapons against us, then we may retort with chemical or nuclear weapons. We have the weapons as a deterrent."[41] The Islamic justification for this attack was also written by Sheikh Nasir bin Hamad in 2003. This document, "A Treatise on the Ruling Regarding the Use of Weapons of Mass Destruction Against Infidels," provides the religious for an American Hiroshima attack.[42] If you wish to see the long list of supporting intelligence that the al Qaeda American Hiroshima threat is on the horizon, go to www.american-hiroshima.info. Former U.S. Attorney General John Ashcroft emphasized the seriousness of this serious threat when he observed that the possibility that al-Qaeda or its sympathizers could have a nuclear bomb is the greatest danger facing the United States in the war on terrorism.[43]

Senior members of the "classified" community are well aware of the very real possibility that an American Hiroshima will occur. Not surprisingly, people with access to this information have relocated so that their children are living and going to school outside these immediate blast zones. For this same reason, the president began the trend of working from locations other than the White House during his first term, and it is likely that the public will see him working far fewer days in Washington during his second term. Special events, where the president's location is known in advance, like the January 20, 2005 inauguration, will continue to have city blocks isolated that mirror the blast zones of a ten-kiloton weapon. For many people this seems hard to believe; but even corporate America has put special plans in place for the locations that are on al Qaeda's target list. It is for this same reason that companies traditionally headquartered in Manhattan with an expertise in risk management, like New York Life, have moved many employees out of Manhattan.[44]

Osama bin Laden has proven to be very patient, capable of executing on what he says he will do, and a master at innovative plans that maximize both their symbolism and destruction. Applying Osama bin Laden's formula of a relatively small weapon compared to the actual destruction achieved, Americans have an opportunity to demand immediate measures to harden all exposed nuclear material and dangerous chemical sites starting with the greatest threat of nuclear power plants and storage facilities. The Committee to Bridge the Gap, a nuclear watchdog organization, has proposed specific common sense changes to upgrade protections against such attacks.[45] To keep costs down for the nuclear industry, the standard of protection established for nuclear facilities is far below the attacking force of the nineteen 9/11 highjackers.[46] If Americans fail to protect nuclear facilities, the destruction from an American Hiroshima will be exponentially greater than the 9/11 attacks. Survivors will surely look back at the decision not to better protect nuclear and chemical facilities with the same regret that people feel today regarding not strengthening airline cockpit doors before 9/11.

IRAN'S AMERICAN HIROSHIMA PLAN AND THE QODS FORCE

An American Hiroshima, independent of or in collaboration with al Qaeda is even more likely to occur if the United States attacks Iran. Unfortunately, the thinking of key insiders like Dick Cheney and Donald Rumsfeld, as derived from the Project for the New American Century, supports that the U.S. or Israel will attack Iran.[47] In March 2005, London's Sunday Times reported that Prime Minister Ariel Sharon's security cabinet gave "initial authorization" in February to attack Iran. The attack would occur if negotiations failed to persuade the Islamic republic to halt its nuclear program.[48] The report noted that Israel has built a model of Iran's Natanz plant to practice attacks on the facility. The plan was coordinated with the United States and would utilize F-15 fighter planes and teams from Israel's elite Air Force's Shaldag unit.

The Bush administration sees the Israeli Air Force destruction, with conventional bombs similar to the destruction of Iraq's Osirak reactor in 1981, as the minimum level of force needed. The fear in Washington is that Iran has moved their nuclear-weapons program underground to multiple sites following the Osirak attack. In response, the Bush administration desired bunker-buster nuclear weapons that could inflict the destruction required to temporarily eliminate Iran's nuclear program.[49] A ground war is the likely next step, especially if the raid does not destroy 100% of Iran's nuclear weapons. As observed during the Iran and Iraq war, Iran currently possesses non-nuclear weapons of mass destruction that would certainly survive an Israeli or U.S. air or ground war.

As President Bush began his second term, it is not surprising that Donald Rumsfeld continued to be the Secretary of Defense.[50] Donald Rumsfeld was deemed absolutely essential by the president to continue Special Access Programs and action team efforts for the next major intervention in Iran. SAPs and action teams are top secret military programs with units that operate using procedures, such as aliases, normally reserved for CIA operatives. Military commanders, even at the regional command level, are unaware of their presence. SAPs and action teams are directed by the Secretary of Defense and to be legal they must operate with congressional oversight. Bypassing Congress is illegal and Congress has been misled about their existence. This is discussed in more detail in Chapter Four.[51]

Donald Rumsfeld obtained presidential authority to use military commandos for covert operations that he would personally control on or before the summer of 2002.[52] As a result of this authority, in July 2002, the secret Gray Fox action team was reassigned from the Army to the Special Operations Command in Tampa, Florida. The team operates under a new secret code name to find and eliminate terrorist organizations. According to reporter Seymour Hersh, the former Gray Fox and other similar teams began conducting secret reconnaissance missions inside Iran in 2004.[53] Iranian Information Minister Ali Yunessi also confirmed that U.S. spy planes have been spotted in Iran.[54] The objective of these spy missions is to identify approximately 36 nuclear weapons-related targets that can be destroyed by an Israeli or U.S. surprise attack.[55] To facilitate military operations in Iran, in September 2004 the U.S. sent 4,500 smart bombs to Israel to use to strike Iran's nuclear facilities and built a base in Afghanistan near its border with Iran.56 Combined with Israel's "initial authorization" to attack Iran, the United States is moving quickly to initiate another major war.[57]

Since Iran has moved at least some of its nuclear-weapons program underground to multiple sites, the likelihood that Donald Rumsfeld's action team efforts will not destroy all of the targets is high.[58] This means Iran will likely be left with at least a dirty bomb retaliation capability after it is attacked. If attacked, Iran may give a nuclear bomb or bombs to Hezbollah, al Qaeda, or Iran's Qods Force. The most likely choice is the Qods Force.

The Qods Force or Jerusalem Force is the most secret of the Iranian regime's numerous military and intelligence organizations. Since its inception in 1990, clerics have kept it under such secrecy that even many Iranians know nothing about it. Responsible for extraterritorial operations, this military unit is Iran's most active, skilled, and elite force. Qods Force members must be devout Hizbullahis, that is, they must be dedicated to the spread of Islamic fundamentalism. The commander of this elite unit, Revolutionary Guards Brigadier General Ghassem Soleimani, reports to Iran's supreme leader, Ayatollah Ali Khamenei.[59]

The Qods Force:

- attracts, educates, organizes and supports sympathizers of the Islamic Revolution and Islamic movements around the world.
- collects military and strategic intelligence.
- develops plans to use nuclear and other weapons of mass destruction.[60]
- assassinates political opponents, writers, and publishers who are opposed to the regime.
- forms Islamic Revolution forces around the world such as the 9th Badr for Iraq, the Lebanon Army or 7th Army, and the Sudan Army.[61]

The Qods Force's major training centers include the Imam Ali University, Shahid Kazemi, Beheshti, and Vali-e-asr garrisons. The Qods Force also operates a college in Qom called Beit ol-Moqaddas, also known as the Melal (Nations) Training Center, because recruits come from around the world. Specific assignments are parceled out to different directorates of the Qods Force. The directorates are:

- Western countries (Europe and the United States)
- Iraq
- Afghanistan, Pakistan, and the Indian subcontinent
- Palestine, Lebanon, and Jordan
- Turkey
- North Africa (Egypt, Tunisia, Algeria, Sudan, and Morocco)
- Arabian peninsula
- Republics of the former Soviet Union[62]

On a related note, the violence in Sudan can better be understood by knowing that Sudan is the Qods Force's headquarters for North Africa. In addition, the insurgency in Iraq can be better understood by knowing that a key Qods Force headquarters was moved from central Iran to the Iran-Iraq border in 2004. Qods Force's commanders oversee their operations inside Iraq from these border bases.[63]

The Qods Force is responsible for gathering information required for targeting and attack planning and has already developed a plan to introduce and detonate nuclear weapons and other mass destruction weapons in the United States.[64] This is why Iran has had Qods Force operatives in the United States, many of whom have been undercover for over a decade. Iran is far more capable than al Qaeda or any other Islamic force to execute an American Hiroshima plan. Iran's Defense Minister Ali Shamkhani indicated that Iran is already capable of implementing such a plan. Shamkhani said in January 2005, "We can claim that we have rapidly produced equipment that has resulted in the greatest deterrent."[65] Western intelligence services believe Iran is anywhere from a few months to a few years from resolving the final technical issues to build a nuclear bomb.[66] Shamkhani's comments are reinforced by Pakistan's acknowledgement that its scientist, Abdul Qadeer Khan, supplied Iran with nuclear centrifuges.[67] In what may be the ultimate "live by the sword and die by the sword" tragic irony, the American Hiroshima nuclear trigger could be a nuclear switch manufactured and sold by an American company as U.S.-made precision triggers have made their way to Pakistan and potentially Iran.[68]

To add to the individual al Qaeda and Iranian American Hiroshima threats, Iran and al Qaeda are collaborating on their American Hiroshima plans. Osama bin Laden's son, Saad bin Laden, is with a small group of al Qaeda and Iranian leaders working inside Iran.[69] Although the U.S. government does not know how Iran will retaliate if attacked, a combined terrorist, military, and diplomat response is expected.

Unfortunately, the policies to fight terrorists by President George W. Bush, as explained later in this book, are actually making an American Hiroshima even more likely. The real danger in such a calamity goes well beyond the four million deaths in the United States that Osama bin Laden has planned. A nuclear attack against the United States would surely lead to retaliation, in which millions of innocent people in the Middle East could be killed. A counter-retaliation could bring even greater death and destruction to America, and the subsequent response could result in retaliation in other regions of the world.

This book focuses on al Qaeda and Iranian American Hiroshima plans. However, threats from additional groups and repeat American Hiroshima attacks are possible. Americans should also remember that an attack within the U.S. may also be initiated by the U.S. government. This is hard to contemplate but previously classified programs like Operation Northwoods prove that the U.S. government is sometimes willing to attack its own citizens. The Operation Northwoods plan was declassified just three months before the 9/11 attacks.[70] The program was proposed by the Joint Chiefs of Staff to Secretary of Defense Robert McNamara on March 13, 1962. This Top Secret plan called for "massive casualty producing events" that would justify a U.S. invasion of Cuba. The proposals included attacking a U.S. commercial passenger plane using a U.S. made reproduction of a Russian made MIG attack aircraft, blowing up a refugee boat, blowing up a U.S. ship, and implementing a series of terrorist attacks in the United States including the capitol. The objective of Operation Northwoods was to concoct a "Remember the Maine" incident and win mass support for an invasion of Cuba.[71]

The most dangerous scenario culminates in retaliation and counter-retaliations and confrontation between major nuclear powers. Al Qaeda sees both the U.S. and Russia as enemies and would like nothing better than to trigger a nuclear exchange between them. A false warning, or a terrorist commandeering and launching a U.S., Russian, or other nation's nuclear weapon could trigger a major nuclear war that could end this wonderful world we all share.

The following chapters explain what we must do to prevent this ultimate disaster.

2

AN UNINFORMED ELECTORATE

"This great informative medium we've got of television is really not fulfilling its obligation to the public."

(Walter Cronkite)[72]

W E THE PEOPLE ARE, INCREASINGLY, uninformed. Sometimes we are unaware of what the United States is doing in other countries because the information is classified. More often, we are unaware because we choose to allow ourselves to shut out new ideas and because the mainstream media inadequately covers events around the world. This chapter defines democracy and highlights why a healthy democracy requires an informed electorate. In addition, this chapter discusses labels that disable, simplistic myths, the need to supplement traditional sources of information, covert propaganda, and power influenced by money, world opinion, apathy, and fear.

DEMOCRACY AND JUSTICE FOR ALL

"Democracy" literally means "rule by the people." The term is derived from the Greek demokratia which, in the middle of the fifth century BCE, denoted political systems existing in Greek city-states such as Athens. Demos translates into "people" and kratos means "rule."[73] Democracy is a government of, by, and for the people, made possible through majority rule.[74] Democracy is not simply the United States' form of government imposed upon another county. A government that mirrored the United States would not be a democracy if the majority of the local people failed to support it. Many of the principles will no doubt be common; but democracy must always be what the majority of the people who are being governed desire. Democracy will take different forms in practice, though it has a common definition. Democracy represents individuals more than any other form of government, and history has shown that democracies are less likely to go to war with each other.[75]

A healthy democracy leverages new ideas, technology, and processes for a government by the people and majority rule. In addition, democracy is something that evolves over time. When healthy, it evolves for the better. For example, the United States initially did not allow women and many others, like

11

African-Americans, the right to vote. This was a contradiction with "a government by the people" and in time was corrected.[76]

Disastrous wars and breeding-grounds for non-democratic movements arise when democracy is imposed on a foreign entity. Where America is going wrong today is failing to recognize that democracy cannot be imposed and must be home-grown to take root. When the United States supports dictators and absolute monarchies in places like Saudi Arabia, America undermines its credibility as a country that supports democracy around the world.

JUSTICE FOR ALL MEANS REDUCING SUFFERING AROUND THE WORLD

Americans often know very little about global poverty. Consider for a moment how a person in the Third World might view the United States. The United States suffered a tragic loss on September 11, 2001. People in the Third World know what it is like to lose thousands of people from preventable events in a single day. Every day preventable disease, such as malaria, kill as many people as perished in the World Trade Towers. Malaria kills one person every 30 seconds, annually accounting for over one million deaths. In Africa, malaria kills one child in twenty before five years of age.[77] Imagine that you live in this world where malaria, hunger, HIV/AIDS, cholera, yellow fever and other diseases often unheard of in the West are common. For the fortunate survivors, life expectancy can be half of what people experience in the United States.

Imagine you know that the World Health Organization can prevent and control malaria in Africa for 2.5 billion dollars. Imagine that you are a poor African living on less than a dollar a day. Your child is sick and you are unable to buy the malaria medicine. Your child dies. Now imagine that a citizen from the United States arrives with malaria medicine. Your child receives the medicine and your child lives. What will the poor African think of America?

Malaria sickens 500 million people sick each year. Do you think having 500 million people and their families with a favorable opinion of the United States would help make the world a safer place? Is it possible that someone who would otherwise be indifferent, or maybe even have anger toward the United States, might volunteer information to help arrest terrorists? I submit the answer is yes and this is an example of how earning the goodwill of the world is essential for America's own security.

While helping people fight malaria would be of great help to the world, many Americans do not realize that hunger is world's number one killer. Hunger is more deadly than malaria, AIDS, and tuberculosis combined. Every four seconds, someone, somewhere, dies of hunger. Today 24,000 people will die of hunger; 18,000 of them will be children.[78] This means that, every month, hunger kills more than three times the number of people that were killed in the December 26, 2004 tsunami. Addressing world hunger is a way for the United States to save over eight million lives each year. Having eight million friends, not even counting their grateful family and friends, would be an incredible aid in defeating terrorists.

A terrorist can extend the hand of friendship to the same people Americans neglect. Every person without clean water or who goes to bed hungry is a victim of injustice. A terrorist can sell the message that the First World does not care about injustice because it provides less clean water, food and health care to the poor of the world than to their own pets. Might not this person be convinced to think that the "wealthier nation" was in part responsible for their suffering? How would you feel if a small fraction of what you needed for clean water, food and health care was spent by a "wealthier nation" on exotic weapons like missiles to shoot down missiles?

Understanding world poverty is important because terror is often rooted in the injustices of poverty. George F. Kennan, the founder of the U.S. policy to contain communism, wrote in 1948: "We have about 50% of the world's wealth, but only 6.3% of its population(...) In this situation, we cannot fail to be the object of envy and resentment. Our real task in the coming period is to devise a pattern of relationships which will permit us to maintain this position of disparity(...) To do so, we will have to dispense with all sentimentality and day-dreaming; and our attention will have to be concentrated everywhere on our immediate national objectives(...) We should cease to talk about vague and(...) unreal objectives such as human rights, the raising of the living standards, and democratization. The day is not far off when we are going to have to deal in straight power concepts. The less we are then hampered by idealistic slogans, the better."[79] George Kennan's description of the inequity of power and wealth over fifty years ago is still applicable today. The United States has 31.5% of the world's wealth and 5.2% of the world's population.[80] The situation for the rest of the world is disturbing, with almost half of the 6.4 billion people worldwide barely surviving on less than two dollars per day.[81]

Americans are often led to believe that world hunger is inevitable. Few Americans realize that what is spent on pet food is about the amount needed to eradicate hunger, or that the amount spent on ocean cruises is the amount needed to provide clean drinking water for the world. The following table from the World Watch Institute illustrates that the funds needed are within reach for the world and even a single wealthy country when addressing global injustice is made a priority.[82]

Product	Annual Expenditure	Social or Economic Goal	Additional Annual Investment Needed to Achieve Goal
Pet food in Europe and United States	$17 billion	Elimination of hunger and malnutrition	$19 billion
Perfumes	$15 billion	Universal literacy	$5 billion
Ocean cruises	$14 billion	Clean drinking water for all	$10 billion
Ice cream in Europe	$11 billion	Immunizing every child	$1.3 billion

While solving these problems is more complex than simply allocating the needed funds, it is critical to highlight that funding is usually the key obstacle. It has been my experience that people barely surviving on two dollars a day will work harder than most people can imagine to break free of poverty. They often simply need a financial hand-up to get started.

A person who truly did not care about suffering and injustice in another country might argue that it is not beneficial to the U.S. to spend its resources to try to help. This same person might say that the suffering of others is not America's concern. I strongly submit that in a world where diseases can spread around the world in days and weapons of mass destruction are already around the world, the best return on America's investment for protecting the United States is to help the poor.

William F. Schulz of Amnesty International summed up why addressing injustice and poverty is in America's best interest. He said "It is in truth a matter of survival–our own survival. Because our welfare is bound up in theirs, and when their dreams die, our health and security die with them."[83] Anything that is done to kill another person's hope for the future is a reason for that person to turn into a terrorist. The motivations to do the right thing have never been stronger. To successfully fight terror, Americans must work against poverty. I know in my mind, heart and soul that the path for a safer world begins with addressing the needs of the poor.

GETTING BEYOND DISABLING LABELS

We like information that reinforces our current beliefs, even at the expense of the truth. New ideas, if attached to the wrong label, are disregarded. Labels like Republican, Democrat, Conservative, Liberal or something sinister with an "ist" at the end (e.g., communist, socialist, terrorist, fundamentalist, elitist, etc.) block openness to fresh ideas. It is hard to get beyond the initial "label to disable" conversation-stoppers.

Labels can be convenient tools to avoid facing the unpleasant reality of

injustice. Labels often not only shut down new ideas but result in gener-
alizations which support incorrect conclusions. I find this happens even
within my own family, as a firm pro-peace position is immediately associated with all things anti-American. If we all seek to understand, we will see
that many of the everyday labels are used to encourage hate, isolation and
misunderstanding.

CHALLENGE POLLYANNAISH MYTHS

In addition to disabling labels that constrain thinking, pollyannaish myths
corrupt the American dialog. The more we want to believe them, the more
they tend to stick. Take the fairly recent myth that Ronald Reagan brought
down communism by initiating a massive U.S. military build-up.[84] This is a
statement that is absurd to people who lived with communism. Georgi Arbatov, head of the Moscow-based Institute for the Study of the U.S.A. and Canada, and George F. Kennan, the former U.S. ambassador to the Soviet Union,
have exposed this myth.[85] However, proponents of increased military spending love to use it to justify military spending.

Why did communism in the Soviet Union really fall apart? Communism
was an economic system that was ultimately not self-sustaining and did not
meet the needs of the people. People demanded freedom of expression, freedom from oppression, and access to the opportunities available in the West.
The expansion of communism to other countries increased the stress on the
inefficiencies of the Soviet Union. When Ronald Reagan took office, the Cold
War was already coming to an end.[86] Ronald Reagan's massive military spending only allowed the Soviet Union to hold its house of cards together longer.
Fear of an external enemy keeps regimes in power, not empower its people
to break free. How else could Fidel Castro in Cuba and Kim Jong Il in North
Korea have stayed in power so long?

Historian Harvey Wasserman's observation about the fall of the Soviet
Union follows:

> *"Beamed in by radio, smuggled in on records and tapes, the "youth
> music" was unstoppable. When, it was at least in partial response
> to the irresistible subversion of the western counterculture. Rock and
> roll was doing to the remnants of Stalin's Russia what it had already
> done to Eisenhower's America. The final blow came not from Ronald
> Reagan's beloved nuclear weapons, but from the Soviets' own Three
> Mile Island.*
>
> *After Chernobyl Unit Four exploded on April 26, 1986, Swedish
> radiation monitors detected huge clouds of radiation pouring out of
> the Ukraine. Gorbachev lied about it. Critical days passed before his*

"open" regime acknowledged the catastrophe. As apocalyptic radia-tion poured over their land and into their bodies, millions of Soviet citizens were infuriated to learn from sources outside their country how horrific the disaster really was—and that their lives were in gen-uine danger. Cancer, birth defects, stillbirths and more soared out of control. Gorbachev's credibility was forever shattered.

Soon a staggering 800,000 draftees –"liquidators"– were forced into deadly manual clean-up at the reactor site. The horrific mael-strom of resulting disease fed a fierce organization parallel to the US's Vietnam Vets Against the War that remains an uncompromising political force throughout the former Soviet Union.

With the fury aimed at Gorbachev came devastating economic fallout. Untold billions went to evacuate and quarantine the Cher-nobyl region. The costs are still escalating. The danger of a renewed melt-down still boils beneath the surface. The epidemic of radiation-related diseases has also taken a huge psychological toll, with count-less evacuees and victims – many of them children – still in pitiable condition."[87]

Wasserman concludes that dissatisfaction at home, further weakened by a cultural revolution and a nuclear disaster, was the straw that broke the Krem-lin's back. President Reagan's military buildup only prolonged and did not precipitate the fall of the Soviet Union.

The lifecycle of a communist government may take three to six generations to burn out, but it will. If a communist government moves toward democracy, it may last longer than six generations. Understanding the process of decline and ultimate breakdown may help you appreciate what really happened with the former Soviet Union.

In general, the first generation embracing communism may be happier if the vast majority of the population experiences real improvements in food distribution, education, shelter, government efficiency, defense, and quality of life. The second generation may also be content, especially if its beliefs are reinforced by parents who share stories of starvation and tragedy in the days before communism. When the third generation comes along, the stories rein-forcing communism are slipping into ancient history. This generation living under communism has a burning desire for freedom and the prosperity of democratic nations. People begin to have a clear picture of the system's flaws, and take small steps in rebellion.

The fourth generation, the catalyst generation, comes along when the focus of the people is on the things that communism does not provide. One of the most important of these "things" is freedom. As the world experienced with the former Soviet Union, the momentum of the change takes time and the final fall can happen in almost the blink of an eye.[88]

The failures of a political system may occur faster or slower, but the key point is that communism unraveled in the Soviet Union because the needs of the people were no longer met by the system and not because of the arms race with the United States. Communism did not reward hard work; it rewarded mediocrity. The fact that the United States had thousands of nuclear weapons versus a lesser number did nothing to promote breaking up the Soviet Union. One could argue that the fear created in the Soviet Union by the massive United States military buildup only empowered Soviet officials to resist change and hold on to power for a few extra years. Did increasing the ability to destroy the Soviet Union with nuclear weapons from one time to over 20 times help bring down communism? Did having a first-strike capability against the Soviet Union help reasonable people within the Soviet Union who were struggling against hard-line decision makers? Hard evidence suggests the answer to both questions is no.

In an economic war, as illustrated by the recent Cold War, success or failure flows from the efficiency of the respective economies. Weapons are bad investments because they create significant inefficient expenditures and maintenance drags on economies. In Chapter Seven on War Profiteering, acquiring weapons that have no purpose other than to establish "overkill" is shown to also hurt America. Not only is this a dangerous inefficiency in the U.S. economy, it is an obvious danger to humanity. A key point to being better informed is we should do our homework, seek information from diverse sources, and not let pollyannaish interpretations of history become historical facts.

SUPPLEMENT TELEVISION, RADIO AND NEWSPAPERS

If you obtain the majority of your information about the world from the major television news outlets, you are a typical American citizen – but, unfortunately, an all-too-often uniformed citizen. This is not meant as an insult, but rather as a reminder that television, radio and newspapers produced from any one country are going to have a narrow perspective – and in fact sometimes incorrect – when compared with the same coverage by the international media. We live in the age of sound-bytes, where the truth is distorted as publishers focus on advertising revenues, biased experts, and double-talk from politicians. Every day Americans are presented with misinformation. One frequent example is the myth that starting a war is, actually, the means to achieve peace.

I first noticed the disconnect between the news and the truth during my military service in South Korea, where I held a Top Secret clearance. Often the U.S. news on television and in newspapers was inconsistent with the classified daily report of incidents that we used to keep commanders informed of regional and worldwide developments. I was left with the shocking realization that the information that was classified was often known by the "enemy" and classified only to prevent the American people from knowing what was really going on. This unhealthy trend continues and helps explain why the news available to the public is often misleading or simply missing major stories that were common knowledge in the classified community. I also realized that the perspective of the classified community was not the same as the truth.

MEDIA IMAGE AND REALITY: THREE PRESIDENTS

Often I find myself speaking with someone who is passionate about a political candidate. I've even heard people comment that they know a person is good for the United States, even though they cannot explain why. They convey a general sense, or gut belief, that I find is often based in large part from obtaining information from television and radio. As an example, Ronald Reagan's image was that of an efficient spender, reducer of big government, concern for the common person, infectious optimism, sunny disposition, amazing jokes, and charisma; this image was effectively communicated both on television and via the radio. His policies contradicting this image were somehow easily forgotten or even unknown. To set the record straight: Ronald Reagan dramatically increased government spending, supported apartheid, suppressed worker rights, traded arms for hostages, created death squads in Central America, and funded secret wars in Nicaragua and Afghanistan. Later, in Chapter Eight, you will learn that he also wasted billions of tax dollars on Star Wars, aided Saddam Hussein with weapons of mass destruction, and supported jihad fighters, including Osama bin Laden.

President William J. Clinton's media image and foreign policies illustrate that harmful foreign policies have been promoted by both the Republican and Democratic parties. Highlighting this point, President Clinton supported the presence of U.S. military bases in over a hundred countries around the world. Said more directly, President Clinton supported imperialism and supported authoritarian regimes in places like Middle East. A few other examples during his presidency from 1993 to 2001 reinforce the point that some of the foreign policies of the U.S. have been harmful, For example, his administration continued economic sanctions against Iraq that resulted in the deaths of hundreds of thousands of people. In 1994 he failed to act to help the people of Rwanda and the resulting genocide killed 500,000 to 800,000 people.[89]

The same disconnect between perception and reality is true today as President George W. Bush is repeatedly presented to the American people as a man with a direct line to God. He can relate to ordinary folks with his plain speaking style. Like Ronald Reagan, he rides horses and works on a ranch to relax. He cares about making America safer for the common person. He is working hard to unite all Americans with affordable medical care, family values and workers' rights. He won election and re-election in part due to his fame from the Texas education miracle in which student scores greatly improved on his watch. How does the "media image of the president" compare with his policies?

President George W. Bush has allowed assault weapons back on the streets, making America less safe. He terminated the Anti-Ballistic Missile Treaty, prompting an international build-up of nuclear weapon arsenals. He has told China that the U.S. supports China's expansion of its nuclear arsenals, and he simultaneously promoted developing new U.S. nuclear weapons.[90] In 2005 he rewarded Pakistan's dictator, one of the leading black-market proliferators of weapons of mass destruction, by announcing the United States would supply Pakistan with airborne nuclear delivery aircraft.[91] In 2002 and continuing to 2005, President George W. Bush instructed the Central Intelligence Agency to overthrow Venezuela's democratic government. In 2003 he invaded Iraq and thereby produced more terrorists throughout the Middle East and in many other countries around the world.[92]

In the United States, more Americans are without health insurance and live in poverty than before his presidency.[93] Even simple changes to help reduce medical expenses, like legislation allowing Americans to buy the same but lower-cost drugs from Canada, have been stalled by his administration. Family values are important, but he did nothing to raise the national minimum wage. In addition, a Bush proposal to weaken clean-air rules put three times more mercury into America's air and water than existing rules would allow. One in six women already has enough mercury in her system to risk her unborn baby having brain damage, mental retardation, blindness, seizures, and speech impediments.[94] Investigations into the Texas education miracle revealed the presence of massive state fraud, which resulted in skewed statistics with no real student improvements.[95] We now know that the Texas Miracle was covert propaganda that manipulated Americans to elect and re-elect a president.[96]

Ask yourself why, on President Bush's first Inauguration Day, the major television networks did not show his limousine being pelted with eggs.[97] Certainly this would be of interest to many people. Who were the networks trying to protect, and why were they afraid of distributing this story? The answer is that corporations own news outlets and sometimes want to avoid making enemies of powerful people like a new president. Major news distributors want to avoid upsetting their advertisers. Media executives also know that if they show information that is objectionable, many consumers will turn them off. The media plays to its audience, whether it is Fox, NPR, or Aljazeera. This dynamic is related to the point at the beginning of this chapter: that we want to hear or see that which reinforces what we already believe.

In addition, so-called "experts" such as former generals, think-tank researchers, and other experts are often included in news reports. The problem is that rarely do these experts come from non-government or non-corporate sponsored organizations. The "money talks" expression is applicable here. The world needs more experts who do not have a financial interest in war or imperialism. Consider the Iraq war for a moment. With the billions of dollars flowing into the war on Iraq, does it make sense that consumers are likely to be exposed to experts who want to keep the revenues coming in?

It is also noteworthy that Americans work longer hours than people in most of the other First World nations. The International Labor Organization noted that on average Americans work 2.5 weeks longer than Australian, Canadian, Japanese and Mexican workers. Compared to Germans, Americans work on average 12.5 weeks more each year.[98] America is geographically isolated and the citizens are much more likely to be monolingual than people in many countries. As a result, Americans are often too busy to concern themselves with global events. For the percentage of Americans who make an effort, coverage of foreign policy issues is increasingly rare. Consider the dramatic decline of foreign coverage by the U.S. media. The time devoted to foreign news on network television, for example, has declined from 45 percent in the 1970s to 13.5 percent in 1995. Time magazine devoted 24 percent of its pages to international coverage in 1985 and only 14 percent ten years later. Newsweek dropped from 22 percent in 1985 to 12 percent in 1995.[99] Today, what little international coverage is presented is primarily consumed by the war in Iraq.

Many Americans say they don't have time to read books. Television is their primary source of information about what is happening around the world. In view of the decline in international coverage, is it any wonder that Americans are often uninformed about U.S. foreign policy? Given all of this, what happens to the news that Americans do receive? Whether on television or from newspapers, it gets watered down; and often facts that would disclose what is really happening are not aired.

Walter Cronkite observed that Americans are highly uninformed and misinformed by the news. He calculated that in a 30-minute news broadcast, only 16 or 17 minutes were available after the lead-in and commercials. Cronkite said, "The material that flows over the newsroom desks each day cannot be handled in the proper detail." Observing that Americans live in a very complex world, he noted that it is impossible to present the important issues of the day in 16 or 17 minutes. He recommended that CBS, NBC and ABC expand their nightly news offerings to one hour from a half hour. He also argued strongly that the networks should use news magazine shows more wisely. Cronkite said, adding that magazine shows focus too much on sex, crime and scandal, "Why don't they take those hours and do instant documentaries, which they are certainly capable of doing?"[100] Mr. Cronkite observed that a very real threat to the American democracy is the uninformed and apathetic electorate. The problem is self-perpetuating as viewers see the news they prefer seeing. The electorate is choosing to be poorly informed.

The electorate also is poorly informed because the media ends up playing the role of propagandist due to invisible forces that are consistently distorting the news.[101] Noam Chomsky and his co-author Edward S. Herman have documented how these information filters distort what is presented by the media. The five information filters are money, advertising, reliance on information by experts, flak or disciplining the media, and anti-communism (now anti-terrorism).

There is widespread belief among people I speak with that the media has a liberal bias. This is the conclusion reached by media personalities Ann Coulter, Bill O'Reilly, Sean Hannity, and Bernard Goldberg. While it is possible to find evidence for an argument that media outlets are biased, the book What Liberal Media? concludes that media representatives are far more conservative and the difference is that conservatives do a better job of complaining about bias. For this reason, media representatives are careful not to project a liberal bias and tend to present a more conservative message.[102]

The sequence and larger context of video images has a tremendous impact on the message delivered. To obtain a powerful appreciation for how television and even documentaries can be spun to promote a specific agenda, I recommend watching Outfoxed, Fahrenhype 9/11 and Michael Moore's Fahrenheit 9/11.[103] The three "documentaries" were created to influence public opinion prior to the 2004 presidential elections. Watching all three will demonstrate that who produces the message controls the message.

Bob McChesney, founder of Free Press, observed in Outfoxed that Fox News successfully distorts the truth. Under the cover of "fair and balanced," Fox assumes the image of a respected news outlet while aggressively pushing biased political viewpoints. Fox's reporting can help you see the very real difference between objective reporting and government propaganda.[104] Propaganda is especially effective when consumers of information limit their understanding of an issue to a headline or listening to a brief broadcast. McChesney believes journalists should be concerned when "the more people consume your media, the less they'll know about the subject and the more they'll support government policy."

Understanding that Fox is heavily biased, you can see why average citizens have such a hard time agreeing on facts. The PIPA/Knowledge Networks poll in October 2003 highlighted just how successful the Fox propaganda has been at misleading Americans.[105] The survey asked:

- Does world opinion favor the U.S. invasion of Iraq? The correct answer is no. Fox viewers who answered yes: 35%. PBS-NPR viewers who answered yes: 5%.
- Has the U.S. found links between Saddam and al Qaeda? The correct answer is no. Fox viewers who answered yes: 67%. Again PBS-NPR viewers were far more likely to know the correct answer with 16% answering yes.
- Has the U.S. found weapons of mass destruction in Iraq? The correct answer is no.[106] Fox viewers who answered yes: 33%. PBS-NPR viewers were far more likely to answer correctly, with only 11% answering yes.

Scary? You bet. What can you do about it? Stop watching Fox. Encourage your friends who watch Fox to view Outfoxed so they can understand how hatred, fear, anger and revenge are packaged to help the presenters turn the truth around.

COVERT PROPAGANDA

Americans will someday be shocked to learn the extent of government produced covert false news that is broadcast on televisions, radios and published in newspapers. The tip of this propaganda iceberg is beginning to be seen. In March 2005 reporters David Barstow and Robin Stein disclosed that at least 20 federal agencies in the Bush administration have made and distributed hundreds of television news segments between 2001 and 2004.[107] These new segments are covert because the source is not identified, the reporters are often actors with aliases, and the information is presented as an actual event and not a staged performance.[108]

The practice of government propaganda inside the United States may be a reflection of the Voice of America success. The Voice of America has produced for decades false new reports for distribution outside of the United States. This is legal under the 1948 Smith-Mundt Act. Today, in clear violation of that act, false news segments are produced for domestic consumption. A leading key source of domestic U.S. government propaganda is a State Department unit called the Office of Broadcasting Services.

On April 9, 2003, a master deception took place when U.S. troops pulled down the statue of Saddam Hussein in Firdus (Paradise) Square. The event was hailed as the equivalent of the fall of the Berlin Wall and was repeatedly broadcast by U.S. television networks. The staged event had multiple serious problems. First, on April 6, 2003 Ahmed Chalabi, the founder of the Iraqi National Congress, was flown into the southern Iraqi city of Nasiriyah by the Pentagon. He was accompanied by 700 of his "Free Iraqi Forces" on four C-17 military transport planes.[109] Upon arrival, Ahmed Chalabi was photographed in Nasiriyah with a militia member who was photographed a few days later as the local Iraqi who welcomed the U.S. soldiers in Firdus Square. His presence suggests that other members of the "Free Iraqi Forces" were in Firdus Square.

Deema Khatib, a journalist, observed that the individuals in the immediate area of Saddam Hussein's statue were uniform in appearance. Specifically she noted they were of a similar age, all male, and had accents that were not from Baghdad.[110] Khatib asked, "how come one of them had the flag of Iraq before 1991 in his pocket? Has he just been waiting there for ten years with the flag on that square? I don't think so. But this is not something that the U.S. like media would talk about...They (the CIA) brought them in with them."[111] Khatib made her observations not knowing that the "Free Iraqi Forces" had been flown to Iraq by the United States just three days earlier.

The Marines reported a lack of Iraqi resistance as they approached Firdus Square.[112] This may have been because with fewer than two hundred people in the square, the other 500 "Free Iraqi Forces" were able to help clear the path and provide additional order for the approach of the Marines. The U.S. soldiers arriving in Firdus Square had no knowledge that they were part of an orchestrated media event. Lacking the ability to notice the different Iraqi accents, they failed to realize they were welcomed by "Free Iraqi Forces" actors who had recently arrived from the United States.

Second, a long-shot Reuters photo revealed not a crowd of celebrating Iraqis but a staged media event with access to the area controlled by U.S. tanks. This perspective was very different from the media broadcasts suggesting that thousands of Iraqis were jubilant that the Americans had taken Baghdad. The Reuters photograph shows much of Firdus Square as empty, with no more than two hundred people crowded around Saddam Hussein's statue. Vice President Dick Cheney and other Bush administration officials were quick to step forward and point out that the U.S. was being welcomed as liberators. In response to the fallen statue of Saddam, Cheney said the advance of U.S. troops into Baghdad is proof that early criticism of the war plans was misguided.[113]

Third, potentially hostile media were removed from the area on April 8th by multiple U.S. military strikes that killed three reporters. As a result of the April 8th killings, the organization Reporters Without Borders demanded an investigation of potential war crimes, with evidence that the reporters were assassinated.[114] British journalist Robert Fisk, in Baghdad at the time, asked: "Was it possible to believe this was an accident? Or was it possible that the right word for these killings – the first with a jet aircraft, the second with an M1A1 Abrams tank – was murder?(...) So the facts should speak for themselves. Unfortunately for the Americans, they make it look very like murder."[115]

Fisk observed that "the U.S. jet turned to rocket the al-Jazeera's office on the banks of the Tigris at 7.45 am local time on April 8, 2003. The al-Jazeera television station's chief correspondent in Baghdad, Tariq Ayoub, a Jordanian-Palestinian, was on the roof with his cameraman, an Iraqi called Zuheir(...) Mr. Ayoub's colleague Maher Abdullah recalled afterwards that both men saw the plane fire the rocket as it swooped toward their building(...) Mr. Abdullah said, 'the plane was flying so low that those of us downstairs thought it would land on the roof – that's how close it was. We actually heard the rocket being launched. It was a direct hit – the missile actually exploded against our electrical generator. Tariq died almost at once. Zuheir was injured.'

The next assault, on Reuters, came just before midday when an Abrams tank on the Jamhuriya Bridge suddenly pointed its gun barrel towards the Palestine Hotel where more than 200 foreign journalists were staying to cover the war from the Iraqi side. Sky Television's David Chater noticed the barrel moving. The French television channel France 3 had a crew in a neighboring room and videotaped the tank on the bridge. The tape shows a bubble of fire emerging from the barrel, the sound of a detonation and then pieces of paintwork falling past the camera as it vibrates with the impact.

In the Reuters bureau on the 15th floor, the shell exploded amid the staff. It mortally wounded a Ukrainian cameraman, Taras Protsyuk, who was also filming the tanks, and seriously wounded another member of the staff, Paul Pasquale from Britain, and two other journalists, including Reuters' Lebanese-Palestinian reporter Samia Nakhoul. On the next floor, Tele 5's cameraman Jose Couso was badly hurt(...) Mr. Couso had a leg amputated but he died half an hour after the operation."

The net effect of the events on April 8, 2003 was the immediate clearing of the Firdus Square area of potentially hostile members of the media. The stage was set for Saddam Hussein's statue to fall the following day. The stage even included the necessary massive American and Iraqi flags to cover Saddam's face so that both U.S. and international audiences could receive the optimal "Berlin Wall Moment" on their local news networks. The performance even included a massive rope for the mock hanging of Saddam. Does anyone really think military units travel around with massive spools of poor quality rope, as exemplified by the giant rope put around the statue's neck?[116]

How can the media be so easily fooled or in some cases directly involved? To answer this question, consider that control of Fox employees is direct, with owner Rupert Murdoch giving specific direction and instructions. Fox experts need to present the Republican party message or their contracts will be terminated. A good example is Larry Johnson, a former CIA agent, who was released from his contract with Fox for saying that invading Iraq might divert resources from the hunt for al Qaeda. Outfoxed also exposes that 83 percent of the guests on Fox's Brit Hume show are Republicans, which should be a concern to any viewer who believe that Fox is a "fair and balanced" news broadcaster.

Unfortunately, Fox's blatant propaganda and substitution of angry arguments for news is spreading to traditional networks. General Electric's NBC (GE is the parent company) and the Disney-owned ABC are also performing a great disservice to the American public by failing to address the issues noted by Walter Cronkite. Until the American people speak up and demand objective reporting, the problem will continue to worsen and America's democracy will continue to be undermined.

As ownership of the media becomes increasingly consolidated, the message turns ever more into the state message. Americans appreciate the need for separation of church and state, and should also demand separation of media and state. America's democracy is seriously undermined by this trend. Consider Rupert Murdoch, whose media corporation owns 175 newspapers, 100 cable channels, 40 television stations, nine satellite TV networks and one movie studio.[117] Though Fox is described simply as a conservative news network, in reality it is a distribution mechanism for partisan Republican propaganda.

In summary, the media is increasing controlled by a few wealthy people. Covert propaganda is no longer broadcast only by the Voice of America. Separation of the media and the state is blurring and this threatens America's democracy. To be informed, America's citizens must actively pursue information, instead of receiving only what the major media distributors present. The Internet, books, world travel, and discussions with others are critical to becoming informed and, thereby, protecting America's democracy.

POWER INFLUENCED BY APATHY AND MONEY

As we enter the 21st century, we find ourselves with leadership increasingly influenced by a wealthy few. America's democracy is undermined when wealthy individuals dilute the power of individual votes. Media outlets enable well-funded efforts to successfully broadcast messages that dilute the power of votes by poorer people. Well-funded candidates are able to flood the airways with negative campaigns having little to do with the opposing candidate's program, but which are extremely critical of the person's personal attributes. The well-financed side wins, as a result of the negative campaigning, if enough people change their vote or simply feel that voting for the attacked candidate is an unproductive exercise.

We have a government of, by, and for, the very rich, made possible through lobbyists, self-seeking politicians and a disinterested population. This may seem "radical," but consider a few supporting points before you let this label disable your thinking. The top one percent now own more than the bottom

90%. Bill Gates alone has as much wealth as the bottom 40% of U.S. house-holds.[118] The point is that one person, with millions of dollars to promote a candidate or issue, can magnify their single vote exponentially.

POWER INFLUENCED BY WORLD OPINION

As hard as it may be for many people who live in the United States to imagine, America is not perceived across the globe as a beacon of light, peace, prosperity and democracy. The United States is perceived as the greatest threat to global peace in many places in the world.[119] America's traditional allies in Europe clearly communicate this when they are polled. The 1999 to 2003 trend discovered by the Pew Research Center is alarming, showing dramatically declining favorable opinions of the United States.

In October 2003, Donald Rumsfeld's stated, "Today, we lack metrics to know if we are winning or losing the global war on terror. Are we capturing, killing or deterring and dissuading more terrorists every day than the madrassas and the radical clerics are recruiting, training and deploying against us?"[120] He was wrong: the metrics do exist. Rumsfeld failed, and he continues to fail to acknowledge the metric of world opinion.

To illustrate a few of the declines from 1999 to 2003, consider Britain, where favorable opinions of the U.S. fell from 83% to 48%; Germany from 78% to 25%; Italy from 76% to 34%; and Turkey went from 52% to 12%.[121] Contrary to President George W. Bush's message that America is hated because of America's democracy, the Pew Research Center 44-nation survey found an appreciation for the free market model and democratic ideals, even in the majority of Muslim publics surveyed.[122] The dissatisfaction of the majority of the world is not with the way Americans think or the way Americans behave at home. The dissatisfaction stems from America's foreign policies.

The Pew Research Center surveys found that President George W. Bush's foreign policies were the source of the dramatic unfavorable opinions. While the finger of blame is pointed first at President Bush, international anger extends beyond one person and is summarized by the Pew research as the United States doing too little to solve world problems and too much to widen the gap between the global rich and poor.

Investigative reporter James Fallow observed that the soldiers, intelligence experts, academics, and diplomats he has interviewed are unanimous in saying they do not agree with the president's "They hate us for who we are" statement.[123] He notes that the danger in believing the president's lazily and self-justifying statement is that it ignores how Islamic extremism has evolved. Michael Scheuer, was the head of the CIA's anti-bin Laden team. He has said, "There are very few people in the world who are going to kill themselves so we can't vote in the Iowa caucuses(...) But there's a lot of them who are willing to die because we're helping the Israelis, or because we're helping Putin against the Chechens, or because we keep oil prices low so Muslims lose money."[124] When I met Michael Scheuer in 2005, he reinforced the latter statements with the observation that not a single CIA Middle East analyst agrees with the reasons President Bush has given the American people for the war on terrorism.[125]

Anger with America's foreign policies is hard for Americans to understand, in part because Americans have a wonderful system of democratic checks and balances at home. Unfortunately, the public is generally unaware of America's foreign policies; and citizens lack a meaningful system of checks and balances for them. In the early years of America's growth, the Atlantic and Pacific oceans served as a geographical check and balance on America's foreign policies. Advances in transportation, communication and information technology have made the world smaller and global business a reality.

Put another way, business globalization, a potentially positive worldwide development for strengthening relationships among countries, is currently a key underlying driver for the decline in worldwide satisfaction with the United States. The connection of big business to the highest office in the land comes from the fact that leaders of corporations make substantial campaign contributions. Corporations can do this because their employees are often encouraged to join Political Action Committees or PACs. PACs pool funds of corporate executives and other employees to pay lobbyists that serve the interests of the corporation. This powerful financial driving force behind those who reach the presidency and Congress is undermining America's democracy. As a result, once in office, leaders are inclined to return the favor with foreign policy decisions favorable to their corporate sponsors. Since only humans can vote, America's democracy would be stronger if elected officials were accountable to voters and not corporations.

POWER INFLUENCED BY FEAR

Fear is routinely used in America's election process and by the government to manage consent. The "fear factor" has morphed from a television show into an essential part of regular news broadcasts. As is done in dictatorships, fear is increasingly being used to control America's electorate. The messages by both candidates in the 2004 presidential campaign were filled with dire warnings. Unfortunately, the policies of the Bush administration are giving Americans real reasons to be afraid, and the American Hiroshima specifics in the prior chapter solidify this point.

An excellent example of power influenced by fear is the U.S. Homeland Security Advisory System. The five-color system starts at level one (the green level). This "low condition" indicates a low risk of terrorist attacks. Level two or the blue "guarded level" is declared when there is a general risk of terrorist attacks. Level three or the yellow "elevated condition" implies a significant risk of terrorist attacks. Level four or the orange "high condition" is declared when there is a high risk of terrorist attacks. The final level, level five, is the red "severe condition." A severe condition communicates a severe risk of terrorist attacks. Americans do not need to live in a world where anything other than a green level is the normal condition. America's policies in the Middle East make a green or blue level impossible, effectively limiting the possible conditions to yellow, orange and red. The power of the Bush administration to wage war is reinforced by what is in practice a three color coded warning system. When Americans wake up and realize that an alternative future is possible, and act to make it a reality, a world where the green condition is common will be possible.

A DILUTION OF AMERICA'S DEMOCRACY

The Electoral College is administered by the National Archive and Record Administration, or NARA. It is essentially a process established by the founding fathers as a compromise between election of a president by Congress and election by popular vote. Under this compromise, the people of the United States vote for electors who then vote for one of the candidates for president. The process for selecting electors varies among the states. In general, the political parties nominate electors at their state party conventions or by a vote of the central committee in each state. The voters choose the electors on the day of the general election when they cast their votes for president.

Why were the founding fathers concerned about a popular vote? They feared that popular rule could result in a loss of their wealth and power.[126] This was not accidental: the richest man in America at the time was George Washington.[127] John Hancock, Benjamin Franklin and the other founding fathers were financially among the top one percent of their day.

The Electoral College is an anachronism that undermines America's democracy and credibility when the U.S. government calls for "fair elections" around the world. Why not put an end to it? You may hear the answer that the Electoral College is part of the original design of the U.S. Constitution and it would be necessary to pass a Constitutional amendment to alter it. This is a fancy way of side-stepping the issue and not answering the question of why America has the Electoral College. A democracy where the president is elected by the people instead of the Electoral College is what the definition of democracy demands.

The 2000 Gore and Bush presidential contest highlighted this deficiency in America's democracy. George W. Bush lost the popular vote to Al Gore, but became the 43rd president by winning in the Electoral College.[128] In 2004,

Colorado tried to lead the way for reform with Amendment 36. Amendment 36 would have made Colorado the first state to allocate electoral votes according to the popular vote rather than giving a winner all of the state's electoral vote.[129] The majority of the people in Colorado voted against Amendment 36 because the majority of the state wanted President George W. Bush to receive all nine and not just five of the electoral votes. Citizens in Colorado seeking to correct the Electoral College dilution of individual votes, while not successful in 2004 with Amendment 36, have demonstrated that bottom-up solutions to protecting America's democracy can be pursued. If citizens in Colorado and other states pass legislation like Amendment 36, the 2008 presidential election will be closer to "one person, one vote."

The continued existence of the Electoral College is a sign of an uninformed and complacent electorate. As more states stop the Electoral College's undermining of America's democracy, the United States benefits internationally with more credibility in calling for fair elections around the world. The time is now to have the Electoral College fade into the history books.

This chapter has highlighted reasons why Americans are often uninformed. Americans need to confront the reality that U.S. foreign policies are unknown to its citizens. These foreign policies, left unchecked by the American people, have conflicted with the same values of free speech, fair elections, the right to assemble, freedom of religion and an impartial justice system that have helped Americans prosper. The point is not to dwell on the negative but stress that strengthening America's democracy at home will help other democracies abroad and thereby make the world a safer place. When Americans become informed and say no to manipulating the internal affairs of other nations, America's democratic values and generous spirit will be welcomed by the world.

3

ADDICTIONS

"Ancient Athens has been one of the most admired of all societies, praised for its democratic institutions and its magnificent cultural achievements...What the experience of Athens suggests is that a nation may be relatively liberal at home and yet totally ruthless abroad. Indeed, it may more easily enlist its population in cruelty to others by pointing to the advantages at home. An entire nation is made into mercenaries, being paid with a bit of democracy at home for participating in the destruction of life abroad."

(Howard Zinn)[130]

LIKE ANCIENT ATHENS, AMERICANS ARE addicted to the American way of life and citizens are quick to turn a blind eye to injustice. Throughout America's history, the country has supported injustice when the economic price of opposing it was seen to be too onerous. Yet Americans have also overcome tremendous challenges and created a better country. History has taught Americans that supporting injustice risks the loss of America's democracy. This point is illustrated by the addiction to slavery that almost destroyed the country. Today, the United States is addicted to oil and the Middle East is thirsting for water. Understanding what America is dependent on, and the fact that wars are being fought to secure these resources, can help you see why America's foreign policies are jeopardizing America's democracy.

SLAVERY WAS ONCE THE FUEL OF AMERICA'S ECONOMY

Slavery was once an addiction that threatened America's democracy. If we step back to the time of Thomas Jefferson, we'll see that, then, the problem of slavery seemed unsolvable – yet it became solvable in time. Thomas Jefferson was born in 1743 and died in 1826. He is the author of the Declaration of Independence and was the third president of the United States (1801-1809). In this period, citizens found a way to rationalize the injustice of slavery.

That slavery could be a normal part of everyday life can seem unbelievable to most people today. Why did Thomas Jefferson and most free citizens in his time perceive slavery as an acceptable practice? Is it possible that we live in a time where we accept equally tragic injustices?

Time often serves as a lens that illuminates the truth. In Thomas Jefferson's time, slaves were the fuel that drove a large part of the economy in the United States. Oil is the fuel that drives today's economy. Money can cloud decision-making. It did in Jefferson's day and it continues to be as powerful a force today. Americans no longer tolerate the evils of slavery, but do tolerate the injustices prevalent in non-democratic oil-producing nations.

A key lesson that we take from slavery is that any policy that treats one human as less valuable than another is unjust. As Jefferson said, "We hold these truths to be self-evident, that all men are created equal; that they are endowed by their creator with certain unalienable rights; that among these are life, liberty and the pursuit of happiness." Jefferson's words are applicable both inside and outside the United States. When America's foreign policy contradicts Jefferson's words, injustice is the result. History has proven that when injustice exists, we need to aggressively promote justice by exhausting all peaceful alternatives.

If we are indirectly or directly supporting an unjust situation, the usual result is an escalation of demands of justice with violence. The violence produces additional suffering which produces more violence. The hearts of the oppressors become harden and their eyes and ears find it more difficult to see and hear the injustice that started the sequence of escalations.

DEPENDENCE ON OIL THREATENS AMERICA'S DEMOCRACY

Dependence on oil is undermining America's democracy. A cab driver once mentioned to me that his family in Egypt loved America because he was able to provide for the needs of ten people back home. He went on to say, "America is great because it helps people all over the world. People in America do not understand the injustice their government supports. The people who are born here are quick to close their eyes when oil is an issue. A foreign state that keeps the price of oil reasonable is a friend even though that same government may persecute citizens that demand the right to organize or to speak freely."

Oil has influenced America's foreign policies in ways that many Americans fail to appreciate. Oil was a major catalyst for war long before the Iraq wars began. Consider for a moment the defining act that motivated the Japanese to attack the United States in 1941. The United States Senate passed an oil embargo against Japan in the summer of 1941. For the Japanese, the oil embargo was the first shot fired, starting the war with the United States. For many Americans, the war with Japan began with Pearl Harbor. The Japanese surprise attack on Pearl Harbor started a cycle of killing people. From a loss of life perspective, the war did start on December 7, 1941. The point here is that the killing often flows from economic reasons that tend to be lost in the fever of patriotism and calls for war.

The war with Japan was a war for control of oil, rubber, tin, nickel and other economic resources in the Pacific.[131] But as we can see, over time, the victor will redefine the original reasons for fighting the war in terms that align with widely-supported values. The war becomes a fight for freedom or to restore justice vs. economic stability or profits.

The impact of oil on America's foreign policy continues to blind America's decision-making. Why did the United States lead the Gulf War campaign to free Kuwait, and yet not intervene in the Rwanda genocide? While the situations are not identical, a reasonable person could conclude that if Rwanda had possessed rich oil fields, the United States response would have been immediate and substantial. Independence from oil will illuminate many of the injustices of America's foreign policies that support authoritarian regimes which are often corrupt and violate basic rights that we often take for granted at home. When we support governments that do not seek democracy, we risk helping create terrorists. The fact that the majority of the 9/11 highjackers were from Saudi Arabia makes this point painfully clear.[132]

The disconnect between America's democracy and America's relationship with the Islamic monarchy of Saudi Arabia drives home this point. We value free speech, yet non-Muslim worshippers in Saudi Arabia risk arrest, imprisonment, deportation, and torture. The simple act of giving a Saudi citizen a Bible is illegal. In a step in the right direction, the U.S. State Department issued a September 2004 report concluding that in Saudi Arabia "freedom of religion does not exist."[133] Persecution of non-Muslim religions is based in Saudi Arabia's Constitution, which is the Koran. Why not demand free speech and freedom of religion of any nation that earns America's most favored trading partner recognition?

Understanding the role of oil and other materials needed by industry is essential in preventing conflict and simultaneously maintaining justice. Justice and peace go hand in hand. If we are to err, then we should err on the side of peace. As Cicero in his Letters to Atticus said, "I prefer the most unjust peace to the justest war that was ever waged." The truth to these words demands that the factors that precede war be understood.

OIL INDEPENDENCE AS A NATIONAL PRIORITY

Americans like to be part of something bigger than ourselves in order to improve the nation and the world for future generations. This is why putting the first person on the moon was supported by a generation of Americans. Yet the current generation has the opportunity to do something even bigger than sending a person to the moon. All Americans can put a foot on this new world that is free from oil wars, pollution from fossil fuels and end America's willingness to support injustice overseas. Just like the Apollo missions, the United States can put the best scientists to work to solve the remaining technological challenges to developing clean coal, fuel cells, solar, wind, geo-thermal, and other yet-to-be discovered efficient sources of energy.

Eliminating dependence on oil and efforts to better use the world's resources is a key lever for moving to a more peaceful world. Is this possible, or an unattainable dream? Simply changing America's fuel efficiency requirements to what is technically possible today would eliminate America's dependence on oil from the Middle East. For example, U.S. vehicles currently consume two-thirds of the oil in the country, with an average of 20 miles per gallon. If Congress raises fuel economy standards for all new cars to 40 miles per gallon – and this is technologically possible right now – by the year 2020, the United States will be saving 4 million barrels of oil every day. That's more than the U.S. currently import from the Persian Gulf.[134]

Americans certainly have the ability to transition to an average of 40 miles per gallon and completely eliminate the need to import oil from the Persian Gulf. New cars would on average be smaller; but it's a better solution than having soldiers and other innocent civilians dying to maintain the status quo. The current hybrid cars already achieve around 50 miles per gallon. Adding plug-in technology where a car is charged by electricity brings the miles per gallon to 75. Replacing a conventional fuel tank with a flexible-fuel tank that can run on a combination of 15 percent petroleum and 85 percent ethanol can result in 400 to 500 miles per gallon of gasoline.[135] Unfortunately, increasing fuel efficiency is rarely discussed as a way to stop the flow of funds to places like Saudi Arabia.

The United States has an abundance of coal, but needs technological advances to seize the energy from coal in a way that is friendly to the environment. Alternatives like clean coal, hydrogen, wind and solar will someday enable a level of clarity comparable to the clarity that grew in the United States when the New England economies started to become "free" of the need for slaves to sustain their economic system.

WATER AS A DEPENDENCY IN THE MIDDLE EAST

We understand America's dependency for oil. Have you ever thought about what you would need but have in short supply, if you lived in many places in the Middle East? The answer is water. The Middle East is home to five percent of the world's population and only one percent of the world's renewable water supply.[136] In addition, the population in the Arab world is approximately 280 million people. This population, comparable to the population of the United States, is on track to double by the year 2025.[137] Iraq is a critical strategic location for both al Qaeda and the United States not just because of Iraq's oil, but because Iraq has the most extensive fresh water system in the Middle East.

A nation without enough water is in a worse position than a nation without enough oil. Understanding the role of water in the Middle East explains why there is no exit strategy from Iraq and why many Middle East experts predict the United States will be in Iraq for decades. Even Donald Rumsfeld, with a track record of being overly optimistic about the cost and duration of the Iraq war, in July of 2005 began to set expectations that the war will continue until 2017.[138]

Iraq's water is as important to the United States as control of Iraq's oil. There is a saying in the Arab world that the person who controls the well also controls the people. Knowing that Iraq's water is a key reason our soldiers are being maimed and killed, can help you evaluate what is really going on in the Middle East. The United States is building 14 "enduring" or permanent military bases in Iraq. Pieces to the puzzle, like the locations of the 14 permanent military bases and likely duration of the American occupation, can suddenly become crystal clear when you consider the locations of the Euphrates, Tigris, Greater Zab and Lesser Zab rivers. One only need look at the Nasiriyah "enduring base" on the Euphrates in South-East Iraq to understand the strategic value of water. A map of Iraq's rivers and the permanent U.S. military bases can be found at the www.americanhiroshima.info site.

Some countries lack both oil and water.. Israel is one nation that needs both and is increasingly having problems providing water for its growing population. Desalination and water imports by air or sea are economically expensive, although, compared to military spending, desalination is actually a bargain. For example, the cost of one jet fighter will pay for a desalination project to provide 100,000 people with water.[139] Israel, with less than 200 millimeters of annual rainfall, has few options for drinkable water.[140] Current overpumping is depleting the main sources of water faster than they can be replenished. Israel's projected water shortage by the year 2010 is 360 million cubic meters.[141]

Water conflicts have been frequent in the Middle East. Israel is another country that needs a new source of fresh water to satisfy the needs of a growing population. As background, Israel and its neighbors, with water-related fighting in 1951, 1953, 1965-66, 1967, 1969, 1982 and 2001.[142] Israel's 1951 conflict with Syria began when Israel started draining the Huleh swamps in the demilitarized zone between Israel and Syria. In 1967, the Six Day War was in large part a result of Israel's construction of its National Water Carrier. The National Water Carrier appropriated much of the Jordan River for Israel's use. The Arab League began to dig canals to divert the Hasbanin and Wazzani

Jordan tributaries. Israel shelled both projects, ending them.[143] As part of this war, Israel also blew up a dam Syria was building on the Yarmouk River. Israel further strengthened its water resources by securing the Golan Heights, Gaza and the West Bank. The Sinai Peninsula was the only property seized that did not provide Israel with new sources of water. The Sinai Peninsula was returned to Egypt in 1979, with the complete pull out of Israeli forces in 1982.[144]

Today, the Palestinian Authority has many villages without any water supply. Access to aquifers is controlled and curtailed by Israel. This began in 1967, when Israel imposed strict quotas on Palestinian water consumption. Palestinians are forbidden to dig new wells or deepen existing ones. Thousands of Palestinian citrus trees were uprooted, cisterns demolished, and natural springs and existing wells blocked.[145] As a result, Palestinians often must collect the occasional rainwater or obtain water from delivery trucks. Palestinian wells are increasingly drying up because nearby Israeli settlements dig deep wells that swallow up the water in the shallower Palestinian wells. Israeli technology enables water wells to be dug to 750 feet, far below the 100 feet depth of Palestinian wells. Author Diane Raines Ward captures the words of one Palestinian, "No one can accept that he does not have water to drink and his neighbor has a swimming pool."[146]

Today, about 30 percent of Israel's water comes from the Jordan, 40 percent from ground water, and 30 percent from treated wastewater.[147] Even if Israel does not withdraw from the Golan Heights, where the Mountain Aquifer is located, the supply of fresh water is insufficient for the area's population.[148] Syria is unwilling and unable to help. Israel is obtaining limited help from Turkey. Israel negotiated to buy 50 million cubic meters of water from Turkey for the next two decades.[149] Turkey's Manavgat River would be the source for this limited relief to Israel's water shortage. Water would be delivered by transporting water in ships from the Manavgat River in southwestern Turkey to the Israeli port of Ashkelton. The problem with obtaining water from Turkey is, without alternative sources of water, Israel will increasing become dependent on a Muslim nation that is not controlled by the United States for a strategic resource.[150]

Iraq, with the region's most abundant water resources, was out of the question as an Israeli source of water prior to the Iraq war. Israel for reasons that include and extend beyond water, hopes that the U.S. will be successful in pacifying Iraq. Control of Iraq's rivers could alter the destiny of the Middle East for decades.[151] While the Bush administration fears that Americans will not support fighting a war to control Iraq's water, Americans deserve to know the truth. The truth is that in addition to oil, water is a real reason for the invasion of Iraq. Our soldiers, their parents, and all citizens have a right to know when the price that is required is in blood and in billions of dollars.

Don't be fooled by the occasional messages that our troops will leaving in a few years. The Pentagon is planning on occupying Iraq for decades. The Pentagon's long-range strategic plan is likely to require an American occupation far beyond Donald Rumsfeld's optimistic 2017 forecast.

4

TERRORISM

"You must be the change you wish to see in the world."

(Mahatma Gandhi)

TERRORISM IS DEFINED AS THE systematic use of violence to achieve an end.[152] By this definition, one can understand why Iraqis see collateral damage to their homes and people as acts of terror. This chapter highlights the fact that all imperial powers have had to fight wars against terror. In many respects, Middle Eastern acts of terror against the United States began to spread like a wildfire after the democratically elected prime minister of Iran was overthrown by the American and British intelligence services. These events in 1953 are discussed, as well as the undeniable connection between the United States' support for Israel and resulting Arab acts of terror. This chapter concludes with foreign policy behaviors that give birth to terrorists.

A BRIEF HISTORY OF RECENT EMERGENCIES

Great Britain has fought many wars against terrorists, because terrorism is a problem that flows naturally from being an imperial power. Britain called these wars "emergencies." The American Revolution was one of these emergencies, and America's founding fathers were considered terrorists by King George III.[153] The need for Britain to fight emergencies declined as Britain's imperial occupations declined. It took Great Britain a long time to learn that you eventually lose when the other force has the home-team advantage. While Tony Blair's administration is having a memory lapse on this learning point: we should learn from past "emergencies."

You may be thinking that the analogy with Great Britain is unfair because you think the United States has not been imperial and has only supported a few corrupt dictators. Perhaps you do not know that the United States has fought in more than 65 countries since 1945. Current fighting in Afghanistan and Iraq follows a long series of interventions after World War II. William Blum's analysis, condensed and supplemented with additions in Appendix D, summarizes a selection of United States interventions.[154]

The following is an updated list of the countries and the dates of the U.S. interventions.

- China, 1945-49
- Philippines, 1945-53 and 1970s-1990s
- South Korea, 1945-53 and 1980
- Vietnam, 1945-73
- Soviet Union, 1940s-1960s
- Marshall Islands, 1946-58
- France, 1947
- Italy, 1947-48
- Greece, 1947-49 and 1964-74
- Eastern Europe, 1948-56
- Albania, 1949-53
- Germany, 1950s
- Iran, 1953 and 1987
- Guatemala, 1953-1990s
- British Guiana/Guyana, 1953-64
- Costa Rica, mid 1950s, 1970-71
- Cambodia, 1955-73
- Middle East, 1956-58
- Indonesia, 1957-58 and 1965
- Laos, 1957-73
- Iraq, 1958-63, 1972-75, 1990s to present
- Haiti, 1959, 1987-94 and 2004
- Cuba, 1959 to present
- Ecuador, 1960-63
- The Congo/Zaire, 1960-65 and 1977-78
- France/Algeria, 1960s
- South Africa, 1960s-1980s
- Brazil, 1961-64
- Dominican Republic, 1963-65
- Chile, 1964-73
- Bolivia, 1964-75
- Yemen, 2002

- Peru, 1965
- Thailand, 1965-73
- Ghana, 1966
- Uruguay, 1969-72
- Australia, 1972-75
- Portugal, 1974-76
- East Timor, 1975 to present
- Angola, 1975-1980s
- Jamaica, 1976
- Nicaragua, 1978-90
- Seychelles, 1979-81
- Grenada, 1979-83
- South Yemen, 1979-84
- Afghanistan, 1979-92 & 2002 to present
- Honduras, 1980s
- El Salvador, 1980-92
- Chad, 1981-82
- Libya, 1981-89
- Suriname, 1982-84
- Lebanon, 1983-84
- Fiji, 1987
- Panama, 1989
- Bulgaria, 1990-91
- Peru, 1990s to present
- Mexico, 1990s to present
- Colombia, 1990s to present
- Kuwait, 1991
- Albania, 1991-92
- Somalia, 1993
- Bosnia, 1994-95
- Yugoslavia, 1995-99
- Pakistan, 2005

- Venezuela, 2002-2005

William Blum concludes, "The engine of American foreign policy has been fueled not by a devotion to any kind of morality, but rather by the necessity to serve other imperatives, which can be summarized as follows:

- making the world safe for American corporations;
- enhancing the financial statements of defense contractors, who have contributed generously to members of Congress;
- preventing the rise of any society that might serve as a successful example of an alternative to the capitalist model;
- extending political and economic hegemony over as wide an area as possible, as befits a great power."[155]

Noam Chomsky and Edward Herman have also contributed significantly to the understanding of U.S. foreign policy in their work on client states. In 1979 they wrote The Washington Connection and Third World Facism. This book provides a detailed account of the United States' key role in the military takeovers of 18 Latin American countries between 1960 and 1976.[156]

TERRORIST ATTACKS AGAINST THE UNITED STATES

Reviewing acts of terror against Americans up to 9/11 is eye-opening. A key theme is that each act of violence is a response to an injustice that occurred far before the attack. United States support for Israel is interwoven into many of the acts.

Middle East terrorism against the United States in many respects begins in 1979, and was a response to the first U.S. overthrow of a foreign government by the Central Intelligence Agency in 1953. Government officials such as Madeline Albright have acknowledged this once highly classified historical event.[157] The CIA's detailed plan is now known to the public. The operation was documented in 1954 by one of the coup's chief planners, Dr. Donald N. Wilber. The document details how United States and British officials plotted the military coup that toppled Iran's elected prime minister.[158]

The planning for the coup began in 1952 when the United States and Britain feared Iran's plans to nationalize its oil industry.[159] Both the Central Intelligence Agency and the Secret Intelligence Service (more commonly known as MI6, or the arm of British intelligence that conducts espionage overseas) selected retired General Fazlollah Zahedi to replace Mossadegh. In early August 1953, Iranians working for the Central Intelligence Agency and posing as communists harassed religious leaders in a campaign to turn the country's Islamic religious community against Mossadegh's government. Shah Mohammed Riza Pahlevi feared overt involvement and he refused to sign the CIA-drafted royal decrees to dismiss Prime Minister Mohammed

Mossadegh and empower General Zahedi. The Central Intelligence Agency arranged for the shah's twin sister, Princess Ashraf Pahlevi, and General H. Norman Schwarzkopf (the father of Norman Schwarzkopf, Jr. who led the United States forces in the 1991 Gulf War) to influence the Shah to sign the decrees. On August 13, the Shah did sign.

CIA efforts to topple Mossadegh became more serious earlier in 1953. Allen Dulles, the director of the CIA, approved one million dollars on April 4, 1953 to be used "in any way that would bring about the fall of Mossadegh."[160] The coup started on August 15, 1953. The coup was prematurely revealed a few hours before it started and General Taghi Riahi, Mossadegh's chief of staff, was informed of the plot. General Taghi Riahi immediately notified the pro-Mossadegh forces. The pro-Shah soldiers sent to Mossadegh's home, having lost the advantage of surprise, were captured. The following morning Iranians learned on the radio that a coup against the government had failed.

The Shah fled the country and went to Baghdad and later to Rome. On August 17, 1953, the C.I.A. organized a "council of war" with General Zahedi, Iranian CIA operatives, and Iranian army officers at the U.S. embassy. The people at this meeting decided to enlist a leading cleric from Tehran to call for a holy war against communism. These same religious people the CIA attempted to manipulate would years later declare the United States "the Great Satan." The secret meeting at the U.S. embassy concluded with an agreement that another coup would begin in two days. On August 19, 1953, General Fazlollah Zahedi succeeded and Mossadegh was overthrown.[161] The CIA covertly funneled five million dollars to General Zahedi's regime on August 21, 1953.[162]

While the 1953 coup was classified and kept unknown in the United States, the operation was, and is commonly known by Iranians. In 1979, 80 Iranian students took over the United States embassy, fearing that the events of 1953 were going to be repeated.[163] The students specifically feared that the United States would restore the Shah.[164] Had the United States not illegally intervened in the affairs of Iran in 1953, the Islamic students would not have kidnapped U.S. embassy personnel in 1979.

Israel's occupation of Palestinian lands is a common catalyst for acts of terror. You may be surprised by how frequently Hezbollah shows up on the following summary of terrorist attacks against the United States. Hezbollah is funded and supported by Iran. Its attacks on United States targets are often attempts to end U.S. support for Israel's occupation of Palestinian lands. As confirmed by the 9/11 Commission, the United States increasingly gets caught up in the mix because of its economic and military support for Israel.[165]

Al Qaeda did not participate in any attacks on Americans prior to 1992. This is because (as discussed in the chapter Alliances With Killers) President Reagan was assisting these same people in their fight against the Soviet Union during the Soviet occupation of Afghanistan that ended in 1989.

The following list is a compiled and condensed summary of notable terrorists acts against the United States from the Frontline Target America[166] and Frontline The Man Who Knew[167] timelines.

November 4, 1979: Fifty-two American citizens were taken hostage at the U.S. embassy in Tehran when students of Islam stormed the U.S. embassy in Tehran. The hostages were released just hours after Ronald Reagan's presidential inauguration on January 20, 1981 after 444 days in captivity.

May 6, 1981: Libyan leader Muammar el-Qaddafi had plans to assassinate American diplomats in Rome and Paris. President Reagan expelled all Libyan diplomats from the U.S. and closed Libya's diplomatic mission in Washington, D.C.

April 18, 1983: An Iranian-backed Hezbollah suicide bomber also supported by Syria drove a pickup truck with explosives into the U.S. embassy in Beirut. Sixty-three people were killed, including 17 Americans.

October 23, 1983: A Hezbollah suicide bomber detonated a truck full of explosives at a U.S. Marine barracks located at Beirut International Airport. The attack killed 241 U.S. Marines.

December 12, 1983: Members of al Dawa or "The Call," an Iranian-backed group, bombed multiple targets in Kuwait. Targets included the American embassy, the French embassy, the control tower at the airport, the country's main oil refinery, and a residential area for employees of the American corporation Raytheon. Five people died in addition to the suicide bomber.

The 1983 al Dawa terrorist attack took place because President Ronald Reagan was supporting Saddam Hussein. Al Dawa was one of the principal Iraqi Shiite groups operating against Saddam Hussein. If the U.S. did not provide military support to Saddam Hussein, al Dawa would have had far less of a reason to attack in Kuwait.

The pattern of terrorism is always the same. People risk their lives committing terrorist acts because something was done to them, not because they have nothing better to do or are "freedom haters."[168]

March 16, 1984: Hezbollah kidnapped and later killed CIA Station Chief William Buckley. Eventually, 30 westerners would be kidnapped during the 10-year-long Lebanese hostage-taking crisis that ended in 1992.

September 20, 1984: Hezbollah sponsored a truck bomb in Aukar, northeast of Beirut, that exploded outside the U.S. embassy annex, killing 24 people.

December 3, 1984: Hezbollah's Imad Mughniyah planned the hijacking of Kuwait Airways Flight 221. Two American officials from the U.S. Agency for International Development were killed. On the sixth day, Iranian security forces stormed the plane and released the remaining hostages. Iran arrested the hijackers and then allowed them to leave the country.

June 14, 1985: Hezbollah hijacked TWA Flight 847 as the plane departed Athens for Rome and was forced to land in Beirut, Lebanon. Robert Dean Stethem, a U.S. Navy diver held hostage on the plane, was shot and his body dumped on the airport tarmac.

October 7, 1985: The Palestine Liberation Front and Libya collaborated to highjack the passenger ship Achille Lauro off the coast of Egypt by four gunmen demanding the release of Palestinian prisoners. Leon Klinghoffer, an American tourist, was killed by Magid al-Molgi.

December 27, 1985: Libya exploded bombs in the Rome and Vienna airports killing 20 people.

April 5, 1986: Libya sponsored the La Belle Discotheque bombing in Berlin, wounding over 190 people and killing an American soldier and a Turkish woman. On April 15, 1986, President Reagan ordered retaliatory air strikes on Tripoli and Benghazi, killing 37 people and injuring 93 others. Two days after the U.S. retaliatory operation, the Arab Revolutionary Cells, a pro-Libyan group of Palestinians, executed three men in retaliation.

December 21, 1988: Libyan intelligence officers bombed Pan Am Flight 103 over Scotland, killing 270 people.

December 29, 1992: The first al Qaeda attack took place when a bomb exploded at a hotel in Aden, Yemen, killing two Austrian tourists.

February 26, 1993: The first al Qaeda act of terror in the United States was the truck bomb in the garage of the World Trade Center. [169]

October 3-4, 1993: Al Qaeda-trained Islamic followers attack U.S. soldiers in Somalia. The "Black Hawk Down" violence results in the deaths of 18 U.S. soldiers and an estimated 500 local people caught in the crossfire.

April 19, 1995: Timothy McVeigh bombed the Alfred P. Murrah Federal Building in Oklahoma City.

June 26, 1996: The al Qaeda organization exploded a gasoline tanker in Dhahran, Saudi Arabia, killing 19.

August 7, 1998: An al Qaeda explosion in the Nairobi capital partially destroyed the U.S. embassy.

October 12, 2000: Al Qaeda suicide bombers in Yemen attacked the USS Cole and killed 17 sailors.

December 29, 2000: An al Qaeda terrorist was captured attempting to enter the United States with a car full of explosives. His intended target was the Los Angeles airport.

September 11, 2001: Al Qaeda attacked the World Trade Center and Pentagon using suicide teams that hijacked commercial airplanes. Over 3,000 people were killed in New York, Washington and Pennsylvania.[170] Original al Qaeda plans included suicide teams to crash airplanes into nuclear power stations and a West Coast skyscraper.

Support of Israel and involvement in oil-rich countries have been key behaviors sparking the prior summary of violence. A pattern that will unfortunately continue is terrorist attacks are now dramatically increasing as a result of the U.S. invasion of Iraq. The U.S. State Department, now refusing to release 2005 and future statistics, previously reported 175 significant terrorist attacks in 2003 and 625 terrorist attacks in 2004.[171]

In the history of the United States and the history of acts of terror, attacks are not because of a democratic form of government or America's freedoms at home. Acts of terror are usually because of something that is done overseas – America's foreign policy. Don't be fooled into thinking that the current wars must be fought for the sake of democracy and freedom. By understanding who is sponsoring terrorists and why, justice can be brought to criminals and injustices can begin to be addressed. The clear message is injustice produces acts of terror and therefore we need to work for justice. As many famous people have noted, if you want peace, work for justice.

SOWING THE SEEDS TO CREATE TERRORISTS

Using foreign militias and economic sanctions to fight terrorists may sound like a good idea, but in practice, they can be disastrous. In August 2004, the Bush administration asked Congress to provide $500 million to fund militias around the world.[172] Paul Wolfowitz, a key architect of the Iraq war and the man who dismissed al Qaeda as a threat prior to 9/11,[173] presented the reasoning for this new strategy in the war on terror. His supporting argument is that local militias can win wars that conventional American armed forces cannot. Perhaps this is why President Bush suggested on August 30, 2004 that the war on terror cannot be won.[174]

During Wolfowitz's presentation to Congress, he failed to mention that al Qaeda is the result of a formerly-friendly militia that the United States armed and funded in Afghanistan in the 1980s. As described in Chapter Five on Alliances With Killers, Osama bin Laden transformed the Afghan jihadists who fought against the Soviet Union in the 1980s into al Qaeda. Paul Wolfowitz also failed to mention that militias often have local enemies that they have been trying to eliminate for hundreds or even thousands of years. As a result, the agenda of the United States tends to quickly fall to the side as local militias pursue their own agendas. The United States gets sucked into conflicts with people and groups Americans are not even aware are combatants.

Funding foreign militias is neither a new idea nor a good one. The United States use of Army Green Berets and CIA ground instructors to train local militias has come back to haunt America time and time again. History is being ignored. The criminal activity and acts of terror that resulted from similar policies in places like Central America have ended up doing more harm than good.

In 1987 to 1988, while in the U.S. Army, I served on a rapid deployment team with special training to intervene in Central America. At that time, the School of the Americas in Fort Benning, Georgia, was training Central and South Americans who fought for their foreign governments and in local militias under the direction of the CIA.[175] In countries like Honduras, a staging ground for the war in Nicaragua, religious leaders and others who disagreed with the government were routinely assassinated by graduates of this school.

In Honduras, a military intelligence unit called Battalion 316 was secretly supported by the Reagan administration. On March 9, 1981, Ronald Reagan signed a presidential "finding" to "provide all forms of training, equipment, and related assistance to cooperating governments throughout Central America in order to counter foreign-sponsored subversion and terrorism." On December 1, 1981, he ordered the CIA to work primarily through "non-Americans" against the Sandinistas in Nicaragua and leftist insurgents in El Salvador. United States military aid to Honduras jumped from $3.9 million in 1980 to $77.4 million by 1984, three years after Battalion 316 started in 1981.[176]

The stories of torture by Battalion 316 are horrifyingly similar to what would occur 20 years later in Iraq when the U.S. military held prisoners at the Abu Ghraib prison. Prisoners in Honduras were hooded, had nooses tied to their necks and wires for shock treatment attached to their bodies. Part of the previously-classified manual the CIA used in Honduras is available at www.americanhiroshima.info. One example of the abuses by Battalion 316, the torture of Ines Consuello Murillo, is presented on page 47 and illustrates the similarities with Abu Ghraib.

A brief review of Abu Ghraib also helps illustrate the convergence of two very different interrogation standards. The U.S. military for decades has aggressively taught soldiers not to torture prisoners. I know this well because I taught soldiers how to interrogate battlefield prisoners when I served as an Army Intelligence Officer. By contrast, the CIA has taught interrogation techniques that – as a result of the Abu Ghraib scandal – are now universally accepted as torture. The reason Americans never realized this is the CIA did a better job of keeping their operations unknown and – more importantly – the CIA interrogation methods were exclusively performed by citizens of other countries.

In Abu Ghraib, Donald Rumsfeld reportedly, in a highly secret operation called Copper Green, authorized torture.[177] Prior to Iraq, he had authorized torture in the Guantanamo detention center to help find the al Qaeda leadership. Donald Rumsfeld was upset to find in 2003 that the intelligence from Iraqi prisoners was far less useful than the intelligence from Guantanamo. He ordered General William Boykin to develop a program to "migrate the coercive techniques" from Guantanamo to Iraq. In simple terms, the order was to start torturing prisoners in the Abu Ghraib prison. This order was significant because it was the first time Regular and National Guard Army personnel, taught a very different understanding of what is permissible under the Law of Land Warfare rules, would observe and participate in torture.

In addition to General Boykin, the Undersecretary of Defense for Intelligence, Stephen Cambone, was a key Copper Green architect. In addition General Richard Myers and Major General Geoffrey Miller were key Cooper Green leaders. In total, fewer than two hundred people were granted a need-to-know for Copper Green. This type of program is called a Special Access Program, or SAP. Alberto Gonzales, the Attorney General that replaced John Ashcroft in President Bush's second term, helped provide the legal guidance for the physical coercion and sexual humiliation of prisoners. To assist President Bush's desire to use "coercive techniques," Gonzales issued a memo saying that the Geneva Convention, as well as treaties signed by the United States banning torture, do not apply to illegal combatants or terrorists. Donald Rumsfeld ran with the legal approval from Alberto Gonzales with reported statements to SAP operatives such as "the rules are, grab whom you must. Do what you want."[178] As a result of this memo, Alberto Gonzales, now the country's leading law enforcement official, had to pledge during his confirmation hearing that he would no longer support torture.[179]

To change from the U.S. military interrogation standard to the CIA standard, General Boykin ordered Major General Geoffrey Miller to Iraq. Not coincidentally, Miller was the leader of the detention and interrogation center at Guantanamo. In short order he transferred the Guantanamo methods to Abu Ghraib. The internal Army report on the abuse charges, written by Major General Antonio Taguba, confirms this point. Taguba disclosed that Miller influenced the commanders in Baghdad to change the interrogation policy and place intelligence officers in charge of the prison. In Taguba's report, Miller was quoted as recommending that "detention operations must act as an enabler for interrogation."[180]

President Bush clearly misled the country about all this in the State of the Union Speech on January 27, 2005. He said "Torture is never acceptable, nor do we hand over people to countries that do torture." On February 28, 2005, Michael Scheuer confirmed that he was one of the authors of a CIA program that performed what they called "extraordinary renditions."[181] He said that he and other members of the CIA knew that they were sending people to countries, such as Egypt and Syria, that employed torture in their prisons.[182] Under this secret rendering program, people can and have been seized by the U.S. around the world, without charges or evidence, for export to a country that practices torture. This also means that any person can be taken from the United States and sent to countries that practice torture.

A CBS investigation found that a jet used by the CIA for the extraordinary renditions program had made at least 600 flights to 40 countries since September 11, 2001. Uzbekistan was visited 10 times, Jordan 30 times, Afghanistan 19 times, Morocco 17 times and Iraq 16 times.[183] In January 2002, William Howard Taft IV raised a red flag in response to the presidential directive that Alberto Gonzales and John Yoo helped create for the president. Jane Mayer reported that Taft urged Gonzales and Yoo to warn the president that he would "be seen as a war criminal by the rest of the world" if he did not abide by the Geneva Conventions. Gonzales and Yoo disagreed. Jane Mayer, in an article for The New Yorker, noted that she spoke with Yoo and he said Congress "can't prevent the president from ordering torture" during a war. "It's the core of the Commander-in-Chief function."[184]

The CIA became concerned that ordinary and "good" soldiers would expose the torture. They feared a widespread investigation that would reveal that these practices have been part of U.S. covert operations for decades. Donald Rumsfeld, in an ongoing saga of poor judgment, did not anticipate the very predictable dynamic that would explode when ordinary soldiers observed obvious Law of Land Warfare violations. With the re-election of President Bush, Americans have rewarded an administration that has secretly promoted torture.

SAP operations are covert, which is different from clandestine. Clandestine is an operation meant to be undetected. Covert means that the U.S. government denies its responsibility or – said more directly – lies. America's democracy would be stronger if Americans made all covert operations illegal and did not permit the government to lie. Under U.S. law, a covert action is subject to very strict legal requirements. Specifically, covert action must be authorized by the president with prompt notification of the senior leaders of both parties in the House and Senate. In other words, Copper Green, the Top Secret program for torture, required President Bush's approval and congressional oversight.

Lawmakers have attempted to learn more about secret intelligence teams and SAPs.[185] The Pentagon sent its top intelligence official in January 2005 to address concerns from Congress that congressional oversight had been bypassed. Larry DiRita, chief spokesman for Defense Secretary Donald

Rumsfeld and Stephen A. Cambone, the Undersecretary of Defense for Intelligence, misled Congress.[186] They correctly acknowledged the existence of the Strategic Support Branch that is managed by the Defense Intelligence Agency's Human Intelligence Service. Lawmakers were told the Strategic Support teams were previously called Humint Augmentation teams. Humint refers to human intelligence and is a standard military intelligence specialty. Lawmakers were misled because the real question was quite different. Were covert Special Action Programs or SAPs being used to bypass Congress? Senator Dianne Feinstein, a member of the Senate Intelligence Committee, sent a letter to Donald Rumsfeld seeking an explanation and requesting a hearing. She and other Democrats were effectively ignored, as the explanation provided by DiRita and Cambone was deemed sufficient by Congress.

Another way to say this is that Strategic Support teams obtain their priority information requirements from the Defense Intelligence Agency through the military command structure. SAP teams obtain their priority information requirements directly from Donald Rumsfeld. By using the military for covert operations, Donald Rumsfeld has the military performing operations normally performed by CIA. When the protocols for covert operations are not followed, specifically obtaining approval from Congress, these operations are illegal. Without congressional oversight or any other checks and balances on SAPs, Donald Rumsfeld could initiate a variety of secret missions, including the assassination of an American citizen, with little risk of anyone finding out.

Illegal intelligence operations, like Copper Green, extraordinary renditions, or Battalion 316 in Honduras, sow the seeds for the abuse of innocent civilians. The Abu Ghraib- like torture in 1983 of Ines Consuello Murillo, a Honduran woman, highlights this point. What is unique about Ines Consuello Murillo's captivity is that her story was reported by The Baltimore Sun and discussed by the 1988 Senate Select Committee on Intelligence.

In June 1988, Richard Stolz, the CIA Deputy Director of Operations, testified before the Senate Select Committee on Intelligence that a CIA officer had visited the jail where Battalion 316 had held and tortured Ines Consuello Murillo. The Baltimore Sun confirmed that Michael Dubbs, a CIA officer, was stationed in Honduras at the time. The CIA did not confirm or deny that this was the "Mr. Mike" who visited Ines Consuello Murillo. The point in making the connection between a CIA officer and a prison that was visibly torturing people is that the CIA absolutely knew that people there were being tortured. This lends some credibility to claims by Hondurans that the torture was at the request of the CIA and performed by locals trained by the CIA.[187]

There are many sad stories in Central America like the Ines Consuello Murillo story. The aid workers and missionaries I work with in Honduras vividly recall the numerous assassinations and disappearances during the 1980s. Much of the violence in Central America during the 1980s was related to the secret war the United States started with Nicaragua. A quick refresher on the specifics of the war with Nicaragua may be helpful. In 1978, the United States attempted to install a new leader in Nicaragua. The transfer of power between Anastasio Somoza and a new leader the United States supported became irrelevant after the Sandinistas seized the capital.

On July 19, 1979, when the Sandinistas marched victoriously into Managua, the United States did not have a rapid deployment military unit that could quickly restore order in Central America. In retrospect, a U.S. battalion inserted in the first 48 hours, followed by a division in the next 72 hours, was believed to be all that would have been needed to defeat the Sandinistas. It was believed that after a few days, only a much bigger military intervention would have been able to set things straight. With Vietnam as a recent public memory, an invasion of this magnitude was unlikely to be supported by the American people. My own military division, the 7th Light Infantry or "Light-Fighter" Division, was created in direct response to what happened in Nicaragua. As a result, in the mid-1980s, the United States could deploy a battalion anywhere in Central America within 48 hours and a division within a week.

The secret war in Nicaragua was in motion with the funding Congress approved for the Contras between 1982 and 1988. The secret war became less secret when the CIA mined Nicaragua's harbors in 1984. The Reagan administration imposed a full trade embargo against the Sandinistas in 1985. In 1986, the full extent of the Reagan administration's secret war was exposed when illegal weapon transfers to Iran were revealed to the world. President Reagan's support and funding for the Contras, the U.S.-formed and supported militia to fight the Sandinistas, resulted in torture, deaths and unnecessary suffering in Central America. His ill-conceived foreign policy, under the pretext of fighting communism, undermined America's credibility and relationships in Central America, South America and even worsened the situation in the Middle East.[188]

ECONOMIC SANCTION HAVE HELPED CREATE TERRORISTS

The seeds for future problems were also planted following the Gulf War, when economic sanctions were led by the U.S. and enforced by the United Nations. The United Nations adopted sanctions in its 1945 charter as a bonafide tool to maintain global order. In total, sanctions have been authorized 14 times, with 12 of the 14 occurring since 1990. Iraq's sanctions were unique in that they were comprehensive, and every aspect of the country's imports and exports were controlled.

If Americans had understood the economic sanctions against Iraq in the

1990s, then they would not be surprised by the ever-expanding insurgency in Iraq. The U.S. turned a program of international governance into a program of revenge because the U.S. government was overly focused on Saddam Hussein. The ineffectiveness of sanctions is demonstrated by the U.S. continuing to have economic sanctions against Cuba. Sanctions against Cuba, still in place because of hatred for Fidel Castro, have only strengthened this dictator's hold on Cuba for decades.

So why would sanctions work against promoting justice, freedom and, ultimately, peace in the world? The comprehensiveness of Iraq's sanctions meant that obtaining even basic necessities was obstructed. Since 1990, the United Nations estimated that at least 500,000 Iraqi children under the age of five have died because of economic sanctions.[189] In 1996, Madeleine Albright, then the U.S. secretary of state, was asked on national television what she felt about the fact that 500,000 Iraqi children had died as a result of U.S. economic sanctions. She replied that it was "a very hard choice," but that, all things considered, "we think the price is worth it."[190] It is noteworthy that this number far exceeds the deaths from the atomic bombs dropped on Japan.

Iraq's sanctions were enforced by the Security Council 661 Committee through the Office of Iraq Program. The Office of Iraq Program operated the Oil for Food Program. The Oil for Food Program was first offered in 1991 and went into effect in 1996. The Oil for Food Program was a $62 billion initiative that allowed Iraq to sell oil to pay for humanitarian goods. Documents surfacing as recently as late 2004 showed that Saddam Hussein used the system to buy political support from the United Nations and other well-placed world officials. The scandal was especially harmful as it further weakened the United Nations.[191]

According to Joy Gordon, a professor of philosophy at Fairfield University, the U.S. strategy since 1991 was to withhold a single essential element, so that approved items were still useless. This policy was to seek revenge for Saddam Hussein's outspoken criticism of the United States and support of Israel. For example, Iraq was allowed to purchase a sewage-treatment plant, but was blocked from buying the generator necessary to run it. As a result, tons of raw sewage poured into Iraq's rivers. The estimate is that 300,000 tons of sewage flowed into Iraq's rivers each day.[192]

Saddam Hussein, oddly enough, actually benefited from economic sanctions. The people of Iraq focused their frustration and hatred on the U.S. and Britain for imposing the sanctions. A population distracted by survival needs such as clean water is in a very weak position to build opposition to a bad government. In addition, Saddam Hussein was able to reach out to the Arab world for sympathy because of the Iraqi suffering that was broadcast throughout the Middle East as a result of these sanctions. It is generally known in the Middle

East that before the Gulf War, the majority of Iraq's population had access to clean water and health care. Iraq's social programs in the two decades prior to the Gulf War brought health care to 93% of Iraq's people.[193]

The 661 Committee operated by consensus and every member had veto power. The U.S. and Britain routinely vetoed proposals by France, China and Russia. Between the spring of 2000 and 2002, the holds on humanitarian goods tripled.[194] Goods blocked by the U.S. included dialysis equipment, water tankers, milk production equipment and dental supplies. While some items, like water tankers, could be arguably a means to move chemical weapons, the U.N. arms experts confirmed that water tankers lacked the necessary lining to be useful for military purposes and therefore were not on the restricted "1051 list." Delegates from Argentina, France and other nations pleaded with the U.S. representatives for flour to be approved because it was an essential element of the Iraqi diet.[195] The U.S. representative, Eugene Young, argued that "there should be no hurry to move on this request." Britain agreed that the flour should be blocked and the request did not go forward.

On March 20, 2000, Anupama Rao Singh reported to the 661 Committee that 25 percent of the children in the south and central regions suffered from chronic malnutrition.[196] She also reported that child mortality rates had more than doubled since the sanctions were imposed in 1991. Many members of the Security Council have been critical of the U.S. decisions to block humanitarian contracts. In April 2000, the U.S. informed the 661 Committee that $275 million in humanitarian holds had been released because the personnel needed to review the contracts had been hired. Another way to look at this is that critical life-or-death humanitarian aid had been stuck in a hold status for many years simply because the United States did not allocate the basic resources to review the requests. As of September 2001, nearly a billion dollars in medical-equipment contracts were on hold for the simple reason that the U.S. had not reviewed the contracts.[197] No matter how you look at this, people were dying.

Key items that the United States blocked included water pipes and the earth-moving equipment to install them. This is critical to note because the number one killer of children and adults in Iraq was the lack of clean water. Prior to 1990, at least 90 percent of all urban households had access to potable water.[198] Since the Gulf War, diseases that had been largely eradicated skyrocketed and child and infant dysentery killed thousands of children. The mortality rate in 1980 for children under five years old was 50 per thousand. In 2002, the mortality rate was 130 per thousand.[199] For the most part, the children died as a direct or indirect result of contaminated water.

In early 2001 the U.S. placed holds on $280 million in medical supplies.[200] Blocked medical supplies included treatments for hepatitis, tetanus, diphtheria, and infant vaccines. Even infant incubators and cardiac equipment were blocked. It was quite certain that preventing child vaccines from entering Iraq would result in the deaths of thousands of babies. To address the negative publicity and international public outcry against the ban on infant vaccines, a new program in 2001 was created called "smart sanctions." In June 2001, the U.S. announced that key contracts would be unblocked.[201] The net effect of this new program was to slow down the approval process. Staff for the new "smart sanctions" program needed to be hired and the new rules learned. The clock kept on ticking and children kept on dying.

The most dangerous item in water purification is chlorine, but chlorine was one of the few items approved to ship to Iraq. Every canister of chlorine for water purification was tracked through arrival, installation and disposal. Why was the most threatening element allowed and humanitarian goods excluded? Does this have anything to do with who is selling the goods? Items sold by the United States or Security Council members had a much greater chance of being authorized and not blocked. The only countries that blocked goods were the U.S. and Britain.

The United States and Britain made the situation worse by introducing retroactive pricing. Iraq's basic ability to sell oil was undermined because the price of the oil was established by the 661 Committee. By delaying approval until after the shipment occurred, the U.S. and Britain could establish the price after the sale. The effect of retroactive pricing was to undermine the entire Oil for Food Program. Buyers did not want to take the risk of knowing the price only after delivery.

With over 500,000 children dead (and a far higher death toll if adults were counted), the average Iraqi on the street was extremely angry at the United States and Britain for the economic sanctions.[202] The massive preventable deaths and suffering were known by President George W. Bush. While no country appreciates being invaded, the massive preventable deaths are a key reason why projections that the invading American force would be welcomed by the Iraqi people were simply lies to help sell the war to the American people.[203] This is also why the senior military commanders who projected the realistic requirement of at least 500,000 U.S. ground forces were quickly forced into retirement.

Imagine the size of the insurgency force in Iraq today if there were just one insurgent fighter for every child under the age of five that died from economic sanctions. The reality is that every person murdered comes back to life in the form of multiple insurgents. The same is true for the adults that died from military operations. If the U.S. government revealed the classified estimate for insurgents in Iraq, the number would likely far exceed one million people.

Time has a way of helping people understand that terrorists and heroes can be the same people, depending on which side of a war you are supporting. This sounds crazy when we apply it to today. However, it makes sense if we apply it to less emotionally charged times.

In 1876, after Custer's famous last stand, Americans clearly saw the Lakota chief Sitting Bull as a terrorist. Officers in the U.S. Army's 2nd Infantry Division wear a patch of an Indian on their uniforms in memory of the "successful" Indian wars. Many officers, including myself, have been given tomahawks upon joining this military unit. The holder of the tomahawk is the "victor" as this was the weapon used by native Americans. Few members of the military are offended or even take a moment to wake up and realize that the tomahawk is really a symbol of the genocide of thousands of children, women and men. An analogy would be for Rwanda's soldiers to be given machetes in the next century to acknowledge the success of the Rwanda genocide.

Today, many Americans now see Sitting Bull as a hero and General Custer as a destroyer of families. As Americans have come to understand that the genocide of native Americans was unjust, the perception of Sitting Bull and native Americans in general has changed to reflect this understanding.[204] As illustrated with Sitting Bull and General Custer, the clarity from stepping out of the economic drivers of war and the calls to hate other people can make anyone who uses violence to promote their cause a terrorist.

5

ALLIANCES WITH KILLERS

CROSS THE GLOBE, THE SO-CALLED "golden rule" is cherished. Many religions and philosophies provide variations on its message.

Islam: "No one of you is a believer until he desires for his brother that which he desires for himself."

Buddhism: "Hurt not others in ways that you yourself would find hurtful."

Confucianism: "Do not do unto others what you would not have them do unto you."

Hinduism: "This is the sum of duty: do not do unto others that which would cause you pain if done to you."

Judaism: "What is hateful to you, do not do to your fellow man."
205

Christianity: "You have heard that it was said, 'You shall love your neighbor and hate your enemy.' But I say to you, love your enemies, and pray for those who persecute you."[206]

This chapter explains the shocking reality of how the United States worked with both Saddam Hussein and Osama bin Laden in the 1980s, and how the results have threatened America's democracy. This may be hard to believe, especially with all the media coverage showing President George W. Bush claiming that a collaborative relationship existed between Saddam Hussein and al Qaeda. While there was never a relationship between Saddam Hussein and al Qaeda, both of them were partnering with the United States in the 1980s. The Reagan administration and President Bush's father, President George H. W. Bush, used U.S. tax dollars to help Iraq fight Iran. The moujahedeen, including Osama bin Laden, were also supported by U.S. tax dollars to fight the

Soviets in Afghanistan. After reading this chapter you may wonder if an Evil Alliance is different from an Axis of Evil.

The golden rule applies for both good and bad, and "what goes around comes around." The historical details are important, so let's start with Saddam Hussein in Iraq. You may wish to refer to the map of the Middle East on page xiv to obtain a better sense for Iraq's borders.

WE STILL HAVE THE RECEIPTS FROM THE WMD
WE GAVE SADDAM HUSSEIN

We gave Saddam Hussein the key ingredients to make chemical and bio-logical weapons to use against Iran. Shocking? Yes and the details follow. First, however, I wish to stress that appeasing Saddam Hussein or al Qaeda is tantamount to giving a criminal more resources to become a bigger criminal. To understand the appropriate path to "fighting" these very different challenges, we need to begin with understanding how these criminals came to power and were helped when they should have been condemned. Americans should also be thinking who are the future Saddams or Osamas that the United States is now helping to create.

Saddam Hussein will no doubt be remembered in history as one of the leading mass murderers of our time. In the 1980s he was a threat to his neighbors and his human rights violations were forgiven by the United States because President Reagan wanted Iraq to inflict as much damage on Iran as possible to seek revenge for the 1979 Iranian hostage crisis. The 1980-1988 Iran-Iraq war was, in many ways, the catalyst for Iraq's subsequent invasion of Kuwait in 1990. The invasion of Kuwait resulted in the Gulf War that started on January 17, 1991. The Iraq war that started in 2003 is, in many respects, a continuation of the Gulf War.

Understanding the interdependencies between these wars requires understanding how Kuwait was created. The border between Kuwait and Iraq has been tense ever since the British Colonial Office established Kuwait as a separate country in 1961. Historically, during the Ottoman rule, Kuwait was a district of Iraq. Kuwait was split from Iraq for profit and strategic advantage because of its oil resources and Persian Gulf waterfront boundary. The country name Kuwait is a diminutive of an Arabic word, meaning fortress built near water.[207] As a result, reuniting Kuwait with Iraq has been a policy of Iraqi leaders since the 1960s.

As a refresher on the Iran-Iraq War, sometimes referred to as the first Persian Gulf War, this war began on September 22, 1980 and ended on August 20, 1988. The war was fundamentally a war over the Shatt al-Arab waterway, which is important for the oil exports of Iraq and Iran. Following the 1979 Iranian Revolution, Iran was a tempting target for Saddam Hussein as it was clear that the United States would not intervene in any conflict there. To start the war, Saddam Hussein accused Iran of attempting to assassinate Foreign Minister Tariq Aziz. In June of 1982, a successful Iranian counter-offensive recovered all Iraqi-held Iranian terroritory.

Concerned that Iran might win the war, the United States aggressively supported Iraq with weapons and economic aid. In particular, the United States provided Iraq with ingredients to make biological and chemical weapons. Donald Rumsfeld met with Saddam Hussein in 1983 as President Reagan's Middle East envoy. His mission was to provide military and intelligence assistance, because the United States feared that Iran would win the war it was fighting with Iraq. The fear of the U.S. was that if Iran won, the Iranian Revolution of 1979 would spread fundamental Islam throughout the Middle East and deny America access to needed oil resources. Perhaps this is why Donald Rumsfeld was so confident when he told the world he knew exactly where the weapons of mass destruction were located.[208]

As part of the program to assist Saddam Hussein, the U.S. Centers for Disease Control and Prevention sent anthrax, the bacteria for botulinum toxin, and the germs to create gas gangrene to Iraq's biological weapons labs in the 1980s. The receipts for supplying Iraq with the key ingredients for weapons of mass destruction are part of a 1994 Senate Banking Committee report. Iraq immediately went to work to make weapons from all of the materials supplied by the United States under President Reagan and Vice President Bush.[209]

Iraq informed the United Nations in 1991 that it had been successful at making anthrax, botulinum toxin and gas gangrene weapons. Iraq disclosed that all biological and chemical weapons had been disposed in the summer of 1991 as demanded by the United Nations after the Gulf War.[210] President George W. Bush, knowing that his father and President Reagan had given Saddam Hussein the deadly ingredients, did not believe Iraq had eliminated all of its weapons of mass destruction. President George W. Bush was surprised when it was discovered that Iraq had actually destroyed, as part of the United Nations inspection effort, all of the weapons that the United States had helped Saddam Hussein make in the 1980s.

What would happen to the president's deceptive cover story now that the weapons were destroyed? For obvious reasons, President Bush did not acknowledge his father's and the Reagan administration's weapons of mass destruction link during the 1980s with Saddam Hussein. He also did not want to acknowledge the United States' role in helping Iraq produce weapons of mass destruction that were used to kill thousands of Iranian soldiers. President George W. Bush certainly did not want to give the United Nations credit for its non-violent success story in Iraq. This was a real dilemma if there ever was one. If he told the truth now, the American public could hold him accountable for his prior deception and war crimes. So why not continue to state to God and the world that Iraq has weapons of mass destruction? In the end, it is appalling but true, Saddam Hussein collaborated to create weapons of mass destruction with the United States and even European countries but not with al Qaeda.

The official U.S. policy during the Iran-Iraq War was pure evil: keep both sides fighting for as long as possible since both were threats to U.S. interests. The U.S. started supplying Iran with weapons, as revealed by President Ronald Reagan's Iran-Contra Affair. This betrayal by President Reagan greatly upset Saddam Hussein, as Iraq was in a life-and-death struggle with Iran. A million people died in the Iran-Iraq War and economic development for both countries was set back decades.

The seeds for the 1990 invasion of Kuwait were planted as Iraq was left with fourteen billion dollars in debt to Kuwait.[211] To further understand Saddam Hussein's motivations for starting the 1990 war, Kuwait was pumping oil from under Iraqi territory prior to the war. Saddam Hussein believed the recently concluded Iraqi war with Iran also provided for Kuwait's defense. At the end of the war, Saddam Hussein expected Kuwait to wipe clean all of the debts Iraq had accumulated from Kuwait as a reward for fighting their common enemy. Kuwait refused to forgive Iraq's Iran War debts. These insults, combined with Kuwait's leadership in driving down world oil prices, was seen by Saddam Hussein as the first shot fired. Kuwait was walking on thin ice and Saddam Hussein just needed approval from the United States to set things straight.

A little over two years prior to the Gulf War in 1988, I was in the 107th Military Intelligence Battalion. I mention this because, even at that time, I was convinced and remain convinced now that the Pentagon saw a war coming in the Middle East. My unit was rapidly undergoing a major makeover from jungle operations in Central America to desert warfare. America's weapons, equipment and uniforms went from jungle green to desert camouflage patterns. I did not know where we were going, but I suspected it would be someplace with lots of oil.

Given my recent desert makeover military experience, I was especially sensitive when I heard the news report given by State Department spokesperson Margaret Tutweiler on July 24, 1990. She sent a mixed message in her answer to a question by a reporter. She was asked, "Do you happen to know if the United States has any commitment to Kuwait, to defend Kuwait or to assist it against aggression?" Margaret Tutweiler replied, "We do not have any defense treaties with Kuwait, and there are no special defense or security commitments to Kuwait."[212] Saddam Hussein's intelligence agents were certainly monitoring the pulse in Washington and immediately passed this on to their leader. This is an almost certainty because Iraq was already on the brink of war with Kuwait.

The very next day April Glaspie, the United States Ambassador to Iraq, was summoned to speak to Saddam Hussein.[213] In this meeting, he sought assurances that the United States would not intervene if Kuwait were attacked. In either a miscommunication of strategic proportions, or a trap for Saddam Hussein, April Glaspie responded to Saddam Hussein's query with, "We have no opinion on the Arab-Arab conflicts, like your border disagreement with Kuwait."[214] The reference to a trap is a reasonable theory that the United States wanted to level the playing field in the Middle East by setting in motion a series of events that would result in the destruction of significant Iraqi military capabilities. Prior to the Gulf War, Iraq had the largest military in the Middle East and Iraq's powerful military was a serious threat to Israel.

After the meeting with April Glaspie, Saddam Hussein did not need further U.S. assurances. Nonetheless, on July 31, 1990, Assistant Secretary of State for Near Eastern and South Asian Affairs John Kelly was testifying before a House foreign affairs subcommittee. Representative Lee Hamilton asked John Kelly: "If Iraq, for example, charged across the border into Kuwait and for whatever reason, what would be our position with regard to the use of U.S. forces?" John Kelly replied, "I cannot get into the realm of what if answers." Lee Hamilton asked the follow-up question, "In that circumstance, it is correct to say, however, that we do not have a treaty commitment which would obligate us to engage U.S. forces?" Kelly responded: "That is correct."[215]

Regardless of the misunderstanding or trap rationale, Saddam Hussein felt betrayed by Ambassador Glaspie's reassurance and President George H. W. Bush's subsequent condemnation. Saddam Hussein made the next strategic mistake by holding the ground he seized in Kuwait. The Gulf War lasted from January 17, 1991 to February 28, 1991. The number of Iraqi deaths reported varies due to the fog of war, but the estimate is 158,000 Iraqi deaths, including 86,194 men (of which approximately 40,000 were soldiers), 39,612 women and 32,195 children.[216] The 158,000 war deaths, combined with economic sanctions that followed, guaranteed that the United States would be hated by the Iraqis.

When President George H. W. Bush decided to end military operations, Saddam Hussein was not expected to hold the reins of power for more than a few weeks. Secretary of State James Baker observed, "Did our Arab allies and everybody else think he would not survive a defeat of the type that we administered to him? Yes, they did not think he would survive."[217] To the surprise of President George H. W. Bush, Saddam Hussein survived and, by surviving, he posed a threat to the Bush family (although he could do little in his country's weakened state to pose a threat to the United States). In April 1993, the United States learned that Saddam Hussein had sent his intelligence agents into Kuwait with the objective of assassinating former President George H. W. Bush. The unsuccessful assassination had been planned to take place during the allied Persian Gulf War victory celebrations earlier that same month.[218]

THE FAILED ALLIANCE WITH SADDAM HUSSEIN AND THE 2003 INVASION

With the previous refresher on how the 1990-1991 Gulf War started, the second Iraq war in 2003 may be less startling. The United States started a war with Iraq absolutely knowing that Iraq was not involved in the September 11, 2001 attacks. A comparison to invading Mexico after Pearl Harbor is applicable here. None of the 19 9/11 highjackers were from Iraq. Iraq did not have a single person in the U.S.-run Guantanamo Bay, Cuba, prison camp. If Iraq was a haven for terrorists, and America was holding terrorists from 43 countries, why were none of the 598 prisoners held at Guantanamo Bay from Iraq?[219] In 2004, the State Department removed the list of 45 countries "where al Qaeda has operated" from their online public information. The previously published State Department list exposed the embarrassing but noteworthy facts that Iraq, North Korea, Syria and Cuba were not on the list.[220] The preponderance of information, well known immediately before and after the 9/11 attacks, dispelled the myth that Iraq had any involvement in the 9/11 attacks.[221]

President George W. Bush and his team were advised in the Central Intelligence Agency's October 2002 National Intelligence Estimate (NIE) that the United States "has no specific intelligence information that Saddam Hussein's regime has directed attacks against U.S. territory."[222] The report also noted that Iraq did not have a nuclear weapon or even the materials to make one. Americans tend to forget that Colin Powell and Condoleeza Rice both stated in early 2001 that Saddam Hussein had been disarmed and was no threat to the United States.[223] The bottom line is that there was no information that an attack by Iraq was planned and no evidence of weapons of mass destruction disclosed.[224] The NIE was very clear on the point that Iraq posed no clear and present nuclear weapons threat because Iraq was years away from developing nuclear weapons.

President Bush's October 8, 2002 speech with its warning, "don't wait for a mushroom cloud," was a lie to the American people in order to use fear to build support for the war he already knew he would start in 2003.[225] President Bush and his cabinet absolutely knew that Iraq never posed a mushroom cloud or any other weapons of mass destruction threat to the United States. The mushroom cloud rationale for invading Iraq was cunningly reinforced by other members of the Bush administration. On January 9, 2003, the president's spokesperson, Ari Fleischer, setting the stage for the president's State of the Union speech later that month, said, "We know for a fact that there are weapons there."[226] President Bush fanned America's fear with his statement that, "the British government has learned that Saddam Hussein recently sought significant quantities of uranium from Africa."[227] We now know that this statement was based on a fraudulent document with forged signatures of officials not in office at the time.[228] The fraudulent forged documents about Saddam's uranium purchase were supplied by Italy's intelligence service.[229]

Colin Powell and Tony Blair added fuel to this fire in February 2003. Colin Powell went before the United Nations and misled the world with a case for war based on fabricated information instead of facts.[230] Even what seemed to be concrete evidence, the Iraqi mobile labs, ended up being proven to be vehicles to inflate balloons.[231] Tony Blair, struggling to sell his people on the need for war, acknowledged the British government was caught plagiarizing a 12-year-old academic paper and presenting it as sensitive real-time intelligence.[232] Prime Minister Tony Blair's intentionally frightening announcement that Iraq could launch weapons of mass destruction in 45 minutes was also fabricated.[233] On the eve of the invasion of Iraq, President Bush told the American people that "intelligence gathered by this and other governments[234] leaves no doubt that the Iraq regime continues to possess and conceal some of the most lethal weapons ever devised."[235]

Once the fog of war clears, the real drivers for war are hard to hide.[236] Given the repeated threat of a clear and present mushroom cloud danger if the United States did not immediately invade Iraq, it is not surprising that three out of four Americans supported the decision for war.[237] Americans now know from leaked classified documents like the British Downing Street Memo[238] that Iraq never had plans to attack the United States. The Bush administration knowingly sold as fact the lies that weapons of mass destruction existed and would be used.

Criticism of how the war was packaged for consumption by the American people is not an endorsement for Saddam Hussein. Saddam Hussein was a ruthless dictator and committed severe crimes against humanity. The point that is critical is that Saddam Hussein did not pose a threat to the United States. While Saddam Hussein deserves to be in jail and tried for war crimes, the United States was not justified in starting a war because Saddam Hussein posed a weapons of mass destruction threat to Americans.

You might be thinking that anyone who would gas his own population is a threat to the United States. While this line of thinking is reasonable, at least one key insider refutes this claim by President Bush and his administration. Stephen Pelletiere, the CIA's senior political analyst on Iraq during the Iran-Iraq War, claims that Saddam Hussein never gassed his own people.[239] It is important to note that there is no question that Saddam Hussein did use gas to kill people in combat operations against Iran. Stephen Pelletiere led the 1991 Army investigation that produced a classified version of the Halabja affair. The Halabja murders were specifically cited by President Bush to illustrate that Saddam Hussein gassed his own people.[240]

Stephen Pelletiere has criticized President Bush for deceiving the American people. The classified investigation of the Halabja gassing found it was Iranian gas that killed the Kurds, not Iraqi gas. The classified information was supported by the condition of the dead Kurds' bodies, which showed signs of death by a blood agent. Iran used a cyanide-based gas or blood agent during the battle in Halabja but Iraq did not possess a blood agent weapon at that time. Pelletiere further stressed that the United States classified investigation did not uncover a single incident where Saddam Hussein used gas against his own people.

Saddam Hussein killed many people in many ways. Perhaps the senior CIA analyst who had access to the best information to determine Saddam's involvement at Halabja will be proved wrong about this and other gassing murders. The point in noting this is not to support Saddam Hussein in any way, but to highlight that the senior CIA analyst is on record as saying that the American people were lied to about Halabja so that President Bush could build a case for a preemptive war. With or without nuclear or any other form of weapons of mass destruction, it is important to remember that U.S. intelligence experts did not see any benefit that Saddam Hussein could incur by starting a war with the United States.

Americans were told that the reason for war was an imminent threat of a mushroom cloud from Saddam Hussein. When the facts could not support this, the next lie was perpetrated: we were going to war because Saddam Hussein had collaborated with the 9/11 terrorists and worked with al Qaeda. When the facts could not support this, the story was respun that Saddam Hussein possessed chemical or biological weapons of mass destruction. When this, in turn, proved untrue, the story was again respun with an even lower bar for war... that Saddam Hussein's removal was the justification. Since one man's removal from power and imprisonment was feared to be seen as a high price for the deaths incurred (and the billions of dollars spent on the war), the rationale in late 2004 focused on an intent by Iraq for a weapons of mass destruction program. As needed and in anticipation of the truth about no weapons of mass destruction, the secondary justification of establishing a democracy in Iraq, to set a good example for other nations in the Middle East, was presented.

The bar for starting a war is now so low that any nation with the means to produce chemical weapons is on warning that a preemptive invasion by the United States is possible. Any nation with a golf course has the means to make, mix and disperse chemical weapons. When you realize that over 30 nations have golf courses, does anyone believe intent to have vs. the intent to use is the appropriate standard for starting a war? President Bush has kept his distance from the intent to use explanation because U.S. intelligence firmly disputed that Saddam Hussein would risk losing power by starting a war with the United States. One simple question that is worth asking yourself is, "Do you believe the United States would have started a war with Iraq if Iraq was not an oil-rich country?"

Walter Cronkite, "America's Most Trusted Person," spoke on the subject of the nature of the current Iraq war on October 23, 2004. He said President Bush's unilateral preemptive policy has made the world a more dangerous place not only for the United States, but for nations around the world. He noted that countries in Africa and the Middle East are preparing to invade their neighbors, using President Bush's preemptive strike policy as justification for their actions. He summarized, "The problem, quite clearly, is we have excited the Arab world, the Muslim world, to take up arms against us." He recommends gathering the most senior U.S. generals who opposed the war from retirement. He would ask this select group of outspoken opponents of the invasion to develop for immediate implementation a plan to withdraw all United States forces from Iraq within six months.[241]

While the American people bought the top two lies for the war (i.e., clear and present danger of weapons of mass destruction and a link to the 9/11 attacks), the real objectives of the 2003 Iraq war are:

1. Continue the existing power structure made possible by near and long-term profits from companies in the energy and war businesses.
2. Ensure a favorable price for oil and eliminate U.S. dependence on oil regimes that can topple overnight, especially Saudi Arabia.
3. Aid Israel by removing a bona fide threat to Israel. Saddam Hussein desired revenge for Israel's bombing of Iraq's Osiraq nuclear plant in 1981. Israel desired a regime change in Iraq as Saddam Hussein was funding suicide bombers in Israel.[242]
4. Solve Israel's need for water. As discussed in the chapter on Addictions, Israel's long-term existence is at risk without access to Iraq's water.
5. Turn water into a weapon by occupying the nation that controls the most extensive river system in the Middle East.[243]
6. Control Central Asia in the upcoming decades as key competitors, China and Europe, become increasingly dependent on resources in Central Asia.
7. Establish permanent military installations for U.S. forces to contain Iran and to fill the strength gap perceived to be created when U.S.

forces in Saudi Arabia were removed. Position 14 permanent U.S. military bases in Iraq in places that will enable control over both oil and water resources.[244]

8. Specifically prevent Iraq from developing or distributing weapons of mass destruction in the 2007 and beyond timeframe to retaliate for the Gulf War and subsequent suffering and deaths from economic sanctions.

9. Revenge for the assassination attempt on the president's father, as well as a fear among the Bush family that Saddam Hussein would one day take revenge on a member of the Bush family.

10. Someday bring democracy and freedom to the Iraqi people, but not now because true majority rule would align Iraq with Iran and interfere with key objectives on this list.

While individual members of the Bush administration would prioritize the list differently, you will note that responding to a clear and present threat of a mushroom cloud from Iraq is not on the list. The immediate weapons of mass destruction threat is also not on the list of a key administration insider.[245] This is because President Bush and his senior advisors knew Iraq was years away from possessing a nuclear weapon. The weapons of mass destruction reason for war and the mental image of a mushroom cloud were selected as the most saleable for promoting the war. After 9/11, the mushroom cloud fear became very real for America.

WE HELPED CREATE THE TALIBAN AND AL QAEDA

Okay, the United States government made foreign policy mistakes by supporting Saddam Hussein in his war against Iran. Well, the United States also supported Osama bin Laden in his fight against the Soviet Union. The link to Osama bin Laden and the Taliban is even more appalling because al Qaeda did attack the United States. The 9/11 Commission Final Report conveniently sidesteps another major foreign policy blunder made by President Ronald Reagan. The main point of this section is that Americans unknowingly helped create the Taliban and al Qaeda. Another way to say this is President Reagan's freedom fighters became Enemy Number One.

As background, the Soviet invasion of Afghanistan began on December 24, 1979 and ended on February 15, 1989. Similar to the U.S. invasion of Iraq in 2003, the Soviet invasion was seen around the world as an unprovoked invasion of a sovereign country. The United Nations General Assembly passed United Nations Resolution 37/37 on November 29, 1982 demanding that Soviet Union forces withdraw from Afghanistan. The Soviet Union justified the invasion as coming to the aid of an ally and a necessary preemptive war against Islamic terrorists. President Reagan saw an opportunity to humiliate the Soviet Union. He instructed the Central Intelligence Agency to support the anti-Soviet resistance. The multi-billion dollar operation not only supported, but also helped create the joint Arab and Afghan resistance against the Soviet Union.[246]

The Central Intelligence Agency and Pakistan's Inter Services Intelligence launched the largest covert operation in history. The CIA funded and recruited almost 100,000 radical moujahedeen from over 40 Islamic countries as soldiers for America's proxy war. The rank and file of the moujahedeen were unaware that their jihad was actually being fought on behalf of Uncle Sam. Weapons like the Stinger ground-to-air missiles which Osama bin Laden was so proud of were paid for by U.S. taxpayers. The Stinger and other weapons enabled Osama bin Laden's Arab and Afghan "freedom fighters," as President Reagan referred to them, to gain the upper hand against the Soviets in 1986. The multi-billion dollar effort – with $600 million allocated in 1987 alone – was funneled through Pakistani intelligence to sustain Osama bin Laden's fighters.[247]

President Reagan failed to consider what might happen when the Soviets left or were defeated. As comedian George Carlin once said, "Well, if crime fighters fight crime and fire fighters fight fire, what do freedom fighters fight? They never mention that part to us, do they?"[248] President Reagan would not have appreciated the truth in this humor. At the time he was unaware that he was financing a future war against America. The CIA's objective of creating a holy war or Islamic jihad resulting in a Vietnam-like defeat of the Soviet Union worked so well that the U.S. proxy resistance leaders began considering how to achieve a Vietnam-like defeat of the U.S. in the Middle East. Therefore, after the Soviets were defeated in February 1989, Osama bin Laden and his Afghan Arab war veterans formed al Qaeda and the native Afghan fighters became the Taliban.[249]

After the war, Osama bin Laden returned to Saudi Arabia as a war hero. He thanked Prince Bandar of Saudi Arabia and the Saudi intelligence chief, Prince Turki, for bringing the United States to help him. Prince Turki was the person who asked Osama bin Laden to lead an Arab resistance force for Saudi Arabia in Afghanistan. The direct quote from Osama bin Laden to Prince Bandar was, "Thank you. Thank you for bringing the Americans to help us to get rid of the secularist, atheist Soviets."[250]

OSAMA BIN LADEN DECIDES HIS FORMER ALLIES ARE ENEMIES

When Iraq invaded Kuwait on August 2, 1990, Osama bin Laden asked Saudi King Fahd Bin-Abd-al-Aziz Al Saud to let him lead his al Qaeda fighters to liberate Kuwait.[251] The Saudi King rejected Osama bin Laden's offer. Osama bin

Laden had recently returned from Afghanistan as a Saudi national hero. His influence was growing and the royal family feared Osama bin Laden might use the opportunity to form an all Arab liberation force not only to repel Saddam Hussein's forces from Kuwait, but to redirect the al Qaeda force to end the royal family's hold on power in Saudi Arabia. King Fahd did not want to take the risk of losing power and he accepted the United States' offer to liberate Kuwait. King Fahd's decision to put the liberation of Kuwait and the defense of the Kingdom in the hands of "infidels" was the "straw that broke the camel's back." Osama bin Laden's allegiance to the Saudi royal family was forever shattered.[252] The King's decision helped Osama bin Laden greatly expand his following because allowing non-believers to establish military bases in Saudi Arabia is a direct violation of the Koran.

Osama bin Laden rallied his al Qaeda organization to begin executing terrorist attacks on Saudi Arabia and the United States. While Osama bin Laden expressed his appreciation in 1989 of United States military aid in the fight against the Soviets, he had been contemplating attacking the United States well before his war with the Soviet Union, primarily because of its support for Israel. The attack on New York's tallest towers was actually conceived in 1982. In 1982, Israel invaded Lebanon, during which towers and buildings in Beirut were destroyed. Osama bin Laden said it was this incident that inspired him to attack the towers of the United States. His comment in 2004 was, "While I was looking at these destroyed towers in Lebanon, it sparked in my mind that the tyrant should be punished with the same and that we should destroy towers in America, so that it tastes what we taste and would be deterred from killing our children and women."[253]

Osama bin Laden's declaration of war against the United States never included occupying or destroying the United States, but was rather meant to draw America into what was essentially an Arab civil war. He was desperate to somehow overthrow the Royal Saudi family. His master plan was to draw the United States into a war in the Middle East, ideally in an oil-rich country. Eliminating an infidel enemy, Saddam Hussein, was a nice side benefit.[254] Osama bin Laden thought Saddam Hussein was an infidel because he followed a false form of Islam and his crimes against humanity were well known. Osama bin Laden's unspoken objective for the September 11, 2001 attacks was to stop disputes among the many variations of Islam by uniting the Muslim world against an external enemy.

Osama bin Laden dreamed of a united Islamic community that would no longer be paralyzed in its efforts to overthrow corrupt dictators in the Middle East. Once united, a sufficient force would exist to establish Islamic control in the region. His specific grievances, stated in his August 1996 declaration of war on the United States, included the presence of U.S. troops in Saudi Arabia, economic exploitation, the deaths and suffering that economic sanctions in Iraq produced, and U.S. support for Israel.

Two years later, in a 1998 decree, Osama bin Laden charged that Americans had declared war on Muslims. He wrote, "For more than seven years the United States is occupying the lands of Islam in the holiest of its territories, Arabia, plundering its riches, overwhelming its rulers, humiliating its people, threatening its neighbors, and using its bases in the peninsula as a spearhead to fight against the neighboring Islamic peoples."[255] Osama bin Laden's plan of attack was to expel the "Judeo-Christian enemy" from the holy lands on the Arabian peninsula. The second priority was Iraq. Iraq would serve as an economically rich base for future operations if Saddam Hussein lost his iron grip on the country. Historically Iraq was especially important because for 500 years it was the most powerful Islamic state. The third priority in his "liberation plan" is Palestine. Palestine is the site of the al-Aqsa mosque in Jerusalem. Muslims believe this is the place where Muhammad ascended to heaven.[256]

On October 29, 2004, Osama bin Laden released a video acknowledging for the first time that he had ordered the 9/11 attacks. In this video tape he states that Bush is misleading Americans by saying the attack was carried out because al Qaeda "hates freedom." He also said, "We fought you because we are free... and want to regain freedom for our nation. As you undermine our security we undermine yours." In the video, Osama bin Laden says peace will come to those who do not threaten Muslims.[257]

President George W. Bush's counter-terrorism czar, Richard Clarke, and many other Middle East experts have been extremely critical of the war in Iraq because the United States fell into Osama bin Laden's trap. Osama bin Laden successfully predicted that American leaders would be enticed by Iraq's oil resources and include an invasion of Iraq in their post-9/11 plans. The U.S. government was further blinded by corporations that stood ready to make billions and incorrect intelligence from Israel, which happens to be the only country benefiting from the Iraq war.[258] The decision to start a war in Iraq will forever be one of the low points in America's history.

Injustices occur and must not be ignored or we will be a party to even greater injustices in the future. How justice is restored is important. When injustices such as the attacks on September 11, 2001 are packaged with an unrelated event, like the war in Iraq, America's credibility is undermined. I submit that in combining the two unrelated events of 9/11 and Iraq into a common war on terrorism, America will never restore justice. In a career-ending move, Richard Clarke went on record saying that the actions by President George W. Bush have made the world a more dangerous place.[259] The body count of civilian bystanders in Iraq alone, not surprisingly a metric not officially maintained by the United States, exceeded three times the number of 9/11 victims in the first year of war in Iraq.[260] How is America restoring justice when the U.S. is creating new 9/11s with innocent people killed in other countries by American bombs?

The combination of no Iraqi plans for violence and no Iraqi weapons of mass destruction make this war an illegal one. This fact is realized by many people around the world including the United Nations Secretary-General Kofi Annan. Kofi Annan said the US-led invasion of Iraq was an illegal act that contravened the UN charter.[261] America's leaders need to be held accountable. This conscious deception has resulted in the deaths of thousands of innocent people in Iraq. This may sound harsh for many Americans, but when a president misleads the country to start a war, he or she needs to be held accountable as a war criminal. At the very least, President George W. Bush should be impeached for the betrayal of soldiers' bravery, loyalty and their unnecessary deaths. The illegal and unnecessary deaths of thousands of Iraqis makes him a war criminal. For President George W. Bush, the golden rule appears to be that there are no golden rules: only profits to be made and perpetuating the economic powers of those who hold them now.[262] America's citizens must hold the U.S. government accountable for the mass murders of thousands of babies, children, women and men.

In conclusion, America's alliances with killers are leading to a major disaster within the United States. President Reagan, Vice President George H. W. Bush and Special Envoy Donald Rumsfeld helped Saddam Hussein develop weapons of mass destruction. President Reagan and Vice President George H. W. Bush also helped al Qaeda and the Taliban come to power. As President, George H. W. Bush gave Saddam Hussein permission to invade Kuwait. In addition to the people killed by Saddam Hussein in Kuwait, the U.S. led Gulf War killed 158,000 Iraqis and the post-war economic sanctions killed 500,000 children and many adults.

President George W. Bush has made the situation significantly worse by invading Iraq. He has abused the loyalty of America's soldiers by failing to acknowledge the real reasons for the invasion. He has lied to the American people and the illegal war in Iraq has helped al Qaeda more than it has hurt it. President George W. Bush's foreign polices have made and continue to make the world a more dangerous place. Innocent people are being killed in Iraq and his policies in his second term are likely to result in additional killings in Iran. A survivor of an innocent person killed in a far-away land may become the person who triggers a future American Hiroshima.

6

UNILATERALISM

"The Multilateral Imperative: Recognize that the United States must provide leadership to achieve the objective of reduced carnage but, in doing so, it will not apply its economic, political, or military power unilaterally, other than in the unlikely circumstances of a defense of the continental United States, Hawaii, and Alaska."

(Robert S. McNamara and James G. Blight)[263]

THIS CHAPTER IS ABOUT THE danger of valuing America's sovereignty at the expense of America's security. The dangers of unilateralism are presented with a review of the death and destruction in the 20th century. The projection of mass deaths in the 21st century is intended to help illustrate that a new way of thinking is needed. This chapter discusses America's role in helping proliferate weapons of mass destruction across the globe. The need for multilateral peacekeeping and justice is discussed, followed by why caring about the suffering of others is in America's best interest. The ultimate unilateral act, the notion that one person should have authority to use a nuclear weapon that could destroy the world, is challenged with an alternative that makes America safer.

THE 21ST CENTURY IS POSITIONED
TO BE THE BLOODIEST IN HISTORY

I am very concerned that America's current foreign policy, and especially America's preemptive war in Iraq, will result in a catastrophic detonation of a weapon of mass destruction within the borders of the United States. Al Qaeda's American Hiroshima project discussed in Chapter One and the previous chapter illustrates that America's foreign policies are making a catastrophic detonation more likely. I am also very concerned that this will lead to a retaliation that will incinerate mass numbers of Muslims.

The 20th century averaged two wars every year for a total of approximately 218 wars with over 160 million people killed. If the 21st century experiences an equal number of wars, over 300 million people will be killed – without adjusting upward for the results of using weapons of mass destruction.[264] At the end of the 20th century, civilians made up 75% of the total war casualties. The trend of predominately civilian deaths is a reflection of the increasing brutality of war. Applying a 75% civilian casualty rate, the forecast for civilian deaths in the 21st century is 225 million.[265] The proliferation of weapons of mass destruction strongly suggests that the percentage of non-combatants killed is likely to increase and the total number of deaths will be higher. A 21st century where eight or nine out of every ten people killed are civilians is a realistic possibility.

Woodrow Wilson feared that people in the 20th century would experience wars even worse than World War I. Wilson wanted Germany to be treated as an equal following World War I. In an address to the Senate in January, 1917, he said, "It must be peace without victory." He feared that punishing Germany after World War I would lead to the deaths of millions and, unfortunately, history proved him correct. He also argued for a multilateral military force via the League of Nations and, had his recommendations been adopted, World War II may never have happened. If we heed his recommendations now, we may be able to prevent future wars.

World War II was born in large part from the hostile treatment of the German people in the 1920s, meant to punish them for the mistakes of World War I. Sanctions and forced war reparations produced hostility in the following generation. Unfortunately, the inverse of kindness begetting kindness is also true. The anger of the German people grew as the years of poverty and hardship continued. The injustices to the German people created fertile ground for an extremist to appeal to their economic needs with policies of hate. Adolf Hitler and his Nazi party directed their anger toward internal and external scapegoats to continue to build their power over the German people.

While the path to World War II was laid at the Treaty of Versailles in 1918, the path for strong allies after World War II was established by the Marshall Plan. Following World War II, the leaders of the United States were able to apply the hard-learned lessons of the two World Wars. The Marshall Plan was a non-violent hand-up restoring the economies and dignity of the Japanese and German people. The Soviet Union unwillingly provided Japan and especially Germany with a constant reminder that things could be worse. The contrast between prosperous free people in the West and impoverished state-controlled people in East Germany did not go unnoticed. The foresight of the Marshall Plan did help facilitate the breakup of the Soviet Union. The Marshall Plan is also responsible for the strong friendship between the United States, Germany and Japan that exists today. An alternative and disastrous future would have been for the United States to punish Germany and Japan with economic sanctions, or to use their soldiers as slaves to fight wars against the Soviet Union on behalf of the United States.

Sadly, we have forgotten the lessons of the first two World Wars, and the post-Gulf War sanctions resulted in preventable Iraqi deaths, as well as severe hardship. The Gulf War repeated the policies of the victors following World War I. If we applied the successful lessons of history to Iraq, efforts to ease the suffering of Iraqi people following the Gulf War would have likely resulted in the local people restoring justice in the decade leading up to the 2003 Iraq war. Just like the Marshall Plan, this "Iraq End Suffering Plan" would be bearing fruit across the Arab world today. Economic sanctions should never be imposed on a country after hostilities cease.

When you consider the reality of 300 million forecasted deaths (or far more if weapons of mass destruction are used), the urgency for the elimination of all biological, chemical, and nuclear weapons becomes essential. Eliminating weapons of mass destruction will remain a difficult challenge as long as the people in the nations that possess them believe their nation is safer because of them. At the same time, often the same people, are horrified when another nation develops weapons of mass destruction. This is of course hypocritical. Until the nations that possess these weapons become equally disgusted by their own weapons of mass destruction, terror will continue to be in the hearts and minds of people across the world.

UNDERSTANDING AMERICA'S ROLE IN WMD PROLIFERATION

This book started with the paradigm-changing fact that weapons of mass destruction have proliferated across the globe. With so many nations possessing weapons of mass destruction, historians will no doubt proclaim that one of the great injustices of our time was the proliferation of weapons of mass destruction. With all the talk about the proliferation of weapons of mass destruction in the Middle East, few people realize that the plans for all of the United States' most advanced nuclear weapons have been stolen and distributed around the world.

Americans are quick to deny or ignore that America is contributing to the problem of proliferation. Whether intentionally or unintentionally, the U.S. is helping lead WMD-proliferation. An intentional example was discussed in the previous chapter in the section titled *We Still Have The Receipts From The WMD We Gave Saddam Hussein.* I will illustrate an unintentional example by reviewing how America's tax dollars are speeding the development of the most dangerous weapons in places like China, Pakistan, Saudi Arabia, Iran and North Korea.[266] In addition, we should remember that stolen U.S. nuclear plans helped make possible the entrance of the former Soviet Union as a nuclear power.

The United States House of Representatives Select Committee on U.S. National Security and Military/Commercial Concerns with the People's Republic of China report in 1999 summarizes how the U.S. is unintentionally spreading weapons of mass destruction. The Commission concluded that China has stolen the plans for every currently-deployed thermonuclear warhead in the U.S. ballistic missile arsenal, as well as futuristic weapons like the neutron bomb that have yet to be developed. China has aggressively marketed the stolen information around the world to North Korea, Saudi Arabia, Pakistan, and Iran.[267] How can this happen, and continue to happen, and yet ordinary citizens are less concerned about this than the hyped-up and untrue statements about weapons of mass destruction in Iraq by the Bush administration?

The Commission concludes that these thefts of nuclear secrets from America's national weapons laboratories enabled the People's Republic of China to design, develop, and successfully test modern strategic nuclear weapons sooner than would otherwise have been possible. China's thefts from the National Laboratories began at least as early as the late 1970s. Significant secrets are known to have been stolen, from the laboratories or elsewhere, and almost certainly continue to the present. This prediction by the Committee in 1999 has proved to be accurate, with the 2004 announcement of the firing of four employees after the recent disappearance of classified information at the Los Alamos labs.[268]

I am certainly an optimist to assert that we have the wisdom and courage to stop designing and developing nuclear weapons. History teaches us that warnings are often ignored. On a pessimistic note, history would suggest that Americans will only change America's foreign policies and help the world become a safer place after a detonation of a weapon of mass destruction in the United States.[269]

MULTILATERAL PEACEKEEPING AND JUSTICE

To a people on the receiving end of war, multilateral peacekeepers are like angels from heaven. They provide security so that the local people and non-government organizations, or NGOs, can do their good work. While the United Nations is not perfect, this organization has more international credibility and objectivity than any single nation. Certainly it would have even more credibility if it were more democratic – or if even a single African, Latin American or Muslim nation had permanent member status.[270]

The reforms proposed in December 2004 to make the United Nations more relevant are a step in the right direction, but fall short of a truly democratic global organization. The authors of the proposed reforms did not address the fact that an individual living in a poor country does not have the same representation as an individual living in a wealthy nation.[271] Nonetheless, the U.N. can accomplish things that individual nations simply cannot. The U.N. is limited in its ability to promote a more peaceful world because it is funded with a tiny fraction of what is spent for defense by even a single nation like the United States. For example, the U.N. funding is 1.5% of what is spent by the world on preparing for or fighting wars.[272] Many in the United States fail to understand this funding discrepancy and see the U.N. as an ineffective organization with a mediocre track record. What critics of the U.N often miss is the fact that the United States and the other permanent members have veto power, which is extremely effective at limiting the U.N. In addition, successes like the weapons inspections in Iraq often go unacknowledged or are even inappropriately defined as failures. If permanent member veto power was eliminated and the representation became more democratic, the possibilities for a more peaceful world are astounding.[273]

We live in a time where no single country has the clarity of perspective to use force independently. History has taught us that nations that go to war against the advice of their traditional allies are often blinded by economic gains and are judged in time to have fought unjust wars. Robert McNamara makes this exact point in the movie Fog of War.[274] Robert McNamara served as President Kennedy's and President Johnson's Secretary of Defense from 1961 to 1968. Robert McNamara observed: "Not one of the United States' major allies—not Britain, France, Germany, or Japan—supported the American decision to intervene in Vietnam. Had the United States applied the multilateral rule, it would have never been at war in Indochina."[275]

What we fail to learn from history is that wars can solve short-term problems, but produce victors that in time solve non-violent problems with violence. Understanding the truism that violence breeds violence is key to understanding why war is the ultimate source of poverty. Opposing a nation's unilateral right to initiate war does not mean turning a blind eye or allowing injustice to continue uninterrupted. Opposing a nation's unilateral right to initiate war does not mean stopping a criminal from committing crimes or allowing genocide to occur. Opposing a nation's unilateral right to initiate war is possible with an empowered multilateral peacekeeping force.

If the world agreed that any individual nation that started hostilities would face retaliation endorsed by all the nations of the world, the century-long worldwide cycle of two wars per year would be broken. Multilateral engagement will lead to exhausting every non-violent alternative. Reducing unilateral wars may seem impossible and unrealistic. The idea suggested here would take time to evolve, but it could begin with no nation having the right to launch a preemptive war without approval of the United Nations Security Council.

To reinforce why the planet has evolved to a point where the unilateral right of a nation to initiate war must end, one must contemplate the killing power and consequences of actually using a nuclear weapon. How can a weapon of mass destruction be used without killing innocent people when it is a weapon that creates massacres? Nuclear weapons are especially evil weapons that also inflict suffering on multiple generations. For instance, in Hiroshima, young people have withheld the fact that their grandparents survived the atomic bomb for fear that a potential mate will lose interest. The thinking is the potential partner may fear a birth defect from genetic radiation damage should the couple have a baby.

Since weapons of mass destruction can only create injustices and not solve them, every measure possible must be taken to prevent their use. Nations may not be able to eliminate them with our current collective lack of courage, but we certainly could work together to reduce the number and implement processes to prevent their use. Multilateral cooperation, another way of saying global teamwork, requires more courage than unilateral actions. Multilateral cooperation also raises the bar for leaders of nations who want to start a war.

Why is the global support for multilateral programs like the International Criminal Court continually resisted by the United States? One answer is that President George W. Bush and other powerful people would be held accountable for their use of force. Sufficient evidence is already present to prosecute the Bush administration for starting the illegal war in Iraq. Leaders are quick to say they are concerned about the average U.S. soldier and this is why they oppose an International Criminal Court. The truth is that leaders are afraid they will be convicted and punished as war criminals. One only needs to reflect on the tremendous harm done to Vietnam during the Vietnam War and the fact that none of the responsible U.S. political leaders were ever held accountable. In fact, responsible political leaders like Henry Kissinger and Robert McNamara were rewarded with wealth and prestigious positions following their war crimes.

Multilateral justice brings justice to the victor, as well as to the defeated nation. In 1971, General Telford Taylor, the chief prosecuting counsel during the Nuremberg trials, said that if the standards of Nuremburg and Manila were applied evenly, and applied to the American statesmen and bureaucrats who designed the war in Vietnam, "There would be a very strong possibility that they would come to the same end Yamashita did."[276] Christopher Hitchens noted that "it is not every day that a senior American soldier and jurist delivers the opinion that a large portion of his country's political class should probably be hooded and blindfolded and dropped through a trapdoor on the end of a rope."[277]

NO NATION SHOULD ALLOW ONE PERSON
TO BE THE SOLE LAUNCH AUTHORITY

I find it amazing that people in nations possessing nuclear weapons strongly believe that their nation needs them, yet these same people are often shocked and upset when other countries seek to develop them. Where is the golden rule in all of this? If you believe in the golden rule, you either oppose all deployment of nuclear weapons or you support nations in their arguments that weapons of mass destruction are needed for national defense.

I predict a time when future generations will look back and wonder how Americans could support the insanity and injustice of policies that have promoted weapon of mass destruction proliferation. They will wonder how the U.S. or Russia could allow one person to have the authority and power to destroy the world in the time it takes to make toast. For future generations, Americans' acceptance of America's nuclear weapon arsenals with single-person launch authority will likely be harder to understand than the acceptance of slavery in Jefferson's time.

We can begin to change this insane situation and set an example for the rest of the world. We need to implement a system of checks and balances for nuclear weapon launch authority. With technology currently available, the following "check and balance" launch approval process leveraging America's three branches of government is possible.

The president initiates a nuclear weapons launch, but the launch is not finalized for 20 minutes. During the 20-minute waiting period, the Speaker of the House of Representatives, the Senate Majority Leader and the Chief Justice of the Supreme Court must agree with the command – or the launch order is canceled. If one of the parties is unavailable, the vice president's vote will serve as the necessary third confirming vote or single veto. With the costs of mistakes so high, it is essential that we implement this potentially world-saving and democratic safeguard.

MULTILATERAL IDEAS THAT COULD SAVE THE WORLD

We can make a difference if we encourage Americans to lead by example and take steps to reduce the risk of nuclear war. Authors Praful Bidwai and Achin Vanaik help put in context the importance of safeguarding against the use of nuclear weapons: "The nuclear bomb is the most anti-democratic, anti-national, anti-human, outright evil thing that man has ever made. If you are religious, then remember that this bomb is Man's challenge to God. It's worded quite simply: We have the power to destroy everything that You have created. If you're not religious, then look at it this way. This world of ours is four billion, six hundred million years old. It could end in an afternoon."[278]

The following weapon reduction measures by the U.S. would have a multilateral domino effect of similar weapon reduction steps around the world. Five changes that would demonstrate real leadership and lessen the risks of unnecessary deaths are:

1. Eliminate the U.S. preemptive nuclear first strike policy and establish a "no first use of nuclear weapons policy." This no first use of nuclear weapons policy would reduce tensions and the potential for accidental wars. A constitutional amendment would strengthen this policy and, when combined with the removal of the president's sole authority to initiate the use of nuclear weapons, serves as a big step forward to a safer world.

A "check and balance" and "no first use policy" launch process would earn the United States the necessary credibility to lead the United Nations to establish common multilateral weapons of mass destruction safeguards across the globe. The world will benefit by not having to defend against a U.S. first strike. This means that nations could maintain smaller nuclear arsenals and the world would have fewer nuclear weapons.

2. Make the use of weapons of mass destruction a multilateral action. While it is unlikely this policy will be supported by the U.S. population at this stage in history, the idea is suggested to prompt debate. America will likely resist this level of multilateral interdependence for another 25 years; or, if sooner, only because we have had a major nuclear disaster. This can happen sooner if we heed what Albert Einstein once said, "Your imagination is your preview of life's coming attractions."

Earlier in this chapter, the idea of requiring the president to initiate the launch request and require supporting approvals from the Speaker of the House of Representatives, the Senate Majority Leader and the Chief Justice of the Supreme Court was presented. Now the multilateral dimension is added to the latter process and thereby adds another level of protection for nations of the world by including the Secretary-General of the United Nations as a launch approver. All would have to concur before a launch decision could be finalized. I realize many Americans will see this as outrageous because we fail to understand why giving up some of America's sovereignty actually improves America's security. In this scenario, the Vice President's vote would continue to serve as a replacement vote for any missing vote by the Senate, House, or Supreme Court leaders. The Secretary-General's vote cannot be replaced. A built-in 20-minute waiting period for all the votes to be received would initiate from the moment the president entered his or her launch codes.

Adding additional approvers to the sole authority process helps make the world safer as current technology facilitates code breaking, voice-morphing, fake video and holographic projection. A multilateral "no first use" and "check and balance" would help protect the world from these technology "advances."[279]

3. Reduce the U.S. arsenal to 384 nuclear warheads immediately and separate the warheads from the missiles to prevent an accidental nuclear launch. The 384 limit is recommended as an initial step since modern day U.S. submarines can carry 192 warheads. One Trident submarine contains 24 missiles that are tipped with eight nuclear warheads. The 192 warheads can destroy every large and medium-sized city in any nation on the planet. This has been true for decades and we still continue to have thousands of missiles with multiple nuclear warheads ready to be launched on a moment's notice. If you imagine a scenario where the U.S. sought a fully-redundant capability to destroy two nations simultaneously, then one could argue 384 warheads are needed.

While reductions in nuclear arsenals have occurred since the end of the Cold War, we still have a ridiculously large arsenal of over 7,000 nuclear warheads. The thousands of extra warheads only increase the risk of mass deaths, hurt international goodwill and waste billions of tax dollars. As additional background on the insane number of nuclear warheads possessed by the United States, consider the destructive power of one U.S. W87 strategic 250 Kt nuclear warhead. This weapon of mass destruction has an explosive force equal to 250,000 tons of dynamite.[280] Warheads beyond 384 only lower America's security: they result in overkill and radiation that could slaughter millions of Americans. Nuclear scientists concluded over 30 years ago that multiple nuclear explosions would threaten life on the planet due to the nuclear winter effect.[281] No one knows for sure the exact point at which a nuclear winter would occur. Scientists believe the risk of a nuclear winter exists if 100 standard U.S. or Russian Federation nuclear weapons are detonated, meaning that even an arsenal of 384 warheads could end human life on our planet. [282]

By any measure, the existing United States arsenal is unjustifiable and a byproduct of simply trying to keep up with, or stay ahead of, the former Soviet Union. You do not have to be a nuclear scientist to understand the compelling evidence that warheads of any number also pose a great risk to the U.S. because of the resulting fallout that would travel around the globe.[283]

4. Upon setting the example with an arsenal of 384 nuclear warheads, work with the world to establish 384 as the global weapons of mass destruction upper limit. This would be far more achievable if we built on the credibility of America's own reduction to 384, which is also in America's best interests independent of what other nations do.

China has been a lot smarter than the United States and Russia in this respect. China has both maintained a nuclear arsenal of a few hundred missiles and kept the warheads unmated from the missiles for years.[284] When you consider that the United States spent $5 trillion since 1945 developing over 70,000 nuclear weapons[285] compared to China's policy of not wasting trillions of dollars on thousands of missiles, the Chinese policy of developing a few hundred missiles has paid off handsomely.

A multilateral international upper limit of weapons of mass destruction would be welcomed around the world. America would work with the United Nations to seek international agreement for a Strategic Arms Treaty of 384 because, for the United States, an arsenal of 384 nuclear weapons is sufficient to achieve the Mutually Assured Destruction (MAD) standard. Weapons of mass destruction would include any nuclear, chemical or biological weapon. This, in practice, would mean the elimination of all chemical and biological weapons in order to retain 384 nuclear weapons.

As part of the Strategic Arms Treaty of 384, nations with weapons of mass destruction would pay $10 million dollars per year for each weapon they possessed. Nations like the United States and the Russia Federation would likely initially keep a full arsenal of 384 weapons and pay out $3.84 billion each year. Other nations would be presented with a strong incentive to keep their arsenals under 100 weapons. These funds would be managed by the United Nations and independently audited. The funds would pay for verification of the 384 limit treaty, promote fissile material destruction, dismantle missiles, multilateral interventions to prevent terrorists from obtaining weapons of mass destruction, fund rescue and clean up operations, and motivate most nations to remain free of weapons of mass destruction.

5. Position the world to evolve to no nuclear weapons, or at least fewer than 384 weapons. This can be accomplished by the United States establishing a policy to always have 10 percent fewer nuclear weapons than the nation with the largest arsenal. In practice this would mean the 384 limit would be reduced by 38 weapons if the Russian Federation reduced its weapons to the 384 limit. If the Russian Federation did not honor the treaty and possessed any number above 384, the U.S. would still unilaterally limit its arsenal to 384. To further illustrate, imagine the Russian Federation had the largest arsenal in the world with 200 nuclear weapons. The United States would lower its nuclear weapons arsenal to 180, or 10% less than 200.

Would you sleep better at night if the ideas in this chapter were aggressively promoted by the United States and the rest of the world? Idea number four alone would provide the multilateral funding needed to help prevent terrorists from obtaining and using weapons of mass destruction. It is critical for citizens of the United States to remember that no single nation can achieve what a multilateral weapons of mass destruction enforcement capability would be able to achieve.

America could throw in a bonus incentive for the world. If the Strategic Arms Treaty limit of 384 is ratified by a specified date, the United States will eliminate all land and air-launched weapons of mass destruction. Only submarine platforms will continue to be deployed and they will never be allowed to operate outside United States territorial waters except during war. As described earlier, very few submarines will be needed because Trident submarines hold 192 warheads, and are extremely difficult for an enemy to destroy. Decoy submarines would further frustrate an enemy's targeting efforts and protect against concerns that, with only 384 nuclear weapons, an aggressor may be encouraged to launch a first strike to disable the U.S. nuclear force.

Other nations may follow, dramatically limiting a terrorist's ability to seize a nuclear weapon. Removing land- and air-launched weapons may also increase the safety of U.S. citizens by eliminating the incentive for an enemy to attack land-based missile sites. Making the U.S. a nuclear weapons- and weapons of mass destruction-free space also reduces the risks of accidents and unauthorized launches. The economic savings and security benefits that flow from unilaterally or multilaterally ending the triad concept of land, air and sea-based nuclear weapons is so compelling that we should end the nuclear insecurity triad before it grows a fourth, space-based leg.[286]

Unilateralism produces a nation of hypocrites. Exceptionalist policies treat people outside the United States as second class humans. Unilateralism and exceptionalism fuel injustice. While America is demanding that other nations not proliferate nuclear weapons, the United States is the source of much of the world's proliferation problems. The U.S. government calls for prosecuting war criminals from Europe, Africa, Asia, Central America, South America and the Middle East but refuses to even consider the notion that Americans are also committing war crimes. Eliminating America's misguided unilateral notions and implementing multilateral safeguards can not only protect America's democracy, they can save the world from nuclear destruction.

7

WAR PROFITEERING

"In strict confidence... I should welcome almost any war, for I think this country needs one."

(President Theodore Roosevelt)[287]

WARS THREATEN AMERICA'S DEMOCRACY. THE concept of starting a "good war" because it will bring peace is oxymoronic. Martin Luther King, Jr. eloquently made the same point when he said, "Wars are poor chisels for carving out peaceful tomorrows. We must pursue peaceful ends through peaceful means."[288] This chapter presents the ideas of Smedley Darlington Butler. His ideas to strengthen America's democracy help put in context the insanity of a military defense system that produces overkill and overspending. Butler's warnings about threats to America's democracy are brought home in the discussion on the United States role in international arms sales. This chapter ends with a warning on the dangers to America's democracy from mercenary corporations, the elimination of a law called the Proxmire Law, and the loss of worldwide support for U.S. policies.

When a country spends hundreds of billions of dollars on a military and no major threats exist, people will naturally think about cutting military spending. After the end of the Cold War, people in the war business (or defense industry, if you prefer this euphemistic label), started to get nervous: a future United States where defense spending could be reduced each year looked possible. Then 19 men, in a misguided pursuit for their idea of justice, killed thousands of innocent people and established the necessary conditions for the next "justifiable" war. The war on terror also happens to be sustainable because it is faceless and without well-defined enemies to defeat or defined end-points.[289]

An understanding of war that deserves attention comes from an amazing person few Americans have heard of. His name is Smedley Darlington Butler, and he was a United States Marine who served at levels from Second Lieutenant to Major General during his 33-year career.[290] He was widely respected in his time by both the political right and left, in part because he won the Congressional Medal of Honor – twice.

Butler is also famous for saving the country from a Fascist plot to seize the United States government in 1934.[291] He reported the plot to Congress, which held hearings that unraveled the evolving coup.[292] Butler's actions saved the United States from a very real potential civil war. Butler retired from the Marines in 1931 and died in 1940. In the last nine years of his life, his views about war were transformed. Some of his thoughts are foundational for our understanding of war. His personal insights about other means of bringing the flag of freedom to places far away are especially applicable for our time. His most famous observation about war was:

War is just a racket. It always has been. It is possibly the oldest, easily the most profitable, surely the most vicious. It is the only one international in scope. It is the only one in which the profits are reckoned in dollars and the losses in lives.

A racket is best described, I believe, as something that is not what it seems to the majority of people. Only a small "inside" group knows what it is about. It is conducted for the benefit of the very few at the expense of the masses. Out of war a few people make huge fortunes. [293]

Like all the members of the military profession, I never had a thought of my own until I left the service. My mental faculties remained in suspended animation while I obeyed the orders of higher-ups. This is typical with everyone in the military service.

I helped make Mexico, especially Tampico, safe for American oil interests in 1914. I helped make Haiti and Cuba a decent place for the National City Bank boys to collect revenues in. I helped in the raping of half a dozen Central American republics for the benefits of Wall Street. The record of racketeering is long. I helped purify Nicaragua for the international banking house of Brown Brothers in 1909-1912. I brought light to the Dominican Republic for American sugar interests in 1916. In China I helped to see to it that Standard Oil went its way unmolested.

During those years, I had, as the boys in the back room would say, a swell racket. Looking back on it, I feel that I could have given Al Capone a few hints. The best he could do was to operate his racket in three districts. I operated on three continents.

The trouble with America is that when the dollar only earns six percent over here, then it gets restless and goes overseas to get 100 percent. Then the flag follows the dollar and the soldiers follow the flag... Why don't those damn oil companies fly their own flags on their personal property—maybe a flag with a gas pump on it.[294]

Smedley Butler stands out among amazing Americans, not only because of his rare accomplishment in winning two Congressional Medals of Honor, but because he had the courage to acknowledge his mistakes. By speaking the truth he has helped future generations see a path to a more peaceful world. He offered a new way of thinking about the defense of the nation.

A central theme Smedley Butler preached was limiting war profiteering. War profiteering is influencing, promoting, starting or supporting the continuation of war for personal economic benefit. For example, if money is going in your pocket to make weapons of war, you are profiting from war. People who profit from war are likely unable to see this fact, as profit clouds decision-making.

To protect against war profiteers, Smedley Butler supported limiting the pay for all workers in defense industries, including senior executives, to the same pay received by soldiers in the trenches. He felt that defense industry workers still had a better deal because they would not be killed or maimed in combat. While this would create a new set of problems, the basic idea of limiting the profit potential is noteworthy. Limiting the profit in war could be improved through more transparency on who benefits and open contract bidding on all business contracts. Perhaps the best way to make war less attractive is to make domestic needs more profitable. Like the Federal Highway Program in the past, we have a national challenge today that is even more exciting and rich with benefits – ending America's dependence on oil. If the United States devoted the same energy and resources into a campaign to end its oil dependence, the military industrial complex might be busy enough to have less interest in war profits.

A little-known fact is that the Bush family became rich and powerful as a result of lucrative war deals. War profiteering in the Bush family started with George H. Walker and Samuel Prescott Bush. Both are the current President's great-grandfathers. George H. Walker was a St. Louis financier who specialized in corporate war contracts. Samuel Prescott Bush led the Buckeye Steel Castings that made weapons. Prescott Bush, the Connecticut senator and grandfather of the current President, was a director of Dresser Industries, which among other weapons is especially remembered for making the incendiary bombs that were dropped on Tokyo.[295] Prescott Bush is famous in history for making millions by helping lead a front company that supported Hitler's war machine. The company, Union Banking Corporation, was shut down under the Trading with the Enemy Act in 1942.[296]

George H. W. Bush is best known as a congressman, CIA director, Vice President and America's forty-first President; he also has a personal history of war profiteering as senior advisor to the Carlyle Group, a major investor in military defense-related companies. To illustrate how incestuous these relationships can be, former President Bush was in Washington D.C. on September 11,

2001 attending a Carlyle directors meeting. The bin Laden family is a major investor in the Carlyle Group. The bin Laden family representative was present at the Carlyle meeting and sitting next to former President Bush as they both watched the twin towers fall.[297] While Americans were in still in shock at the horror of this mass murder, the Carlyle Group decided to take a company it controlled, United Defense, public in order to reap the near-certain 9/11 market boost. The Army's fifth-largest contractor, United Defense, went public on December 14, 2001.[298] In one day, Carlyle earned $237 million selling shares in United Defense Industries. The percentage of this profit that went to former President Bush has been kept secret so as to minimize the political damage and public outcry.[299]

Another widely-respected American war hero, President Eisenhower, also warned about the military-industrial complex. In his farewell address he said, "We must guard against the acquisition of unwarranted influence, whether sought or unsought, by the military-industrial complex."[300] This has been criticized by some as so vague as to be meaningless. Yet one would have to think long and hard to find a better and more specific example than a dad, like former President George H. W. Bush, who is profiting financially from the policies of a son who also benefits when he inherits his father's wealth. While the decision to invade Iraq was influenced by several factors as discussed in the chapter on Alliances With Killers, the influence of economic gain should not be disregarded.

Smedley Butler also proposed that a declaration of war could only be valid if approved by the people subject to conscription. Conscription or the draft, unlike today's volunteer military, requires services from the children of the rich and powerful. He wanted safeguards against accidentally starting a war and to specifically prevent politicians from sending U.S. soldiers into a situation where they would be massacred and thereby become the catalyst for a call to war. For these reasons, in peacetime, he wanted Navy operations limited to 200 miles from the U.S. coastline and military aircraft restricted to 500 miles from the U.S. coast. During peacetime, the Army would be prohibited from leaving the United States.

Smedley Butler's key conclusions are just as poignant today. "To summarize: three steps must be taken to smash the war racket. We must take the profit out of war. We must permit the youth of the land who would bear arms to decide whether or not there should be war. We must limit America's military forces to home defense purposes."[301]

OVERKILL AND OVERSPENDING

It is unfortunate that compassionate conservatism has nothing to do with prudent government spending. The war business rewards government insiders and the privileged benefactors. America's representatives tremble in fear at the thought of opposing a military spending bill because such a stand is guaranteed to be used by political opponents when seeking reelection. We are bombarded with constant messages that the answer is more money for the military, the intelligence community and development of weapons of mass destruction.

The United States and Russia both continue to carry a bigger nuclear stick than anyone could ever conceivably need for a deterrent or any other reason.[302] Robert McNamara and James Blight observed that between 1987 and 1998 the United States has reduced its nuclear force from 13,655 strategic warheads to 7,256 strategic warheads, and the Soviet Union and then Russia have moved from 8,619 strategic warheads to 6,340 strategic warheads.[303] Of the 7,256 U.S. nuclear warheads, 2,200 are on hair trigger alert. Missiles on land are ready for launch in two minutes, and missiles on two submarines in the Atlantic and two submarines in the Pacific can be launched in 15 minutes.[304]

The United States has spent over five trillion dollars on nuclear weapons since 1945. During this time more than 70,000 nuclear weapons have been developed.[305] This fact is widely unknown and multiple presidents have been shocked at the cost and size of the U.S. arsenal. When President George W. Bush received his initial security briefing on the U.S. nuclear arsenal, he replied, "I had no idea we had so many weapons... what do we need them for?"[306] The common rationale supplied is this massive arsenal was needed to defeat communism. This response was ridiculous then, but continues to be told – and believed – today. As each year passes, more people will likely realize that communism fell apart, not because of the number of missiles we developed, but because the system was fundamentally flawed. To fail to recognize this fails to acknowledge the reason the United States opposed communism in the first place. The myth that massive U.S. military spending won the Cold War is not supported by the opinions of the former U.S. Ambassador to the Soviet Union or Soviet experts and is discussed in the chapter An Uninformed Electorate.

Consider the money that could have been kept in taxpayers' pockets or directed to support programs to benefit America's citizens. The total Pentagon spending between 1940 and 1998 exceeded $19 trillion. The magnitude of this amount can be appreciated when compared to the second highest government expenditure for the period, which was $7.9 trillion for Social Security payments.[307] What would schools, transportation systems, health care options and employment opportunities be like if a portion of the trillions of dollars for nuclear weapons had been spent to improve the United States? Some may argue that defense spending is only a small percentage of the total U.S. Gross Domestic National Product. When billions and trillions are at risk of being wasted and furthermore create nuclear overkill that lowers U.S. security, the percent of U.S. Gross Domestic National Product becomes irrelevant. When it comes to defense spending, what is relevant is asking if the dollars spent have made people safer. For additional information on how tax dollars are spent, the www.americanhiroshima.info site has a summary of the federal budget.

History teaches us that wars are routinely projected to cost a fraction of their true cost. To illustrate, the Civil War was estimated by Lincoln's Secretary of the Treasury to cost $240 million, or seven percent of the U.S. Gross Domestic Product. The actual cost for the North was $3.2 billion. The official projection was 13 times too low.[308] Why are overly optimistic war costs routinely put before Congress and the American people? The reality is that most people would not support going to war if they understood the real cost of war. As Senator Hiram Johnson said during World War I, "The first casualty when war comes is truth."[309]

Imagine what the public reaction would have been to the Vietnam War if citizens knew the Pentagon's war estimates throughout the 1960s were in error on the low side by 90%.[310] The Pentagon's error is compounded when the actual costs, including inflation and other post-war factors, are considered. Of course, the real cost is in lost lives and human suffering, but realizing that financial costs are not honestly projected or disclosed is important. A good rule of thumb is take the initial "official cost of war projection" and multiply it by ten. If you multiply by ten you will still be on the low side but at least you will have a more realistic starting-point.

Unfortunately, the rule of thumb for Afghanistan and Iraq is guaranteed to far exceed ten times. The real multiple is likely to be more than thirty times what was sold to the American people. Donald Rumsfeld knowingly lied when he said "Well, the Office of Management and Budget has come up with a number that's something under $50 billion for the cost. How much of that would be the U.S. burden, and how much would be other countries, is an open question."[311] Readers should remember that Lawrence Lindsey, President George W. Bush's chief economic adviser, was fired prior to Rumsfeld's statement because he calculated the cost of invading Iraq at $100 billion to $200 billion.[312] America has already far surpassed even Lindsey's calculation. At the time of this book's publication, the cost of the Afghanistan and Iraq wars was roughly $300 billion, or six times more than the Bush administration calculations.

The likely total costs will exceed $1.9 trillion.[313] The $1.9 trillion is close to the amount, when compressed into a single year, that the United States spends on everything. The $1.9 trillion projection assumes an active United States involvement over a ten-year period in an environment with insurgency disruption. If the $1.9 trillion expense is the final tally, how do we pay for this? In the business world, if a corporation missed their financial estimates for investors by a factor more than six times, they would likely be prosecuted for misleading the public. If they missed their financial estimates by more than thirty times, they would be considered another Enron.

I will make a low risk-prediction that you will see increasing arguments by the Republican party to "privatize" Social Security. Yes, it is true that the number of workers making contributions into Social Security is decreasing relative to the number of people receiving benefits. Therefore, something should and can be done to ensure that Social Security will continue to serve everyone. What Americans are not being told is Social Security would be self-sustaining well beyond 2040 by simply repealing the tax reduction for very wealthy Americans. In addition, Social Security would be fixed for a far longer period of time if the money spent on fighting in Iraq had been used to shore up Social Security.

The Bush administration's strategy is to use the "urgent problem" of Social Security to divide Americans. The generational anger between young and old will occur if privatization takes the form, and I suspect it will, where one group has to sacrifice its interests for the other. As I see it, the issue is receiving a lot of media attention to take the focus off the problems in Iraq and bring young people into the Republican party. If concern for young or poor Americans was really the issue, the tax break for the rich would simply be repealed. As presented by President George W. Bush, the primary group of Americans that will benefit from his privatization plans are wealthy Americans as the infusion of a massive amount of Social Security funds into common stocks would increase the value of common stocks.

Overkill and overspending can be better understood when contrasted with opportunities to help the world. How many Americans realize that the $350 million in tsumani aid the United States pledged is the same amount spent on current U.S. wars in just two days?[314] How many Americans realize that Africa has more people dying from hunger and malaria each week than died in the December 26, 2004 tsunami? Sadly, the United States has repeatedly missed opportunities to end worldwide hunger and help break the cycle of poverty by buying unneeded weapons and fighting unneeded wars. What would the world look like today if the five trillion dollars that the United States wasted on additional nuclear weapons after 1945 was invested in programs to break the cycle of poverty at home and around the world?

The U.S. will achieve a dubious milestone no later than 2006 by spending more on its military than the combined military spending of the rest of the world.[315] This is already true when black budget accounts and intelligence spending are added to the totals. Is America the land of the brave or the land of the afraid?

All Americans should try to imagine what the U.S. would look like if over half of all spending by Congress did not go to the war business. Just a small fraction of this spending could mean the difference in a number of important programs of social uplift (e.g., improving U.S. schools, increasing the accessibility of health care, and drug rehabilitation programs just to name a few). When you view the chart on the following page, also note that the trend indicates that even a greater portion of total U.S. government spending will be allocated to the war business in the upcoming years. The price of imperialism is high and military overspending risks bankrupting the entire country in the future. Even more important, imperialism resulting in overkill, puts the entire human race on the endangered species list.

Military Spending ($ Billions)

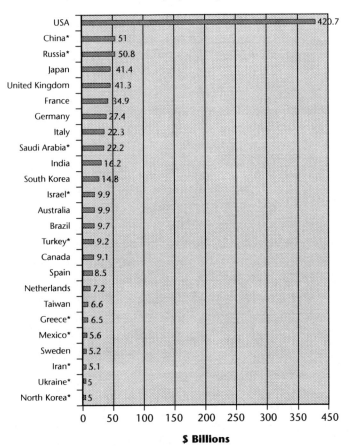

Country	$ Billions
USA	420.7
China*	51
Russia*	50.8
Japan	41.4
United Kingdom	41.3
France	34.9
Germany	27.4
Italy	22.3
Saudi Arabia*	22.2
India	16.2
South Korea	14.8
Israel*	9.9
Australia	9.9
Brazil	9.7
Turkey*	9.2
Canada	9.1
Spain	8.5
Netherlands	7.2
Taiwan	6.6
Greece*	6.5
Mexico*	5.6
Sweden	5.2
Iran*	5.1
Ukraine*	5
North Korea*	5

$ Billions

The graph of worldwide military figures are from 2005 for the U.S. and the latest year available for all other nations.[316] The graph illustrates only part of what is being spent by the U.S. on war and defense. The 2005 $420 billion figure does not include the full expenditure. Money spent on the Energy Department nuclear weapons programs, military-related activities of other agencies, international military financing and training, expenses paid for the wars in Iraq and Afghanistan, mandatory spending for military retirement and health care, veterans programs, and the estimated portion of interest paid on the national debt are not included in the $420 billion. The total as calculated by the Friends Committee on National Legislation equaled $715 billion in 2004.[317]

Does it make sense to you to have a U.S. military budget that exceeds the rest of the world combined? Does it seem necessary that the U.S. military budget is more than 30 times than the combined total of the U.S. declared "rogue" states (Cuba, Iran, North Korea, Sudan and Syria spent a total of $13.6 billion)?[318] When a nation seeks to dominate the earth by spending more on weapons than all nations combined, the price paid by its own citizens is very high. Martin Luther King, Jr. saw this clearly when he said,

"A nation that continues year after year to spend more money on military defense than on programs of social uplift is approaching spiritual death."[319]

Almost every American knows someone who makes their living from the war business. Smedley Butler's observations earlier in this chapter are important to remember. If you are involved in the war business, you are blinded by your conflict of interest and may not realize this until after the conflict of interest ends. While people in the war business are often not bothered by international weapon sales, many young people are quick to see that this is wrong. America's number one export, weapons, is not going unnoticed. They see the hypocrisy of the U.S. government and the people around them who are supporting this injustice. This dynamic can strain family relationships and leave parents wondering why their children do not value their advice.

Another dubious milestone is likely to happen in 2006. The U.S. is on the track in 2006 to spend more money on the military and obligations from past wars than on all other government programs combined.[320] This means even more Americans will be frustrated when seeking services for public health, aid for the poor, and even programs to strengthen homeland security. Currently, over 44 million Americans already lack health insurance[321] and nearly one in five U.S. children live in poverty.[322] The price of dominating the world with weapons is endless wars, increased preventable suffering, and the spiritual death of the country. Overkill, overspending, and the true cost of war have already hurt America's democracy and could someday end it... as well as life on our planet.

INTERNATIONAL ARMS SALES

"We should not keep weapons that our military planners do not need. These unneeded weapons are the expensive relics of dead conflicts. And they do nothing to make us more secure. In addition, the United States should remove as many weapons as possible from high-alert, hair-trigger status—another unnecessary vestige of Cold War confrontation."

(Presidential Candidate George W. Bush)[323]

Once in office, President George W. Bush had a change of heart. He promoted efforts to become the world leader of international arms sales and simultaneously cut programs that would have eliminated nuclear weapons at home and abroad. He also initiated efforts to obtain Congressional approval for a new class of "mini-nukes."[324] The campaign promises in May 2000 that sounded so wonderful were, in retrospect, just "lines" to get people to vote for him. He did not even bother to address this topic when he campaigned for reelection in 2004.

Countries worldwide purchased at least $26 billion in new arms in 2003.[325] With 57% of the world market, the dominant seller and distributor of weapons is the United States.[326] Throughout the 1990s, the biggest buyer in the international market was Saudi Arabia, followed by Taiwan.[327] The United States' market share continues to increase each year. In addition to the United States, Russia has 17% of the market, Germany has 5% and France has 4%. All other nations (e.g., North Korea, Iran, Israel, Pakistan, China, etc.) have very small slices of the weapons of death pie and together they account for 17% of the world market.[328]

The Middle East is a major focus of this book. The Middle East is not the only place in the world that weapons producers are actively promoting their products. Understanding what creates markets for selling weapons, illuminates an important dimension in U.S. foreign policy. One region of the world that illustrates this point is the Asia Pacific region. The tension between Taiwan and China is already a key hotspot that could result in a conventional and ultimately a nuclear war.[329] United States military war plans in the 2017 timeframe indicate the expected increased tension in this part of the world as China is often the enemy in these futuristic war simulations.[330] Some see the current Middle East wars as linked to the future management of China. This analysis views the bases the U.S. is establishing in Central Asia to secure oil and other resources as a means to "managing" China over the next five to twenty plus years.

Ultimately, China will reclaim Taiwan. Will the United States honor the One China policy endorsed in 1972 by President Nixon and Chairman Mao Tse-tung in the Shanghai communique? Will the American people realize that this very dangerous game is being played and the price paid could escalate into a major nuclear war? Whether a unification of the two is to happen peacefully as the July 1, 1997 unification of Hong Kong, or after a war killing millions, China will be successful in uniting Taiwan. In the meantime, a dangerous marketing plan remains in place so that the insecurity flowing from this open issue keeps Taiwan, Japan and South Korea hungry for U.S. weapons.

In general, the official United States policy is to promote weapons sales as aggressively as possible everywhere in the world. A chaotic and insecure world is the ideal state for selling weapons. Raymond Mabus, a former ambassador to Saudi Arabia, summed this up when he said: "It is our job to do everything possible, and legal, to make sure they buy American."[331] Unlike economic aid, when military aid is given, Congress is not required to vote. A study by Lora Lumpe of the Federation of American Scientists found that the U.S. shipped some seven billion dollars' worth of free military equipment abroad between 1990 and 1996.[332] U.S. foreign aid is substantial, but not after military aid is subtracted. U.S. foreign aid as a percentage of gross national product (GNP), excluding military aid, ranked last among the world's wealthiest countries in 2003 at about 0.1 percent.[333]

Major General Smedley Butler offered a perspective on selling weapons that is worth remembering. He said: "Do you really think that if you start handing your Democratic friend ammunition, you won't get into it, too? You can't help it."[334]

Butler's concerns about selling weapons remain true today.[335] He concluded that if you sell weapons to the winner, the winner will hate you because you took advantage of them in their time of need. If you are selling weapons to the loser, you need to get in the fight because losers don't exist after they lose or are so bankrupt that they cannot pay for the weapons you sold them. In any event, nations selling weapons do not remain neutral in the war business. Promoting weapons, one of the United States' top exports, will keep America's defense factories warm but someday will come back to haunt the country.[336]

While in general I do not support taxes that hurt business, a worthy exception would be to take the profit out of war with a "weapons of death" sales tax. If the United Nations put before the assembly a proposal to tax international arms sales, with the proceeds going to feed and care for the world's poor, perhaps war would become less profitable.

MERCENARY CORPORATIONS

Companies that sell mercenary combat forces are far from new. What is new is that the United States is increasingly leveraging its mercenary corporations. If there is anything good about the war in Iraq, it is that Americans are becoming aware of mercenary corporations as they hear the odd and unfamiliar names of the companies operating in Iraq. Often, and unfortunately, the name of the company is revealed when an employee is taken hostage or has just had his head chopped off. It is also noteworthy that people tend to care less about mercenaries than they do when soldiers are killed. Often the dead mercenary does not even show up in the news, although the Iraq war with its head-chopping executions is proving to be an exception. The bottom line is that the capture or murder of mercenaries carries almost no political risk.

President Bush likes mercenaries because combat teams outside the normal chain-of-command offer plausible deniability and an opportunity to help big business campaign supporters with their bottom line. For the military, the situation is a mixed bag. Companies like Military Professional Resources, Inc. (MPRI) can quickly send out twenty former U.S. colonels in the matter of a day. MPRI, founded in 1987 by retired Army General Vernon Lewis, is one of the largest mercenary training firms. As currently configured, significant command voids would be created if the U.S. Army had to group twenty former field officers for an assignment in just a few days' time.[337] The military has to give up some control; but it is worth it for many senior commanders who are only a few years away from retirement, with lucrative retirement years ahead made possible by working for mercenary corporations.

A summary of one private mercenary corporation will help illustrate the privatization of the military. Vinnell, a company started in 1931, came on the defense scene in 1946 as a government contractor. In 1975 Vinnell won a massive contract to train Saudi Arabia's National Guard. In 1992 the company was acquired by BDM. A joint venture with Saudi Arabia, called Vinnell Arabia, was started in 1995. BDM at the time was owned by the Carlyle Group. Senior U.S. former officials who have had leadership positions with Vinnell include former Secretary of State James Baker, former White House budget chief Richard Darman, and former Secretary of Defense Frank Carlucci. In 1997, Vinnell was acquired by TRW. TRW was acquired in 2002 by Northrop Grumman Corporation.[338]

In 2003, Vinnell was awarded a $48 million contract to train the nucleus of a new Iraqi Army. The $48 million figure is significant, as Congress receives notification only if a contract is worth more than $50 million. A visit to the Vinnell Internet site is interesting. On the Vinnell site you can even send online condolences to some of the Vinnell employees that have been killed on the job (private mercenary corporations don't use the killed in action or KIA abbreviation).[339]

Other firms like Booz-Allen & Hamilton, one of the biggest consulting firms, oversees the Saudi Marine Corps. Booz-Allen also runs the Saudi Armed Forces Staff College. They teach senior-level military skills and tactical training. Another firm, DynCorp, is active in Latin America, Africa and now Iraq. The company has over 17,000 employees, over 550 operating facilities around the world, and annual revenues of $1.3 billion. DynCorp, like many of the private mercenary corporations, has its corporate office in Virginia.[340] The Virginia headquarters is convenient as it is widely understood that the larger mercenary corporations often receive their operating instructions directly from Langley[341] and even have people assigned to work with them from the Central Intelligence Agency.

THE DEATH OF THE PROXMIRE LAW

The revolving door between the people that serve the United States and the defense contractors that sell these same people weapons is a practice that is undermining America's democracy. Senior members of the military and Pentagon sometimes have an incentive to help war businesses because they are remembered when they retire with significant salaries and bonuses in the defense industry. The limited efforts in the 1990s to monitor the revolving door quickly illustrates how widespread the revolving door has become.

In the 1990s, a law sponsored by former Wisconsin Senator William Proxmire provided information on the conflict of interest between the military and defense contractors. The Proxmire Law required former Pentagon employees to file a disclosure report upon taking a position in the defense industry paying more than $25,000 a year. The Proxmire Law was repealed and no longer exists. The Pentagon wanted the law repealed even though it never prevented anyone from taking a position with a defense contractor. All Proxmire Law records were shredded by the Pentagon except for the years 1992 to 1995. In that time, 2,482 officers above the rank of lieutenant colonel went to work in the weapons and war business.[342]

One of the best reports on the revolving door is in the book Private Warriors. Author Ken Silverstein, observes, "The Defense Security Cooperation Agency (DSCA), the Pentagon bureau that oversees the government's Foreign Military Sales program, is a prime example of the revolving door." Nine out of ten of the last DSCA leaders went on to work in the arms industry after leaving the DSCA. With the growth of private mercenary corporations, the conflict of interest issues are dramatic and embarrassing. America's democracy needs not only the Proxmire Law restored, but also measures to shut down the privatization of the military.

BECOMING DARTH VADER

America's own actions can and have resulted in massacres. Contrary to what many people may wish to believe, Vietnam and the native Americans are not America's only "massacres" and Americans are not exempt from torturing people or sponsoring massacres. Massacres or the killing of civilians, including women and children, are becoming increasingly accepted. A media story about U.S. bombs falling in a far-off place to counter terrorism may not even result in the listener thinking about what this means to the innocent people who happen to be near the explosion.

Americans see movies like Black Hawk Down and leave the theater thinking about the two UH-60 Blackhawk helicopters that were shot down and the daring fighting the movie portrayed.[343] Others leave the theater stunned by the poverty of the people in Somalia or the loss of the 18 Americans who were killed in Mogadishu. Why is it that only a few Americans realize that Somalia is 99% Muslim and the mission in Mogadishu was ill-planned and counterproductive to the objective of preventing widespread starvation in the country?[344] Even fewer Americans leaving the theater would likely be thinking about the five hundred local people massacred and the thousand more who were injured. Even today, the fact that hundreds of innocent women and children were killed in the crossfire is unknown to most Americans.

How many Americans see the events in Somalia on October 3, 1993 as a massacre? Americans should consider how we would react if a foreign power flew in with helicopters to arrest a local leader. To give a historical perspective for how American might feel, we can go back to March 5, 1770, when British soldiers killed five colonists. We teach high school students about this event, known as the Boston Massacre, to illustrate the evils of being occupied by a foreign power. How will the event be viewed in Somalia as the story is told from one generation to the next? Will the story live on in Somalia as the Boston massacre lives on in the United States today? How does the son or daughter of one of the many local people killed fighting "foreign invaders" feel about the United States? What will they say to their children? Have we planted the seeds of future violence and helped produce a breeding ground for terrorists in Somalia?

The answers to the preceding questions are not promising for Americans wishing to travel or do volunteer work in Somalia in the next twenty years.

Michael Vlahos, a political scientist and former Cold War policy analyst observes, "We, the United States, may become the Darth Vader wearing the black helmet. We've created an industrial system that works for us and some allies but is imperial and seems oppressive to many others. We increasingly will find ourselves in the same position as empires of the past, the Persians and Romans, Spain under Phillip II, the British in the late nineteenth century. Any great empire trying to ride herd on the world in an age of major change is in danger." [345]

The United States as Darth Vader is a reference to the science fiction movie Star Wars. Specifically, Darth Vader starts off as a good person or "force" and becomes corrupt. He eventually becomes the lead agent of evil in the empire. This analogy may initially sound crazy. When you consider America's far and away number one leadership of weapons sales around the world, disdain for international systems of justice like the International Criminal Court,[346] massive arsenal of nuclear weapons,[347] military bases in over 130 countries,[348] torture programs like extraordinary renditions, use of depleted uranium weapons, and policies of preemptive wars, the observation is no longer worthy of a chuckle. The Pentagon even has an active program underway called the Death

Star.[349] President Eisenhower was concerned about a military-industrial complex that in time would defend its own economic interests even if it contradicted America's national defense. Such a time has arrived and it is fair to say, from the perspective of the Pew Research reports reviewed in the chapter on An Uninformed Electorate, that the United States is now seen as the world's Darth Vader.

8

WEAPONIZING SPACE

"Every gun that is made, every warship launched, every rocket fired, signifies in the final sense a theft from those who hunger and are not fed, those who are cold and are not clothed."

(President Dwight D. Eisenhower)[350]

THIS CHAPTER EXPLAINS WHY WEAPONIZING space threatens the United States and makes the world a more dangerous place. Weaponizing space means putting offensive weapons in space. While the final mix of weapons deployed in space will depend on the results of current and future testing, the weaponization or militarization of space literally threatens the survival of everyone. Imagine one nation dominating all other nations by mastering the "high ground" of space with weapons that can kill targets on earth or in orbit. How would you feel if a foreign country was in a position to dominate the planet because they were the only nation that had militarized space?

The process of weaponizing space has its roots in the final days of World War II. In a secret program called Operation Paperclip, one hundred Nazi rocket scientists were brought to the United States.[351] The head of Hitler's team that built the V-1 and V-2 rockets, Wernher von Braun, was made the first director of NASA's Marshall Space Flight Center in Huntsville.[352] Major General Walter Dornberger was Hitler's military liaison to von Braun's rocket team.[353] He came to the U.S. as part of Operation Paperclip. Dornberger is the person who created the idea of "missile defense" as an offensive program that would have nuclear powered satellites that could destroy targets on earth.[354] I strongly recommend anyone wishing to learn more about the origins of the U.S. space program to view the documentary "Arsenal of Hypocrisy."[355]

The idea of missile defense became well known to Americans on March 23, 1983, when President Ronald Reagan announced his vision of a world safe from nuclear threats.[356] Many nations depend on nuclear missiles for deterring attack. If Nation A develops first strike weapons capable of knocking out Nation B's deterrent, Nation B will be insecure. Nation B will still have a deterrent since it is unlikely Nation A could knock out all of Nation B's nuclear missiles. But if Nation A also develops ballistic missile defenses, other nations will be very apprehensive that Nation A's missile defenses will be used after a preemptive first strike to mop up the small number of remaining Nation B missiles. This makes Nation B and other nations around the world less secure, and will force them to go to a hair trigger launch status to better insure they could launch their nuclear weapons before being attacked. Unfortunately, missile defense ultimately increases the chances of a nuclear war due to a false warning and everyone becoming less secure.

President Reagan's Strategic Defense Initiative or SDI was later called Star Wars because of the popularity of the Star Wars movie. President Reagan made this public appeal because he needed approval from Congress for what would be a multi-billion dollar funding request. In March 1985, the Reagan administration launched SDI and asked Congress to appropriate $26 billion to support the program for a five-year period.[357] Even when adjusting for the time value of money, this appropriation of funds meant the U.S. missile defense effort had cost over three times what was spent on the Manhattan project to create the atomic bomb.[358]

We live in a time where it is possible to keep space weapons-free in a way that is highly verifiable. This can be accomplished because it is possible to inspect, track and monitor all equipment launched into space. The nations capable of putting weapons in space have pleaded with the United States to keep space weapons-free. They see the danger in weaponizing space and also a need to use the funds that would need to be allocated to address critical domestic programs. If America fails to establish a multilateral and verifiable agreement to keep space weapons-free, America will not only waste its precious resources, but also will dramatically weaken the safeguards that currently help protect the world from destruction.

WHY IS SPACE WEAPONIZATION BEING KEPT SECRET?

Would the U.S. public support the billions of dollars needed to create a new department of the military, when no other nation is seeking to control space?[359] Would Americans rather have the billions and ultimately trillions of dollars that are being spent on space weapons used to strengthen Social Security? What would the U.S. public say if they knew that China and the Russian Federation want space to be kept weapons free?[360]

One reason that this effort is kept classified is the fear of some experts, that without a clear and present danger of a potential enemy simultaneously seeking to place weapons in space, the U.S. population will not support increases in the defense budget for space weapons. If a national debate on the low-cost and verifiable non-proliferation alternatives to missile defense became widespread, President Bush's support for missile defense would be understood to be wasteful and to actually decrease America's national security. The missile defense cover enables President Bush to sidestep public opposition, political attacks and condemnation from the international community.

Imagine if President Bush publicly declared his real intentions to put weapons in space. While U.S. Air Force planning documents do directly declare that weapons will be put in space, the president only talks about scientific and peaceful space exploration because a public announcement could enable other nations to take the issue to an international court to oppose U.S. efforts. The issues of who owns space and the negative worldwide public opinion could stall current efforts to build and deploy space-based weapons. Billions of dollars of current space-based commerce could come to a standstill if a court prohibited satellite orbits, since virtually all satellites could be deemed to be weapons and therefore prohibited from orbits over protesting countries. Distinguishing non-commercial satellites with hidden weapon systems from commercial satellites could be impossible without a verification program to inspect them before they were put into orbit. An international court would certainly raise questions, and could determine that space-based weapon orbits over other countries are acts of war. Many questions like the latter would surface and in the end the U.S. fears that an international court would outlaw space-based weapons on the grounds that no single nation owns space.

Many other roadblocks to developing space-based weapons would flare up. A U.S. Space Force announcement would likely result in a protest from the Russian Federation on the grounds that Article IV of the October 10, 1967 Outer Space Treaty is being violated. Article IV prohibits the placement of an offensive capability in orbit around the Earth.[361] One roadblock the administration fears is the public could become informed about the risks that are presented when nuclear powered satellites are launched into space. At least 34 nuclear reactor cores are in satellites currently orbiting the earth.[362] Nuclear powered satellites are essential in order to generate the needed power to destroy targets from space either on earth or in orbit. The U.S. government seeks to continue the perception that the nuclear power industry is safe and secure. This is one reason why al Qaeda's American Hiroshima has not been discussed by the U.S. government as it results in a person coming to the conclusion that nuclear power is far from safe.

NATIONAL MISSILE DEFENSE DEFINED AND FLAWS THAT SHOW ITS TRUE PURPOSE

National Missile Defense is defined by the Bush administration as a collection of high-tech components that create a shield over the U.S. from intercontinental ballistic missiles with nuclear warheads. Intercontinental ballistic missiles are sophisticated rockets capable of traveling through space to reach their targets. The land, sea, air and space-based components of the National Missile Defense program include detection sensors, engagement radars, interceptor missiles and lasers.[363]

The stated goal of the program is to detect and destroy intercontinental ballistic missiles from the world's most unstable leaders. Until 9/11, the thinking in the Bush administration was that the primary threat to the U.S. was a nuclear weapon delivered by an intercontinental ballistic missile. This program is unlike Ronald Reagan's Star Wars or Strategic Defense Initiative, which focused primarily on threats from the former Soviet Union. Due to the significant problems in the Strategic Defense Initiative cover story, the National Missile Defense program is not initially intended to protect the U.S. from Russia, China or any other country with an arsenal of intercontinental ballistic missiles that exceeds a few dozen missiles.

FIVE FLAWS IN THE PROPOSED NATIONAL MISSILE DEFENSE PROGRAM

The five major flaws in the proposed National Missile Defense program illustrate why missile defense is only a cover story to conceal weaponizing space and simultaneously create a first strike weapon. If missile defense were really the objective, these five flaws illustrate that it is the wrong solution to the wrong problem. The stated problem requiring National Missile Defense is protecting the U.S. from a rogue nation or terrorist deciding to use weapons of mass destruction. A true solution to this problem must provide protection from the far less expensive and far more likely alternative means of delivering weapons of mass destruction.

1. Missile Defense Protection Only From Missiles That Fly Above The Shield

What if a terrorist used a technology that flew under the shield or defensive umbrella? Short-range missiles and cruise missiles that do not fly through space would defeat the proposed National Missile Defenses. While it is possible that the program could be redefined to include a short-range missile entering its boost phase, the focus of the National Missile Defense is exclusively on long-range missiles.

If the primary objective of America's missile defense efforts is to control space by creating a capability to destroy orbiting enemy offensive satellite platforms, the limitations of flying under the shield becomes irrelevant.

2. Low Cost Alternatives To Long-Range Missiles Are Available

Why would a rogue nation or terrorist bother with the effort, potential for reduced accuracy, and expense necessary for using intercontinental ballistic missiles when these enemies could use an airplane, ship, boat or truck to serve as their delivery vehicle? Why bother with the expense of exotic weapons required to protect against a subset of missiles when a variety of more likely delivery vehicles exists?[364] Consider the difficulty of preventing tons of illegal drugs from entering the U.S. each year. If an enemy of the U.S. wants to blow up a major city, why not achieve pinpoint accuracy and smuggle the bomb into the city on a moving truck?

If the objective is securing space, then exotic and expensive weapons are needed.

3. Countermeasures Can Defeat National Missile Defense

A country capable of developing an intercontinental ballistic missile can certainly be expected to develop countermeasures. Missile defense will be good for Russian and Chinese arms suppliers, because both have already developed many countermeasures that they would likely sell to other nations.[365] The General Accounting Office February 4, 1992 report on the Patriot missile failure at Dhahran, Saudi Arabia highlights the fact that no room for error exists when trying to hit a missile with a missile.[366] During the Gulf War, the Patriot missile failure rates ranged from slightly under 40 percent to over 90 percent.[367] Had Iraq had access to the sophisticated countermeasure technology that Russia and China have developed to counter anti-missile technology, the Patriot missile failure rate during the Gulf War would have reasonably been higher.

If securing space is the objective, satellites that remain in space have more predictable paths or orbits than intercontinental ballistic missiles and are therefore easier to destroy with a missile or laser.

4. Terrorists And Rogue Leaders Would Avoid Immediate Attribution

If a rogue leader or terrorist wanted to prevent a counterattack on their nation, they would certainly not launch a missile, because a missile launch can be traced back to the point of origin and guarantee immediate retaliation. A terrorist or rogue leader would prefer to frustrate U.S. efforts to retaliate by delivering the weapon through means that could not be traced.

If securing space is the objective, the fact that terrorists and rogue leaders have low-tech options to deliver a weapon of mass destruction and avoid immediate attribution is irrelevant.

5. No Protection For Biological And Chemical Weapons

The singular focus on nuclear intercontinental ballistic missiles fails to offer protection for easier-to-produce biological and chemical weapons of mass destruction. Biological and chemical weapons probably would be detonated as bombs, but even missiles could defeat the National Missile Defense by deploying hundreds of submunitions into the atmosphere. A missile defense interceptor might have to destroy hundreds of targets to defeat each biological or chemical missile instead of a single or few nuclear warheads in each nuclear missile.

Ignoring biological and chemical weapons, when the real objective is space, is logical because biological and chemical weapons are ineffective weapons in space.

WHY U.S. AND GLOBAL SECURITY DECREASES

THE SAFETY WINDOW SHRINKS

One reason foreign nations and the allies of the U.S. are against the National Missile Defense is that the safety window of several minutes to an hour that existed in the mutually-assured destruction world becomes a few seconds or minutes in a missile defense world. Critical to the first layer of protection in the National Missile Defense program is the ability to knock out the incoming missile when it leaves the ground and begins its boost phase. Boost-phase missile defense interceptors require near-instantaneous authorization to respond to a missile launch and must be located in space, otherwise the brief boost phase will be missed. Space-based weapons, especially high-powered lasers, may be able to hit earth-based targets or missiles much faster than earth-based missiles and this can reduce the safety window and lead to a mistake.[368]

The Cuban missile crisis of 1962, or even the 1995 Norwegian weather rocket incident, show us that the chain of mutually-assured destruction would have likely engaged if decisions needed to be made in seconds instead of several minutes. Put another way, if National Missile Defense existed twenty years ago, you would not be reading this book. Consider how fast events unfolded in the 1995 Norwegian weather rocket incident. The Norwegians launched a weather rocket after informing the Russians of the launch. Unfortunately, the Norwegian notification never made it to the Russian missile command. Thus the Russian military thought that a U.S. Trident submarine had launched a first strike attack and President Boris Yeltsin activated his nuclear briefcase.[369] Fortunately for the world, the flight of the missile was monitored for several minutes and a Russian technician determined that the missile was moving away from Moscow.[370] Had the extra minutes vanished, and President Yeltsin ordered a counter-attack, the Norwegian weather rocket could have triggered the escalation necessary to destroy the world.

U.S. Representative Edward J. Markey, a democrat from Massachusetts, stressed the brief window of time concern by sending toasters to all 535 members of Congress. Markey and a group of other concerned citizens wanted to remind policy makers that "in the time it takes to make toast, we could all be toast."[371]

INCREASED WEAPONS OF MASS DESTRUCTION AND A NEW ARMS RACE

National Missile Defense, because of first-strike fears, will guarantee a new arms race by promoting the development of additional weapons of mass destruction around the world. Specifically, the basic math of how many nuclear weapons are needed for a nation's security is now increased by the number of missiles forecasted to be destroyed by the U.S. missile defense system. For example, China is likely to double the size of its existing arsenal to deliver the same killing power to U.S. targets that it was prepared to launch prior to U.S. missile defenses.

U.S. efforts to build a National Missile Defense capability have already resulted in the reversal of Russia's "no-first-use if attacked" nuclear weapons policy by President Vladimir Putin.[372] President Putin's announcement was a major step backward and yet few Americans even noticed. Americans are thrilled that the Cold War was won and this event suggested that America's relationship with Russia could quickly go from cold to burning hot.

President Bush actually invited China to build more nuclear weapons and guaranteed that the U.S. would not protest, in order to help win China's support for National Missile Defense in 2001.[373] Sometimes America's foreign policy is stranger than fiction, unless you realize that these behaviors increase weapon sales. While nuclear weapon nations increase their arsenals, non-nuclear weapon nations have a new incentive to join the club. Non-nuclear weapon nations, when insecure, can become motivated to join the ranks of nuclear weapons nations.

ATTRACTIVE ALTERNATIVE TARGETS

If the U.S. could counter a missile threat from a rogue nation or terrorist, and a rogue nation or terrorist did defy logic and decide to use a missile, would the rogue nation or terrorist be more likely to choose a target outside the U.S. umbrella? Would a U.S. base in another country be more attractive? The answer to both questions is yes, and it clearly highlights one of the reasons America's allies fear missile defense. In addition, a National Missile Defense capability would actually undermine the shared-risk concept that currently binds the North Atlantic Treaty Organization (NATO) nations, since it shifts risk from the U.S. to the allies. National Missile Defense could result in the weakening of NATO and therefore motivate NATO nations to refuse to support us.

A National Missile Defense does not offer allies any hope for missile defense protection in the foreseeable future. The system is currently not being built to include allies; and, even if it ultimately included allies, few allies are willing to believe that the missile defense system would prevent missiles from reaching their country. After all, if a missile were shot down in its boost phase, it would land short and this might land on an ally.

Rogue Nations Will Create Alliances And Thereby Become Stronger

One of the more bizarre likely outcomes of National Missile Defense is strengthened relationships between North Korea, Iran, China and Russia. The early signs of proof that these unusual alliances will form have already appeared. In July of 2001, a friendship pact was signed between China and Russia that strengthens military cooperation between both countries.[374] Both Chinese and Russian authorities have noted a greater need to cooperate because of mutual concerns that the U.S. National Missile Defense program threatens their nations. NATO allies may also be more willing to collaborate with nations the U.S. considers high risk or rogue nations.

A President May Believe Missile Defense Will Work And Pursue Risky Strategies

On January 29, 1991, President George H. W. Bush, in his State of the Union address, cited the "remarkable" success of the Patriot anti-missile system.[375] The Army and Raytheon supported this notion of tremendous success. During testing, the Patriot anti-missile system had a perfect record of 17 successes out of 17 attempts.[376] When fired in combat, according to 1992 investigations by both the House Government Operations Subcommittee on Legislation and National Security and the General Accounting Office, the Patriot missile defense failed on almost every occasion.[377] Theodore Postol has argued the Patriots did more harm than good in the Gulf War because they added to the number of missiles that fell on Israel.[378]

A National Missile Defense system would need to be 100 percent effective in order to protect millions of Americans from annihilation. If just one missile made it past the shield, millions of Americans could be killed. The expectation by a president that a complex National Missile Defense system would work with 100 percent accuracy the first time the system was fully stressed in a combat environment could be the first in a series of unrecoverable mistakes.

In Time Other Nations Will Create Missile Defenses

If we do not make space an offensive and defensive weapons-free zone, there is no reason to believe that in time the other nations of the world will fail to put weapons in space in the name of missile defense. The world will follow the U.S. example and in time, one of these complex systems will fail and could start a major war. How does sparking the proliferation of weapons in space make sense when we are the only country in the world that can provide the leadership to make space a weapons-free zone? I prefer to see economies growing without the additional economic strain of purchasing a new class of space weapons. As the U.S. weaponizes space, very poor nations may make difficult tradeoffs and choose space weapons at the expense of programs to feed their people. It is important to remember that the world opposes this program because it increases the likelihood of the end of the world.

Cooperative Programs Unravel

Will non-proliferation programs that require cooperation with nations stall or terminate? During the Clinton administration, the Nuclear Cities Initiative, Defense Threat Reduction Agency and other cooperative threat reduction programs helped increase global security. As a result of the Nunn-Lugar-Domenici Cooperative Threat Reduction program, the Ukraine, Belarus, and Kazakhstan were denuclearized. This cooperative program funded the deactivation of 4,838 nuclear warheads and the elimination of 387 nuclear ballistic missiles, 343 ballistic missile silos, 136 nuclear submarine launch tubes, and 49 long-range nuclear bombers.[379]

Non-Proliferation Agreements Unravel

The Anti-Ballistic Missile Treaty and subsequent arms control efforts that played a major role in the reduction of weapons of mass destruction are either already terminated or are in the process of being terminated. The Anti-Ballistic Missile Treaty was initially entered into force in 1972 because ballistic missile defense systems could undermine confidence in retaliatory capabilities. The Anti-Ballistic Missile Treaty, now terminated by the United States, limited the U.S. and the former Soviet Union to "two anti-ballistic missile deployment areas that prevented a nationwide anti-ballistic missile defense capability.[380] The idea was each country would leave unchallenged the penetration capability of the other's retaliatory missile forces."[381] For Russia, the Anti-Ballistic Missile Treaty signed by Leonid Brezhnev and Richard M. Nixon was the foundation for all other arms control agreements.

Now that the Anti-Ballistic Missile Treaty has been canceled by the United States, the Intermediate-Range Nuclear Forces Treaty may also unravel, enabling other countries to reintroduce shorter range missiles that could easily defeat the National Defense System by flying under the shield.[382] During prior administrations, the Anti-Ballistic Missile Treaty was credited with directly enabling reductions in both the U.S. and Russian nuclear arsenals.

Following the Anti-Ballistic Missile Treaty termination, will the non-nuclear nations take the next step and begin abandoning the Nuclear Non-Proliferation Treaty? Sadly, I am convinced that the answer is yes. The Nuclear Non-Proliferation Treaty is supported by 187 countries and has served to motivate the vast majority of countries to not develop nuclear weapons based on a pledge from the nuclear nations that they will continue efforts and eventually become nuclear-weapons-free.[383] International agreements have proven that they are one piece of the broader solution to prevent and slow the proliferation of weapons of mass destruction. The already too high price we must pay in dollars and America's security for a National Missile Defense system is further increased as fifty years of non-proliferation agreements unravel.

MISSILE DEFENSE IS EASILY DEFEATED

The ultimate issue is not whether missiles or lasers can be created to destroy missiles. If we let history be America's guide, we will see that if we spend hundreds of billions of dollars, the U.S. could accomplish the technical miracle of hitting a missile, but someone else will find a way to defeat America's system to destroy a missile. History, as illustrated recently by the Patriot anti-missile system in the Gulf War, has also shown us that perfection in the laboratory and chaos on the battlefield are normal outcomes.

Given the split-second launch authorization necessary for a missile defense and the history of system failures, one could predict that the only successful use of the U.S. missile defense program will be to counter an unauthorized launch of a U.S. missile. Consider that the U.S. has the largest number of active strategic nuclear weapons on "trigger alert status" and missile defense is more likely to work when the flight path and operating characteristics of the missile are known.

Before a multi-billion or trillion dollar system is built, the objective should be discussed in a free society. The obvious flaws in the National Missile Defense should be addressed and the economic expense evaluated. Research efforts to counter weapons of mass destruction are prudent, but building a system that will not accomplish its objective is wasteful. What good did the $22 billion spent to deploy a missile defense system in the early 1970s (to protect the missile base at Grand Forks, North Dakota) accomplish?[384] Has Secretary of Defense Donald Rumsfeld forgotten that the first time he was Secretary of Defense he ordered the Grand Forks missile defense system shut down in 1976 because it was ineffective?

We can learn from the Grand Forks experience: building a weapons system with major flaws produces an ineffective system. On October 15, 2004, leading missile defense experts concluded the Bush administration's missile defense system provides absolutely no protection for Americans. The rush for deployment was primarily influenced by the upcoming November 2004 presidential election.[385] Unless the currently deployed system is scrapped, the American public will be hearing new stories about problems and failures of the U.S. National Missile Defense system at least until the year 2025. This is because insiders who understand the system problems, and the test cycles needed to correct the existing problems, expect it will be at least 20 years before the current flaws are addressed.

With respect to the Comprehensive Test Ban Treaty, Anti-Ballistic Missile Treaty and National Missile Defense, the U.S. is appearing as a rogue nation to the rest of the world.[386] We are back-stepping at a time America should be exerting leadership with a robust array of non-proliferation programs. Non-proliferation efforts have proven to be more effective, less expensive and more consistent with a people who believe in doing the right thing. These actions would make the world a far safer place. Fear in the Bush administration and financial gain by war profiteers has created a barrier to rational thought on what is needed to increase U.S. security. Unfortunately, regardless of how we label what is happening in the Bush administration, America's own actions are decreasing its security and threatening the world.

Missile defense makes a lot of sense to people who see war profiteering opportunities. Charles E. Wilson, a former President of General Electric, was so happy about the wartime situation that he suggested a continuing alliance between business and the military for "a permanent war economy."[387] His wish came true when the Truman administration created a war economy that continues to this day. A war profiteer sees not only the vast sums of money from building missile defense, but also the profit-rich opportunities of countries wanting products to defeat missile defense. Weaponizing space is opening up a new market for the military-industrial complex. A basic business marketing principle is to create demand. If terrorist and rogue states disappeared tomorrow, the focus of fear and justification for increased military spending would shift to space-based threats from China, the Russian Federation and others.

THE STEPS TO WEAPONIZE SPACE

What would be needed if the president decided to weaponize space? The president would want to promote a "space vision" for the public to strengthen the classified cover story.[388] He would want an infrastructure of space-based sensor systems, engagement radars, and satellite or missile interceptor devices. Next, he would need to restructure the Army, Navy and Air Force so that reductions in personnel would help offset the additional expenses of weaponizing space. Massive funding would also be required from Congress. The president would also want to evolve an existing organization that could transform itself into a U.S. Space Force. The November 2003 U.S. Air Force Transformation Flight Plan provides insights on the transformation to the U.S. Space Force.[389] The U.S. Air Force Space Command Strategic Master Plan FY06 and Beyond directly calls for the U.S. to dominate space with approximately 500 billion dollars in space weapon systems between now and 2030.[390] In the report, General Lance W. Lord says, "This plan is the command's roadmap to ensure our military remains dominant in space, in the air, on the ground and on the sea."[391]

The Space Command Strategic Master Plan FY06 and Beyond is packed with so much detailed offensive space weaponization information that it is amazing that it is not classified. Another U.S. Space Command resource that describes the weaponization of space is the Vision for 2020.[392] In the notes section of this book you can find the Internet address for the full Vision for 2020 and Space Command Strategic Master Plan FY06 and Beyond reports.[393] The Vision for 2020 states "the U.S. Space Command will dominate the space dimension of military operations to protect U.S. interests and investment." This document, mirroring the opening of a Star Wars movie, goes on to state: "Integrating Space Forces into warfighting capabilities across the full spectrum of conflict."

A key justification for weaponizing space is explained in the Space Command Strategic Master Plan FY06 and Beyond. The report states: "Just as the advent of airpower greatly enhanced military operations of the time, space forces, likewise, greatly enhance modern military operations across the spectrum of conflict. Air Force doctrine views air, space, and information as key ingredients for dominating the battlespace and ensuring superiority. Effective use of space-based resources provides a continual and global presence over key areas of the world ... satellites permanently "forward deployed" add another dimension to the capability of our force's ability to quickly position themselves for employment. Military forces have always viewed the "high ground" position as one of dominance and warfare advantage. With rare exception, whoever owned the high ground owned the fight. This capability (space) is the ultimate high ground of US military operations."[394] President Bush's space vision statements in 2004 are certainly laughable when one reads these military documents.

The United States Strategic Command (STRATCOM) is the organization that will someday morph into a separate branch of the military. As discussed earlier in this chapter, the Pentagon objective of keeping the attention away from the militarization of space, is served by keeping space weaponization within the Air Force command structure. One current component of STRATCOM is the Air Force Space Command (AFSC).[395] STRATCOM, headquartered at Offutt Air Force Base in Nebraska, has authority over all nuclear weapons[396] and all space weapons.[397]

STRATCOM is currently aggressively developing space-based weapon platforms. Going back to the Reagan Administration, government officials have downplayed the multi-year plan to create the U.S. Space Force. Because of the classification of these plans and distraction of public attention on the war in Iraq, the weaponization of space has received little debate by citizens. In addition, the September 11, 2001 terrorist attacks also diverted the public's attention and simultaneously created support for significant increases in military spending. With a citizenry focused on terrorism, current space exploration and missile defense programs provide a convenient cover for this multi-billion and ultimately multi-trillion-dollar effort to weaponize space.

While overall defense spending is increasing, the military is being restructured and was being downsized before the 2003 Iraq war. The plan was fewer armed forces personnel so that more money would be available for the U.S. Space Force. Military planners forecasted an increased reliance on technology and a lesser need for personnel. Now that there is an insurgency in Iraq requiring a large U.S. ground force, many in the Pentagon wish the 1985 military staffing levels were not severely cut. The Army had 800,000 people in 1985, 480,000 people in 1999 and planners understandably failed to consider that the United States might start a ground war requiring over 100,000 troops.[398]

The downsized military combined with the privatization of the military creates the potential for an over-stretched force that commits atrocities. This is because the accountability of the U.S. government is degraded.[399] While a privatized military creates the potential for select corporations to profit, the U.S. military has proven to be extremely professional, ethical, and capable of protecting against corruption and internal espionage.

Another key piece President George W. Bush would want to evolve into a U.S. Space Force department is the National Reconnaissance Office or NRO. While the Central Intelligence Agency and National Security Agency are generally more known to the American public, the NRO is America's largest spy agency. The NRO was created in 1960 and its existence was classified until 1992. Today the NRO receives over $6 billion a year in funding.[400] To help put the $6 billion in perspective, most nations spend less than $6 billion on their entire defense budget. The NRO's intelligence, defense, and space capabilities combined with the existing U.S. Space Command is in the process of becoming a solid launching pad for the U.S. Space Force department.

THIS GENERATION CAN MAKE SPACE A WEAPONS-FREE ZONE

This generation has the opportunity to make the world a safer place by keeping space a weapons-free zone and simultaneously keeping our resources focused on programs that bring justice so that the world remains a safer place. The true purpose of National Missile Defense and the broader space program has always been first and foremost for the weaponization of space. The U.S. is now consciously sabotaging global disarmament so as to remove barriers to mastering space. Decades of meaningful nuclear disarmament agreements are now being undermined as protective barriers, like the Anti-Ballistic Missile Treaty, are removed. Worldwide security is decreasing with each step toward becoming "masters of space." The U.S. Space Command bold "master of space" objectives have ideological similarities with Hitler's

"Germany over all."[401] The language of dominance is littered throughout the Air Force's space plans. Insiders in the Air Force are so used to using this language that they fail to see that America is all about promoting freedom and protecting against Hitler-like "over all" dominance.

In Chapter Six, the fact that the United States has spent over $5 trillion developing over 70,000 nuclear weapons was presented.[402] Think of the many more billions or even trillions the United States will spend on space weapons in the next few decades. A verifiable weapons-free space is in the hands of the United States and, specifically, our generation. Do we make the world safer with a piece of paper that can be enforced across the globe or do we continue to start the space weapons race? The European Union, Russian Federation, Canada, China and other nations of the world are pleading with the United States to keep space weapons-free. The world will gladly endorse a weapons-free space if the United States is part of the agreement.

In 1961 President Dwight D. Eisenhower warned the American public, "In the councils of government, we must guard against the acquisition of unwarranted influence, whether sought or unsought, by the military industrial complex. The potential for the disastrous rise of misplaced power exists and will persist. We must never let the weight of this combination endanger our liberties or democratic processes. We should take nothing for granted. Only an alert and knowledgeable citizenry can compel the proper meshing of the huge industrial and military machine of defense with our peaceful methods and goals, so that security and liberty may prosper together."[403]

Only one nation in the world is working to dominate the planet by placing offensive weapons in space. The United States is using the Trojan Horse of National Missile Defense to secretly weaponize space. The Pentagon has helped keep public attention away from the militarization of space by managing the military space program from inside the Air Force. Several years from now, when the system of offensive weapons is ready to be unveiled to the public, the United States will announce a new branch of the military called the U.S. Space Force. People will be presented with information that this is a natural evolution just as the formation of the U.S. Air Force from the Department of the Army. Keeping space free of weapons is an opportunity to prevent the theft from humanity that President Eisenhower so wisely observed at the beginning of this chapter. Americans have time to stop this dangerous and misguided new frontier for weapons and, in the process, direct the billions and ultimately trillions of dollars that would have been wasted to programs that really can bring about a more peaceful world.

The time has come for all Americans to keep space free of weapons and end this serious threat to our survival.

9

DRAWING THE WRONG CONCLUSIONS FROM HISTORY

"The problem after a war is with the victor. He thinks he has just proved that war and violence pay. Who will now teach him a lesson?"

(J. Muste)[404]

WE ARE LEARNING THE WRONG lessons from history. As a result we think violence can solve our problems. The problem with this thinking is that in a world proliferated with weapons of mass destruction it leads to our destruction. A new multilateral way of thinking is required to deliver security. This chapter makes known, even though it is extremely unpopular for Americans to hear, why the first atomic bombs dropped on Hiroshima and Nagasaki were horrendous mistakes.

VICTORY SOMETIMES REINFORCES THE WRONG CONCLUSIONS

History is an opportunity to learn and avoid past mistakes. History is also often written from the perspective of the victor. When this happens, key learning points fade away. One of the startling things I learned from history is that there is a direct correlation between anti-American feelings and the use of air force power after World War II. This seems obvious now; but every bomb dropped by the United States is a reason for people around the world to disapprove of our country.

The hidden cost of bombing is collateral damage and collateral damage produces new enemies. Collateral damage is the innocent bystander who loses a child, or has his house destroyed by a bomb. This person will understandably be angry at the country that killed his child or destroyed his house. When innocent people are killed, we have just made an enemy of the surviving family for at least the current – and likely the following – generation.

The fact is that we have dropped a lot of bombs on at least 24 countries since the end of World War II. Here is the list from 1945 to 2005:[405]

China 1945-46 and 1950-53, Korea 1950-53, Guatemala 1954, 1960 and 1967-69, Indonesia 1958, Cuba 1959-60, Congo 1964, Peru 1965, Laos 1964-73, Vietnam 1961-73, Cambodia 1969-70, Grenada 1983, Libya 1986, El Salvador 1980s, Nicaragua 1980s, Lebanon 1983, Iran 1987, Panama 1989,

Kuwait 1991, Iraq 1991-2005, Bosnia 1994, Sudan 1998, Afghanistan 1998 and 2001-2005, Yugoslavia 1999 and Yemen 2002.

Historian William Blum observed that in none of the above bombings did a lasting democratic government develop.[406] While there were certainly other contributing factors that prevented democracy, zero out of 24 countries would suggest to most people that dropping bombs is contrary to bringing democracy, peace and prosperity. Consider a central teaching of Buddhism:

> *Hatred never ceases by hatred.*
> *But by love alone is healed.*
> *This is an ancient and eternal law.*[407]

THE FIRST ATOMIC BOMBS – TWO PERSPECTIVES

On August 6, 1945, the atomic bomb was dropped on Hiroshima. An estimated 140,000 Japanese people died. On August 9, 1945, another atomic bomb was dropped on Nagasaki, where an estimated 70,000 people were killed.[408] Citizens of the United States have been taught that violence, even the violence of using a nuclear weapon, can pay. Many Americans have a "fact set" on the history of the first atomic bombs that consciously or subconsciously can affect opinions about nuclear weapons and their potential use in the future. The "lifesaver" and the "unnecessary mass killings" perspectives are presented here to illustrate the point that the victor writes history. We are drawing the wrong conclusion on this major learning point and as difficult as it may be to imagine in 1945 or even today, the world would be a safer place today if the atomic bombs had never been used.

MYTHS TO SUPPORT USING ATOMIC WEAPONS

I find in speaking to U.S. citizens, especially those who lived through World War II, that three key points have become embedded in the history of the first atomic bombs. First, the atomic bombs in World War II ended the war quickly with the minimum number of people being killed. The logic for this claim is that since the war ended quickly, an invasion of Japan was avoided and over a million American lives were saved. Secretary of State Byrnes estimated a half a million U.S. soldiers and President Truman claimed the number provided by General George Marshall was closer to one million.[409] Second, the bombs were dropped with adequate time between them for the Japanese to surrender. Third, the targets chosen were primarily military targets and the U.S. made a reasonable effort to minimize civilian casualties.

President Truman's statement immediately after the Hiroshima bombing helped establish the collective understanding. He said, "The world will note the first atomic bomb was dropped on Hiroshima, a military base. That was because we wished in this first attack to avoid, insofar as possible, the killing of civilians."[410] The saving lives theme has been expanded to include not only American but also Japanese lives, by speeding up the surrender. Many years later, retired Air Force General Paul Tibbets, the man who dropped the atomic bomb on Hiroshima, actually received a Humanitarian Award for piloting the Enola Gay.[411] Truth is indeed stranger than fiction.

Robert Oppenheimer, the father of the atomic bomb and the other Manhattan Project team members should therefore, in a tremendous twist of logic, be credited for being "lifesavers" because they created a weapon of mass destruction. The "lifesaver" thinking is commonly accompanied by the fact that Japan terrorized the Chinese and Korean people and started the war by killing over 2,000 members of the U.S. military at Pearl Harbor.

UNNECESSARY MASS KILLINGS

A more critical analysis of the atomic bombs dropped on Japan challenges the "lifesavers" historic justification. Without question, the first atomic bombs ended the war quickly and the American people were uniformly thrilled that they had been used to end the war. Did another "quick" alternative that would have killed fewer people also exist? Were the estimates of lives saved communicated by President Truman created from thin air and primarily designed to justify the massacre of civilians?

A minority of Americans know that the United States Strategic Bombing Survey interviewed hundreds of Japanese leaders after the war and concluded with absolute certainty that Japan would have surrendered in 1945 without the use of the atomic bomb, a U.S. invasion, or Russia entering the war.[412] Few Americans know that the Emperor had decided to surrender on August 8, 1945 even before the Soviets announced their declaration of war or the Nagasaki bomb was dropped.[413] The fact that the Japanese leadership was seeking a way to end the war through diplomacy in the weeks before the atomic bombs were dropped, makes one wonder what the world would be like if the bombs were never used. American leaders were aware of these facts in early 1945 because the Japanese code had previously been broken by U.S. intelligence.[414] The United States Strategic Bombing Survey concluded that to end the war in July 1945, Truman only needed to offer the Japanese a conditional surrender. The one condition required was that the Japanese emperor, a holy figure to the Japanese, would not be dishonored.

Would the war have ended quickly if President Truman had invited the Emperor to send representatives to witness a test bombing in July of 1945? In retrospect, these suggestions may seem absurd, especially when engaged in a life-and-death battle with a formidable enemy. However, should not every effort be made before thousands of people are burned to death or condemned to die slowly from burns and radiation? Had President Truman demonstrated the power of the atomic bomb without killing civilians, the war may have ended in July or August of 1945. Certainly the world perception of the United States as a force for peace would be very different in the decades and centuries after 1945.

Evidence exists to support the idea that the key timing issue for the use of the bombs was to end the war before the Russians declared war against Japan. British scientist P. M. S. Blackett believed that the United States was quick to deploy the bombs before the Russians could enter the war against Japan.[415] The Russians had promised the United States to declare war on Japan ninety days after the European war ended. The date the Russians were to enter the war was August 8, or two days after the first bomb was dropped. Blackett is supported by American historian Gar Alperovitz who notes a diary entry for July 28, 1945, by Secretary of the Navy James Forrestal, describing the Secretary of State James F. Byrnes as "most anxious to get the Japanese affair over with before the Russians got in."[416]

To challenge the second "lifesaver" myth that the Japanese had plenty of time after the first bomb to surrender, consider the following: the two bombs were dropped three days apart to accelerate Japan's unconditional surrender and test the effect of two types of bombs. The Hiroshima bomb was a uranium bomb, the Nagasaki bomb was a plutonium bomb. The U.S. had tested a plutonium bomb on July 16, 1945 at the Trinity site in New Mexico.[417] Prior to Hiroshima, a uranium bomb had never been detonated. Did both bombs serve as a scientific experiment to determine the suffering that would be inflicted on real buildings and people? The answer is yes and Air Force chief General Hap Arnold specifically instructed his generals to keep Hiroshima and Nagasaki undamaged from conventional bombing attacks for this reason.[418] It is important to remember that the time between August 6 and August 9 was extremely short. The Japanese were in a total state of confusion after the first bomb. No one had ever in the history of the world been on the receiving end of an atomic bomb. Japan's scientific teams needed until August 11, 1945 to confirm for the Japanese government that an atomic bomb had been used.[419] Waiting eight days instead of three may have prevented the horrible deaths of approximately 70,000 people in Nagasaki.[420]

Third, the targets chosen were primarily civilian targets and chosen because of the concentrated populations. Suitable targets without innocent civilians were plentiful. Truman's statement about avoiding killing civilians was purely to calm the fears of concerned citizens at home, because almost all of the 210,000 people killed in the bombings were civilians. The U.S. Strategic Bombing Survey further contradicted Truman with the disclosure that "Hiroshima and Nagasaki were chosen as targets because of their concentration of activities and population." Tokyo was not chosen so that the government could surrender before the Russians declared war, plus a previous saturation bombing raid with conventional bombs in Tokyo had already burned the city to the ground and killed over 80,000 people.

The fact that U.S. intelligence notified the launch group that twelve U.S. navy airmen were in the Hiroshima jail had no impact on the target selection. The airmen were subsequently killed in the bombing. Further troubling is the fact that the War Department received intelligence on July 31, 1945 that U.S. prisoners of war were also being held in Nagasaki. The reply from the War Department was "Targets previously assigned for Centerboard remain unchanged."[421] The fact that the first two atomic bombs also killed U.S. soldiers raises additional questions about the target selections.

WHAT WE LEARNED FROM THE FIRST ATOMIC BOMBS

The war with Japan was primarily an economic war that was set in motion when Japan threatened potential U.S. markets by attempting to take over China. The U.S. imposed a total embargo on scrap iron and oil in the summer of 1941, and a military attack by Japan was recognized in Washington to be a likely outcome by the end of that year. Japan's bombing of military targets at Pearl Harbor was a terrible crime and unfortunately ultimately served only to fuel the anger of a powerful nation and lead to atomic bombs being dropped. Osama bin Laden can still learn this lesson from history because his 9/11 attack, and a future American Hiroshima attack, will only bring even greater mass deaths to the Middle East. From where I stand, we are only beginning to see the long-term price that may need to be paid for using atomic bombs in World War II.

Since the saturation bombings in World War II, we have somehow lost sight of the fact that innocent people are killed by weapons of mass destruction. Wars are primarily started for economic reasons and many people, especially in the U.S., see bombing and the resulting death of innocent people, including children, as acceptable. By failing to question the first use of the atomic bombs, we also fail to see the primary catalyst for the subsequent global development and proliferation of weapons of mass destruction.

President Truman realized he had opened a Pandora's box by authorizing the first use of an atomic weapon. In his last State of the Union address, he said: "For now we have entered the atomic age, and war has undergone a technological change which makes it a very different thing from what it used to be... The war of the future would be one in which man could extinguish millions of lives at one blow, demolish the great cities of the world, wipe out the cultural achievements of the past—and destroy the very structure of a civilization that has slowly and painfully built up through hundreds of generations. Such a war is not a possible policy for rational men."[422]

John F. Kennedy's assessment of the threat on July 26, 1963 sums up the evolving problem as if it were written today. He said, "I ask you to stop and think for a moment what it would mean to have nuclear weapons in so many hands, in the hands of countries large and small, stable and unstable, responsible and irresponsible, scattered throughout the world. There would be no rest for anyone then, no stability, no real security, and no chance of effective disarmament. There would only be the increased chance of accidental war, and an increased necessity for the great powers to involve themselves in what otherwise would be local conflicts."[423] Little did John F. Kennedy know at the time that he was describing the present.

To go on record opposing the use of atomic bombs against Japan is a very unpopular thing for an American citizen to do. I realize that this is an offensive statement to many people who believe the first two atomic bombs saved American lives in World War II. With a keen eye on the facts and the benefit of time, I submit that the bombs dropped on Japan were unnecessary and have created more problems then they solved. I understand why people feel the decision to use atomic bombs against Japan was justifiable. We did not have the complete set of facts that we do today. How were the leaders at the time to know that the Japanese did not have their own "new and powerful" weapon? Making the right decision in the midst of a war is certainly harder than after the dust has settled and more facts are known.

For the record, General Eisenhower wrote to Secretary of War Stimson, "Japan was at that very moment seeking some way to surrender with minimum loss of 'face.' It wasn't necessary to hit them with that awful thing."[424] Admiral William D. Leahy was even stronger in his condemnation of the use of atomic weapons on Japan stating the "use of this barbarous weapon at Hiroshima and Nagasaki was of no material assistance in our war against Japan. The Japanese were already defeated and ready to surrender ... in being the first to use it, we ... adopted an ethical standard common to the barbarians of the Dark Ages."[425] Even J. Robert Oppenheimer, known as "the father of the atomic bomb" and the scientific leader of the Manhattan project, went so far as to personally tell President Truman, "Mr. President, I feel I have blood on my hands."[426] Oppenheimer then went on to oppose the development of the hydrogen bomb in 1949. Why did people like Eisenhower, Leahy and Oppenheimer feel using the bomb was a horrendous mistake? The answer is they had access to classified information that the American people would not see for decades.

As difficult as it is for many to hear, using the first atomic bombs was a horrendous mistake. The lessons from history that the atomic bombs saved lives and paved the way for a more peaceful world are untrue. We are now faced with the terrible situation of weapons of mass destruction proliferation that John F. Kennedy feared. Realizing that there has never been a just use of a weapon of mass destruction can help us break free of thinking that allows arsenals of nuclear weapons to exist. American citizens, as the creators of this destructive capability, carry an extra burden in terms of finding ways to end this threat to the world.

10

HOW INDIVIDUALS CAN PROMOTE PEACE AND HELP AMERICA'S DEMOCRACY

"Darkness cannot drive out darkness; only light can do that. Hate can-not drive out hate; only love can do that. Hate multiplies hate, violence multiplies violence, and toughness multiplies toughness in a descend-ing spiral of destruction…The chain reaction of evil-hate begetting hate, wars producing more wars-must be broken, or we shall be plunged into the dark abyss of annihilation."[427]
(Martin Luther King, Jr.)

THE COLD WAR HAS ENDED and instead of enjoying the long anticipated peace, Americans are now fighting an endless series of "Hot Wars." This chapter explains how individuals can help wage peace to prevent and end current conflicts. Several key forces for peace are highlighted along with a rec-ommendation for a Department of Peace to balance the Department of War. Recommendations for transformational change are also provided together with a methodology for where to start strengthening America's democracy. This chapter concludes with thoughts about the secondary allegiance to a country and a far more important allegiance to God and humanity.

FORCES FOR PEACE AND INNOVATIVE THINKING

Becoming a force for peace requires individuals to be informed. To learn about U.S. foreign policy and obtain ideas for a more peaceful world, I recom-mend joining a local peace organization. The budgets of these organizations are minuscule compared to that of the military-industrial complex, but their contribution to strengthening our democracy far exceeds any dollar for dollar comparison. The Internet addresses for each organization in this chapter can be found in notes section at the back of this book. While hundreds of organi-zations could be commended for their good work, the following organizations are highlighted because these are the organizations that have most helped me make sense of complex issues.

NUCLEAR AGE PEACE FOUNDATION

The Nuclear Age Peace Foundation's (NAPF) vision is a world at peace, free of the threat of war and free of weapons of mass destruction. NAPF is an amazing organization that started in Santa Barbara in 1982. The NAPF's President, David Krieger, J.D., Ph.D., is a global leader in the campaign to abolish nuclear weapons. He and his team produce a constant stream of thought-provoking educational materials to abolish nuclear weapons, strengthen international law and use technology responsibly and sustainably. This non-profit, non-partisan advocacy organization is one of the most insightful information providers on how to strengthen our democracy.[428]

WORLD AFFAIRS COUNCILS OF AMERICA

World Affairs Councils are a group of 85 non-profit, non-partisan organizations open to all who wish to join. The organization has 484,000 participants and 28 affiliated organizations. It reaches over 20 million people each year through its 2,500 events, radio, TV, and school programs.[429] The largest affiliate is the northern California chapter which has over 10,000 members and was founded in 1947. In northern California alone, projects include the Global Philanthropy Forum, a Schools Program helping more than 150,000 students, a Young Professionals group, the Asilomar foreign affairs conference, and the Helen Brown Lombardi Library of International Affairs.[430]

ARMS CONTROL ASSOCIATION

The Arms Control Association (ACA) was founded in 1971. The organization is a national nonpartisan membership organization dedicated to promoting public understanding of, and support for, effective arms control policies. The organization benefits from a number of retired military leaders who, seek peace through educating the public and exposing threats to our democracy. Arms Control Today (ACT) is published monthly and provides policy-makers, the press and the interested public with authoritative information, analysis and commentary on arms control proposals, negotiations, agreements, and related national security issues. ACA is a respected force in Washington and offers politicians, journalists and scholars insightful perspectives.[431]

NATURAL RESOURCES DEFENSE COUNCIL

The Natural Resources Defense Council (NRDC) is widely viewed as the nation's most effective environmental action organization. The organization has more than one million members working to protect the planet's wildlife and wild places and to ensure a safe and healthy environment for all living things.[432] I especially value the analysis from their Nuclear Weapons and Waste team. The experts on their staff are scientists and lawyers who have dedicated their lives to making the world a safer and better place for all of us.

CARNEGIE ENDOWMENT FOR INTERNATIONAL PEACE

The Carnegie Endowment for International Peace is a powerhouse of talent. The organization, founded in 1910, is a nonprofit organization dedicated to advancing cooperation between nations and world peace. Joseph Cirincione leads the Non-Proliferation Project. The Endowment publishes Foreign Policy, one of the leading magazines of international politics and economics. The Endowment helps to shape new policy possibilities that span geographic regions, governments, businesses, and international organizations with a focus on the forces driving global change.[433]

PHYSICIANS FOR SOCIAL RESPONSIBILITY

Physicians for Social Responsibility (PSR) was founded in 1961 to educate the public about the dangers of nuclear weapons and nuclear war. In the following decades, PSR's efforts to educate the public about the dangers of nuclear war grew into an international movement, with the founding of the International Physicians for the Prevention of Nuclear War (IPPNW). PSR shared in the Nobel Peace Prize awarded to IPPNW in 1985. In the 1990s, PSR worked to end nuclear testing and succeeded in bringing about the first U.S. nuclear test moratorium. Today, PSR's Sensible Multilateral American Response to Terrorism or SMART is a well constructed platform for peace. The PSR organization notes that "It's time to stop acting out of fear, and to start acting from core American values that respect life, the environment that sustains it, and the freedoms that allow for a full and healthy debate about the future of our nation."[434] SMART Security means pursuing policies that effectively prevent acts of terrorism, the spread of nuclear and other weapons of mass destruction, and the devastation of war. With nuclear proliferation well beyond the point of being put back in Pandora's box, PSR's work to prevent a nuclear holocaust is more vital than ever.[435]

While the previous six organizations and many other organizations work to promote peace, more is needed. Our government needs a new internal arm for peace. In order for peaceful solutions to be able to go head-to-head with military alternatives, a Department of Peace is needed to counter the Department of War. Many Americans forget that the Department of War was renamed the Department of Defense after World War II.[436]

U.S. DEPARTMENT OF PEACE

George Washington introduced a Department of Peace bill into Congress in 1793. The African-American freeman Benjamin Banneker, a brilliant astronomer and mathematician, wrote in his 1792 Almanac about a Department of Peace to "balance" the Department of War. Banneker's friends, like Dr. Benjamin Rush and Thomas Jefferson, supported the idea. Yet over 200 years and over one hundred bills later, we still do not have the Department of Peace or the U.S. Peace Academy.[437] How many wars like Vietnam and now Iraq would have been prevented if this balancing force to the War Department existed?

The Secretary of Peace would be a mandatory presidential cabinet level position. A cabinet level position is required in order to position the Secretary of Defense and the Secretary of Peace as equals. Presidents should establish a common practice of consulting the Secretary of Peace before authorizing any arms sale or weapons shipment. In peacetime, both budgets should be required to equal each other. The power of authority as a cabinet officer with an equal budget would help prevent the Department of Peace from being sidelined as a program in existence, but with no real muscle to offset the Defense Department. On the international level, the Secretary of Peace would work to reduce international conflict, sponsor regional conflict prevention and be a watchdog agency for U.S. military, CIA, and other U.S. organizations working in other countries.

A two-year tour of duty in the Department of Peace or a teaching assignment at the U.S. Peace Academy could be part of the U.S. military career development. This rotational assignment for our protectors of freedom would help develop leaders of the military with a broader perspective than constantly focusing on the use of force to solve problems. The military currently has a policy of rotational assignments from command and combat positions to prevent burnout. The idea of a rotation to the Department of Peace would also have the benefit of increasing retention of the best soldiers and sending into retirement people less likely to be won over by the military-industrial complex.

The mission of the U.S. Peace Force would include assisting people who are suffering and delivering education programs to enable self sufficiency. The current Peace Corps would naturally continue and could help lead this arm of the Department of Peace. Specifically, this would include building bridges, sewage treatment plants, clean water facilities, hospitals and other infrastructure projects around the world. When you build a bridge or a hospital, people have a favorable thought of appreciation when they use it. We will build friendships and frustrate efforts by terrorists to fuel hatred of the United States. Approximately one-half of the Department of Peace would be the U.S. Peace Force with the mission of feeding the hungry, aiding the sick, removing land mines, cleaning contaminated areas from depleted uranium weapons, rebuilding infrastructures, and sustainable development. Fighting hunger, malaria, AIDS, and lack of clean water would be top priorities.

The other half of the Department of Peace funding would be focused on education. The Department of Peace would promote alternatives to violence with programs designed to educate from kindergarten to graduate school. The Department of Peace would develop future leaders in the government and industry through the U.S. Peace Academy. In a positive twist of history, we should close down the Western Hemisphere Institute for Security Cooperation at Fort Benning, better known as the School of the Americas, and use the buildings to start the U.S. Peace Academy.

A Department of Peace with the U.S. Peace Force and U.S. Peace Academy components would offer a check and balance to save lives and reduce suffering. This arm of government would likely promote international justice by supporting, rather than opposing, an empowered international system of justice like the International Criminal Court. Innovative democratic ideas, like enabling citizens to opt out of paying taxes that go toward weapons of mass destruction, could be spearheaded by a Department of Peace.[438]

A bill, not as comprehensive as what I am proposing, but nonetheless a big step in the right direction, was sponsored by Representative Dennis Kucinich, a Democrat from Ohio. The bill for a Department of Peace was introduced on April 8, 2003 but has not been approved. Congress seems to be too busy with the wars that we are currently fighting to consider creating a Department of Peace.

STOPPING HARMFUL BEHAVIORS IS TRANSFORMATIONAL

Why not create an alternative and more prosperous future for everyone? We can transform ourselves and potentially our country if we start asking why not. Consider the difference between a to-do list and a not-to-do list. To-do lists are good, but not-to-do lists are transformational. To illustrate this point, you may have a dozen or so tasks on a to-do list. Putting a check mark next to each to-do list task that is completed feels good and helps accomplish objectives. Putting a check mark next to a list of not-to-do behaviors changes your life. Whether it is stopping smoking, stopping swearing, or some other behavior, you are transforming who you are. Consider the transformational changes that are possible if the United States stopped selling or giving weapons to other countries.

Hopefully you are asking, "Why not stop missing opportunities for a more peaceful world?" Three important why not questions further illustrate how transformational this can be are:

1. Why not eliminate our dependence on oil?
2. Why not recognize that addressing human suffering is in our best interest?
3. Why not make the true costs of war known?

The above and other key why-not questions for reflection or group discussion are listed in Appendix F.

These actionable questions can produce actionable answers that strengthen our democracy and leave our children with a legacy of a world with less hunger, suffering, and violence.

The magnitude of the above and the financial waste on unneeded weapons alone can rally both fiscal conservatives and liberals. One example is acknowledging that we and the world do not need additional nuclear weapons. Recovering the five trillion-plus dollars that the United States has already spent on nuclear weapons is not possible. The thought of how more peaceful our world would be if the majority of these funds went to help educate and care for people makes me sad. The good news is that it is possible to stop wasting the future trillions of dollars for weapons that we do not need and in the process improve our economy and the world.

WHERE DO WE START?

With so many opportunities, where do we start? David Krieger in the Foreword of this book answered this question. He observes, "Each of us by our daily acts of peace and our commitment to building a better world can inspire others and help create a groundswell for peace too powerful to be turned aside." I recommend focusing on the mistakes that are getting people killed – which also happen to be the top-dollar mistakes. Starting with billion dollar mistakes is sufficient to arrive at a workable list. Appendix C also provides a list of 15 activities individuals can engage in to protect our democracy from being undermined.

A world without weapons of mass destruction is possible in our lifetime. The majority of all Americans already believe that no nation, including the United States, should have nuclear weapons.[439] The U.S. is in the unique position, should Americans provide the leadership, to make a nuclear-weapons-free world possible. The combined reduction of weapons of mass destruction and the necessary trust-building measures may take many years to accomplish, but even accomplishing half of this goal would be wonderful. Bringing the total arsenal of weapons of mass destruction to half, a third or perhaps a tenth of the current levels would help position a future generation to achieve a nuclear-weapons-free world.

Do you believe kindness begets kindness and violence promotes additional violence? If you do, help the U.S. pursue kinder and gentler policies. Do you believe that dialogue leads to understanding and secrecy promotes mistrust? If you do, call for open dialogues to resolve differences. Do you believe in love your neighbor? If you do, would you agree to supporting a policy whereby the U.S. would never initiate a first strike with nuclear weapons? Do you believe thou shall not kill? Even if you believe in the just war doctrine, how can anyone justify nuclear arsenals that kill millions of innocent civilians? Basic questions, but nonetheless the answers to these questions can provide clear guidance for helping make the U.S. a better and safer country.

The principles of a just war are commonly held to be: having just cause, possessing right intention, declared by a proper authority, having a reasonable chance of success, and the end being proportional to the means used. Another way of looking at the concept of a just war is that, in it, life is taken only to save life. In a world with weapons of mass destruction, weapons that kill millions of innocent people can never pass the test of the just war doctrine.

It would take tremendous courage to eliminate weapons of mass destruction. A nation that is afraid may only be able to support no biological or chemical weapons and reducing its nuclear arsenal. I ask you to imagine that you are at the gate to heaven and you are asked "Did you support nuclear weapons or did you oppose them?" Perhaps it takes less courage to oppose them when you consider that your soul is more important than your life. As Thomas Jefferson said, "The rights of conscience we never submitted, we could not submit. We are answerable for them to our God."[440]

In a world where only one out of four people has running water, it really is a crime against humanity to build and maintain weapons of mass destruction. With history as our guide, increased weapons buildup results in other nations increasing their weapons buildup. This also is consistent with the kindness begets kindness and inverse theme.

Jimmy L. Spearow, a speaker for Physicians for Social Responsibility Sacramento Chapter, has created a diagram to illustrate the factors driving the nuclear and conventional arms race.[441] Notice on the diagram (on next page) that Nation A has a perceived threat from Nation B. The perceived threat generates an insecurity and the natural reaction for Nation A is to develop weapons and build nationalism. This helps Nation A feel more secure. Nation B becomes fearful of Nation A and as a result develops more weapons and fuels additional nationalism. The diagram concludes that war is the ultimate outcome of this cycle of developing weapons and increasing nationalism.

When you consider that weapons of mass destruction, especially nuclear weapons, change the paradigm of what it means when war is the ultimate outcome, we must passionately act to rid the world of these weapons. Until we realize that weapons of mass destruction do more to empower the weak than to protect the strong, the shadows of death and destruction will continue to advance upon us.

Without the courage that can come from an informed electorate, the cycle continues producing endless and ever increasingly deadly wars. For religious people, upon reflection you may find that your religion demands that you step outside this cycle of death and destruction. For all people, the courage to turn the other cheek, is hard to accept, but the cycle of subsequent violence is dramatically less. Albert Einstein once said, "you cannot simultaneously prevent and prepare for war."[442] The wisdom in Einstein's words is graphically captured by this diagram, especially since a nuclear war has the potential to kill everyone.

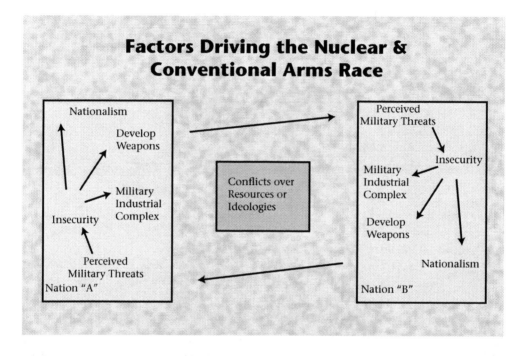

Imagine a new way of thinking. A multilateral police force would be needed to help prevent the spread of weapon of mass destruction and intervene to stop atrocities. Envision a world where money spent on weapons seeking to dominate the world is no longer a priority. The peace dividend could employ millions of people and tackle tough challenges ranging from providing health care to the uninsured to solving world hunger. Acts of kindness would be followed by acts of more acts of kindness. The following diagram illustrates this new way of thinking and specifically the key factors that help drive peace and goodwill. In the diagram, Nation A perceives no threat from Nation B. This leads to security in Nation A. Nation A is able to invest in foreign aid, improve their domestic services like health care, and in general help others. Nation B, receiving kindness from Nation A, is also secure. Nation B uses their peace dividend from not having to buy weapons to improve domestic programs and help others around the world. The natural outcome of this repeating cycle is endless peace.

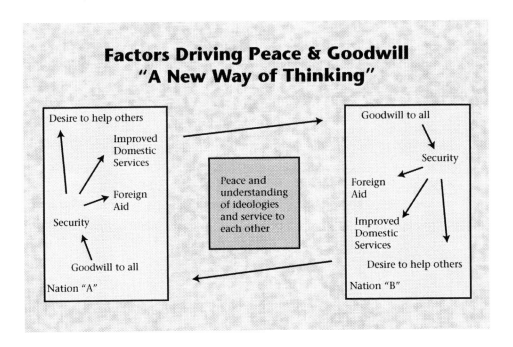

The world has been fortunate in that the last atomic weapon used in a war was in 1945. As a result many people have a false sense of security and think nuclear war is unlikely to happen. History has already proven that atomic weapons were almost used at several points in the last fifty years. Today we now know that during the Kennedy administration the U.S. was considering a first strike against the Soviets in 1961. The first strike was recommended by members of the U.S. Joint Chiefs of Staff to thereby prevent an even greater anticipated future disaster as the former Soviet Union arsenal was still a fraction of its size a few years later. Fortunately, a first strike on the former Soviet Union never occurred and after this meeting with the Chiefs of Staff Kennedy said, "and we call ourselves the human race."[443]

Perhaps another analogy can provide some insight of why doing the right thing yields ongoing benefits for future generations. As military officers (unlike CIA officers at that same time), we were taught not to torture captured prisoners during interrogations. I found myself asking the tough question: "Would I restrain myself from torturing a prisoner if the knowledge from a prisoner would save my unit?" As I wrestled with this question, I came to the same conclusion that the U.S. military continues to teach to this day. If a soldier tortures another person, the immediate unit might be saved – but, in general, many more people will die in this war and in future wars because enemy soldiers will continue to fight when they know they cannot safely surrender. Doing the right thing may cost lives in the short run but will save lives in the long run. One only need look at the mass surrender of Iraqis during the Gulf War for proof that treating prisoners well will save lives. The price of the Abu

Ghraib torture is already being paid in Iraq as many current combatants fear what will happen after they surrender more than fighting to the death.

The key point in these stories is finding ways to stay true to a value system of right and wrong pays off in the long run. Waging peace is not only more humane, it is also more effective than projecting our military power to secure our well being.

NO FALSE ALLEGIANCES

I am convinced that in heaven there are no national flags. The saying, "my country right or wrong" is itself wrong and can lead to terrible abuses of power. A suicide bomber who kills people is never right, regardless of whether his or her country is Palestine, Israel, Iraq, the United States or anywhere else.

If you support the concept "my country right or wrong," think about how popular this statement would be in Germany following World War II or read Inside The Third Reich by Albert Speer. While external examples may help make this point, you do not have to look at other countries for examples.

Consider for a moment the United States war in Vietnam. Many Americans now realize that Vietnam was one of our most painful lessons that "my country right or wrong" is misdirected. The truth of "my country right or wrong" and how the betrayal by key leaders can occur are especially clear in Robert McNamara's writings in the years after the war. Robert McNamara's reflections on Vietnam illustrate how national ego, disregard for the positions of traditional allies, detachment from the soldiers in the field, and a failure to understand the enemy resulted in a country sending its soldiers to be killed and maimed in an illegal war.[444]

Another way to look at the question of my country right or wrong and the broader issue of patriotism is to reflect on the statement "God Bless America." While hearing "God Bless America" is pleasing to my ear, I feel God would prefer we say "God Bless The World," or "God Bless Us All." Nations are created by people, the world was created by God. All life is equally valued in God's eyes and therefore why limit God's blessing? Too much patriotism leading to too much nationalism, again along the absolute power theme expressed earlier, can result in a disconnect between the equal value of all life inside and outside the United States.

11

WAGING PEACE NOW —
HOW TO PREVENT AN AMERICAN HIROSHIMA

"If you succumb to the temptation of using violence in your struggle, unborn generations will be the recipients of a long and desolate night of bitterness, and your chief legacy to the future will be an endless reign of meaningless chaos."

(Martin Luther King, Jr.)[445]

THIS, THE FINAL CHAPTER, EXPLAINS how the United States can prevent an American Hiroshima and protect America's democracy from domestic and foreign threats. The words "waging peace now" are important because "waging peace" demands a nonviolent and passionate campaign for justice. We must all have courage and perseverance to fight for justice right "now" because failing to do so will result in the horror of an American Hiroshima.

HOW TO DEFEAT TERRORISTS – WORK FOR JUSTICE

The founders of our country rooted for the underdog, sought protection from the dangers of absolute power, and exercised care not to use force overseas.[446] Today, the United States has become the closest thing to an absolute power the world has ever known. If absolute power corrupts, have we become corrupted? Our failure to see what our government is doing around the world, combined with our lack of concern, strongly suggests the answer is yes.

Al Qaeda and other terrorist groups can be defeated. Americans, and especially the president, need to understand that terrorism is a method, and not an enemy, in order to transform today's reactive war on terror into a proactive pursuit of justice. Defeating terrorists requires that we recognize that U.S. foreign policies following World War II have eroded America's image, moral authority, and given birth to movements that seek its destruction. Americans need to know how the U.S. government helped create the leading terrorists of our time, including Saddam Hussein and Osama bin Laden. Recognizing these mistakes is a step toward defeating terrorists and correcting the problems that flow from becoming an absolute power.

An essential step toward defeating terrorists is to withdraw from Iraq. The invasion of Iraq was counter-productive to defeating terrorists and this war was already lost the day it started. Consider for a moment the chance of success if a primarily Islamic military force occupied territory in the United States following a decade of economic sanctions that resulted in having 500,000 American children die from preventable causes? Yes, the war was lost on the same day it started. In addition to being a lost cause and illegal by any standard, the preemptive invasion and occupation is continually increasing the number of terrorists and preventing moderate Muslims from denouncing future 9/11 like attacks. Denial of these facts prolongs the waste, suffering, and casualties.

As simple as this sounds, the United States needs to pursue actions that will reduce the number of terrorists. If we fail to do so, the country will win most military battles but lose the war. One only need consider the worldwide opposition to the U.S. use of force in Iraq, as measured by the Pew Research Center and discussed in Chapter Two, to see this dynamic.[447] The current strategy is absolutely guaranteeing a more dangerous world for everyone, especially our children.

Terrorism as a method of violence can be stopped and the recruiting pipeline shut down. To do so requires commonsense measures like identifying the terrorists and understanding the real reasons for their acts of terror. We greatly undermine terrorists when legitimate injustices are addressed. This is the fastest way to shut down the terrorist recruiting pipeline. The long-term way to keep the recruiting pipeline shut down is to aggressively wage war on hunger, malaria and other diseases spreading poverty and death. When combined with programs to help educate the poor, the United States will do more to defeat terrorists and the spread of violence than is possible from military campaigns.

If you feel addressing valid terrorist needs is fueling more terrorism, know that justice is ultimately the medicine for terrorism. In the end, justice prevails when the injustice that fueled the violence is no longer fueled and the people who used violence to seek justice are prosecuted for their acts of terror. To achieve justice, Americans need to understand that supporting the International Criminal Court is essential for justice to prevail. Terrorists, sentenced by the International Criminal Court for harm done to others, would in time be seen as criminals from all vantage points.

Defeating terror requires no double standards. Anyone, regardless of religion or country of origin, who kills an innocent person, has committed an act of terror. To be blind to this reality guarantees ongoing acts of terror. Holding others to a different standard creates terrorists. We can start by not threatening and executing wars based on other nations developing weapons of mass destruction for deterrence, especially since the United States possesses the largest arsenal in the world. Strengthening the Biological Weapons Convention, Chemical Weapons Convention, Non-Proliferation Treaty and Comprehensive Test Ban Treaty are other logical steps to defeat terrorists.

The world must make the United Nations more democratic so that all people in all nations have a voice. A democratic and strengthened United Nations can implement measures to deny all nations the right to possess weapons of mass destruction. This far-reaching idea of justice and lasting peace is acknowledged to take time, but we must act quickly; the Pandora's box is open and proliferation is already with us. As we seek this necessary step to defeat terror, near-term measures, like the proposed limit of 384 weapons of mass destruction, can help the world slow and in some cases stop proliferation.

A multilateral non-proliferation task force is needed immediately. The United Nations has proven around the world, in places like Liberia, that it can rally and lead successful peacekeeping forces. The best of the best from the world's military services could join forces to police the global market for highly enriched uranium and plutonium. Unfortunately, how to make a nuclear bomb is no longer a well-kept secret. Fortunately, producing new fissile material requires a massive effort, one with at least some opportunities for a talented multilateral peacekeeping force to detect and stop proliferation.

These aggressive actions to defeat terror must be accompanied with an end to America's dependence on oil. If the United States can put a person on the moon, America can certainly find a way to eliminate its dependency on oil from the Middle East. Continuing to support corrupt governments like Saudi Arabia empowers terrorists and brings us closer to the time when terrorists possess weapons of mass destruction.

The United States must assist the cause of justice in the Israeli and Palestinian dispute. This dispute has been the single greatest fuel for fundamentalist Islam in the world. Both sides have suffered but the poverty of the Palestinians suggests that they have suffered the most. They have endured three generations of displacement and poverty. If hope for the Palestinians continues to be denied, Israel is guaranteed to experience nuclear terrorism. This is especially true if the United States implements the prior recommendations in this book to defeat terrorists, as Israel will regain its position as the primary target of terrorists.

Just compensation for Palestinians who are unable to return to their homes is essential. This will cost billions of dollars but is cheap relative to the inevitable price tag I see in Israel's future. The Israelis who were forced from their homes in Arab lands will also need to be compensated for their loss. If the United States led the creation of this international commission, the goodwill engendered in the Islamic world would serve to further frustrate terrorists.

Finally, and certainly not to be forgotten, America can defeat terrorists by continuing to provide justice, freedom, and opportunity for the millions of people that come to our country. The goodwill that occurs when a person from another nations sends money home, often to help family members struggling on a dollar or less a day, greatly undermines people who seek to harm the United States.

The following is a recommendation of what President George W. Bush should say to the world:

> *The time has come to successfully end the war on terrorism and bring our soldiers home. I recognize that acts of terror are not because people hate our freedom. Terror is a response to something, and that something is injustice. Our choice, in this age of nuclear weapons, is not between nonviolence and violence, but between nonviolence and nonexistence.*[430]

> *Today, I announce an end to our wars. Peace is only possible by ending the escalating cycle of violence and aggressively working for justice around the world. I am starting the process of justice by apologizing to every person who is a victim of United States-sponsored injustice. I will therefore, on behalf of the United States:*

> - *renounce our right to declare unilateral war and will work passionately with other nations so that they do the same.*
> - *bring our brave and loyal soldiers in Iraq and around the world home. In today's world with aircraft, submarines and missiles that have a global reach, no U.S. forces should be stationed outside our country in a time of peace, except as members of an United Nations peacekeeping force or to perform specific operations to deny terrorists access to nuclear weapons and nuclear materials.*
> - *protect our nuclear facilities in the United States. We must ensure that if a nuclear bomb or accident occurs, the highly radioactive materials are protected so that large portions of the United States do not become uninhabitable for future generations.*
> - *start the process to free our nation from oil wars, fossil fuel pollution and end our willingness to support injustice overseas by putting our best scientists to work to solve the remaining technological challenges to developing clean coal, fuel cells, solar, wind, geo-thermal, and other yet-to-be discovered efficient sources of energy. We currently have the technology to develop vehicles that are powered by a combination of electricity and alcohol-based fuels, with petroleum as only one element among many. My administration will provide the leadership so that the United States is no longer dependent*

on petroleum from the Middle East by the year 2015.[449]

- promise not to intervene in the political process of other nations or to seek the overthrow of democratically elected leaders.
- stop military funding and arms sales to other nations.
- lead an international commission to resolve the Israeli and Palestinian dispute.
- cut the military budget in three parts and use one part for defense, one part for to help the people of Iraq and Afghanistan rebuild their countries, and the last part will stay at home to provide education, health care assistance, create the U.S. Peace Force, and strengthen the Social Security system.
- end hypocritical policies by no longer holding other nations to a standard different than we hold for ourselves. This will allow us to regain our credibility as we seek to solve our most pressing challenges, especially stopping the proliferation of weapons of mass destruction.
- agree to aggressively work to eliminate weapons of mass destruction proliferation by immediately reducing our nuclear arsenal to 384 weapons.
- protect future generations by exercising great care to safeguard our environment. High on this list is stopping the creation of nuclear waste that poses a health hazard and terrorist threat for future generations.
- endorse the International Criminal Court and honor the Universal Declaration of Human Rights.
- and, champion a weapons-free space nonproliferation agreement. Independent of this agreement, the United States will end all missile defense funding. We can learn from the past and not repeat wasting billions of dollars on weapons that only make everyone less secure by keeping space free of weapons.[450]

Throughout our history we have hated and fought with many nations. In time these same countries have become our friends. We need only think of our wars with England, Germany, Japan, Vietnam, and the Cold War with the former Soviet Union to realize that it is not a specific people that we must hate, but hate itself. If we kill for peace we will have war forever. A great American, Martin Luther King, Jr., once said:

"A true revolution of values will lay hands on the world order and say of war: This way of settling differences is not just...

A true revolution of values will soon cause us to question the fairness and justice of many of our past and present policies...

A true revolution of values will soon look uneasily on the glaring contrast of poverty and wealth...

A nation that continues year after year to spend more money on *military defense than on programs of social uplift is approaching spiritual death."* [451]

Because we desire peace and justice, the time has come to end exceptionalist policies. We must ask for and give forgiveness as we are all part of a common humanity. We must become the example we expect to see in return. We do this for ourselves and for humanity.

God bless us all!

If the president had the courage to set forth the above policies and aggressively enforce them, justice would result and terror groups would be defeated. Immediately attacks against Americans at home and overseas would decrease at a far faster pace than allowed by the current strategy. An American Hiroshima would be prevented by this change in foreign policy as America would be seen by the Islamic world as correcting great injustices and a subsequent terrorist attack would backfire on the ultimate objective of expanding terrorist movements. Tensions that could produce a nuclear exchange in places like North Korea and Iran would be decreased, allowing reasonable people to find new peaceful solutions. America's economy would be saved from the devastating costs of war and the black hole of new expenses associated with space weapons. Members of the U.S. military would stop being killed and maimed in counter-productive wars. America's mercenaries could go back to being productive citizens. Americans could address the many other important opportunities to improve our country... maybe even finally make assault weapons illegal to own and create the U.S. Department of Peace!

Thank you for considering the ideas in this book on how we can wage peace now. God bless us all!

APPENDIX A

FORMATIVE EXPERIENCES FOR WRITING "AMERICAN HIROSHIMA"

THE FOLLOWING EXPLAINS HOW A former military person and conservative Republican became motivated to write American Hiroshima.

In 1981, I joined the military because I believed that the United States was the greatest source of peace and prosperity in the world. In 1982, I had my first overseas military Temporary Duty Assignment. My unit, the 104th Tactical Fighter Squadron, was sent to Turkey to participate in exercises to help prepare us in the event of a war with the Soviet Union. I had my first experience with terrorism during this assignment. Our officers said we did not have to worry about hostility from the Turkish people; but Turkey had several hostile neighbors. We were warned that U.S. service people in Turkey had to be aware "that they were not in Kansas anymore."[452] The warnings about potential terrorist attacks proved to be accurate. One day we left a market in Bursa and later a terrorist bomb exploded there.[453]

When I returned to the United States and college, I started to think seriously about nuclear weapons. My Air Force Reserve Officer Training Corps commander often talked to me about becoming a missile officer. The Air Force needed officers to be prepared to launch land-based nuclear warheads. As a reminder of that time in my life, I still have my Why Serve In The Missile Branch book and "Missile Branch Certified" medical report. My inner voice was loud and clear that this was not my purpose in life. My thinking at the time was that sitting in a hole to turn a key that would incinerate millions of innocent people was cowardly. I could not then – and still cannot now – see how using a nuclear weapon that would result in the mass deaths of innocent people could ever be approved by our Creator. While clearly a contradiction, killing a person with a rifle was acceptable at the time because I thought the judgment of saving a life before pulling the trigger would be present.

When I finished college, I transferred to the Army. To change branches of the military is unusual but the Army was the better path for me. I dreamed of becoming a paratrooper and serving as an Army Intelligence Officer. I recall thinking that, in the Army, I could represent the best of America in peacetime and war. My selection of the Army was also motivated by an uneasiness with dropping bombs that were bound to kill innocent bystanders versus the more direct use of force by Army combat units. I envisioned myself in combat situations where missions could be carried out without losing sight of protecting innocent people. I remember thinking that my soldiers would never fire on villagers or mistreat prisoners of war. We would protect freedom, and even risk death before we ever would fire blindly into a village and inflict harm on non-combatants.

Looking back on that nineteen-year-old's thoughts, I now realize that the nature of war and the lack of clarity in combat situations would have made the level of non-combatant care I wished to guarantee impossible.

After completing my Army officer, Intelligence and Airborne (parachute) training, I was assigned to South Korea. One of my instructors at Intelligence school at Fort Huachuca in Arizona said, "South Korea is the last place in the world where you can go and the people genuinely like you." This comment, made in 1985, had an impact on me because I firmly believed the American military was admired in most places. Prior to arriving in South Korea, I had a hard time imagining that people around the world disliked the U.S. military.

In 1985 I went to South Korea and experienced my first exposure to why people both love and hate the United States. I expected the majority of South Korean people to like U.S. soldiers because we were putting our lives on the line for their defense; logically they should appreciate our presence. What I witnessed instead were mass protests against the U.S. military presence. As a 21-year-old second lieutenant, I started to question what I believed to be true about our military presence and broader foreign policies.

My year in South Korea continues to be a source of powerful memories for me. As far as peacetime military assignments go, day-to-day life in South Korea was difficult. The conditions were tough, and missions in the heavily-mined Demilitarized Zone or DMZ, were dangerous. Most Americans were stationed 20 miles or more south of the DMZ. Other United States soldiers served in a one-mile sector of the border with North Korea, at Panmunjom.[454] However, intelligence officers and their teams were assigned to work in the other 150 miles of the border with North Korea.

My team was assigned to the Chorwon sector in the Kangwon Province, which is in the middle of the 151 mile border. Since North and South Korea were then – and are still now – technically at war, the DMZ was and is a tense place. At night, North Korea occasionally sent spies and military teams across the border. Night-time operations through the landmine littered territory leads the thinking person to conclude that the "D" should be removed from DMZ. My team's basic routine was to perform communication intercept intelligence and serve as a forward warning element in the event of a North

Korean invasion.

Kim Il Sung, who had led the surprise invasion of South Korea in 1950, was still in charge at the time. He was in power until he died in 1994 at the age of 82. His regime illustrates how badly a country can be run. Starvation of thousands of people and abject poverty for the bulk of the population continues to this day under his son, Kim Jung Il.

When President George W. Bush visited South Korea and the DMZ on February 19, 2002, he stated that North Korea has an evil government. He has been criticized for this statement, but he was correct. North Korea has suppressed freedom and allowed its population to starve for decades. If Kim Jung Il's government made an effort to feed its people, starvation would cease immediately. Unfortunately, peace continues to be only a dream in the Koreas and the DMZ continues to be one of the most dangerous hot-spots on the planet. North Korea's June 2, 2003 announcement to U.S. representatives that it has joined the nuclear weapons club only makes the current situation more volatile.[455]

With or without nuclear weapons, if war were to break out in Korea, the American soldiers in the DMZ know that they are dead. They will either be overrun by the North Korean divisions or killed by friendly fire directed against the invading forces.[456] In any event, we knew that our mission was to warn our command and then dig in and fight for as long as we could before being killed.

In the DMZ, we could see the North Koreans, and they often broadcast messages and music in English to us over loudspeakers. I'll never forget the North Koreans threatening to kill us one day and offering us beautiful women the very next day. The North Koreans also liked to drop propaganda from balloons that would float into South Korea. Over the years, a few American soldiers have accepted this offer of a better life in North Korea. North Korea made good use of these Americans in propaganda movies and as instructors for their spies. North Korea also used these Americans to father children that would be groomed to be spies in the West.[457] News about the exchanges of fire, captured spies, and the sunken spy boat that were very real never made it back to the United States; or, if it did, I never saw it covered by the media when I returned home.[458]

The contrast between the prosperous South and the starving North was dramatic. The South is prosperous while North Korea is one of the poorest places on the planet. Without question this contrast speaks well for de-mocracy and condemns communism. Given this obvious contrast, clearly still visible today, why were the South Koreans demanding that the United States leave the country? During my first six months in the country I was still puzzled by this contradiction.

I started to be exposed to South Korean people when I was reassigned as the intelligence officer for an armored battalion. During this time I routinely made use of a skill that I was taught in intelligence school. This skill – or framework for organizing information – is called Intelligence Preparation of the Battlefield, or IPB.[459] It makes sense of numerous pieces of related and unrelated information. IPB is equally helpful in an information society, as it organizes information and makes sense of what could otherwise be information overload. Unorganized information can be useless, or even cloud the truth, resulting in tremendous error. In combat situations, intelligence personnel need to quickly filter out the noise, capture the meaningful pieces of the puzzle and prevent distortion between insignificant information and what is really going on.

My time as an intelligence officer was valuable beyond solidifying my IPB skills. I was able to make sense of the love-hate feelings that South Koreans have toward the United States. This love-hate dynamic exists not only in South Korea, but everywhere foreign soldiers are deployed overseas.

I remember South Korean children waving to us from the side of the road. At first I thought these kids really like us. I thought back to what I heard in intelligence school; "South Korea is the last place in the world where you can go and the people genuinely like you." Several weeks later, I learned enough Korean to realize that while the kids smiled and waved, they were swearing at us as they shouted to give them the bubble gum from our Meals-Ready-To-Eat or MREs.

I recall the South Korean man who saw his Gin-Zing field destroyed by our tank battalion. I was told that he would be reimbursed by an indemnification program that the United States had with South Korea; but from the way he cried, the monetary reimbursement must have been a fraction of what he lost. Over the years, every incident like the Gin-Zing field destruction, an outright theft, or more serious incidents such as rape would remind local Koreans that these foreigners should leave. South Koreans are understandably angry when they see U.S. soldiers in public who are drunk or with prostitutes.[460] The occasional story of a crime committed or a murder of a local person by a soldier further sours the approval of the United States military presence.[461] Over time, serious resentment and hatred are natural results. When this happens, the United States military presence becomes perceived by the local people to be the United States military occupation.

By the time my tour of duty was completed, I was not surprised that many South Korean people wanted the American soldiers to leave. Older South Koreans would sometimes tell me that the United States saved their country from the communists. As the population became older, this sentiment toward the United States was clearly changing. Younger South Koreans saw the United

States as an obstacle to reunification and peace with North Korea. Students especially hated American soldiers and intense protests in Seoul were common. The decline in approval for the U.S. military has further declined in the last 20 years. Today "many Korean restaurants refuse to serve Americans."[462] Some South Korean stores display signs that state Americans are not served. For Korean War veterans who experienced a overwhelmingly positive reaction from the Korean people, this change in attitude is mind-boggling.[463]

I was offended then, but now understand and actually agree with the perspective of the then younger and now middle-aged South Koreans. If I were in their shoes, I would evaluate the United States' military presence on the combination of the good accomplished by the United States that my grandparents and parents may have shared with me along with my first-hand experiences. After all, even the people who are 50 years old today were not born when North Korea invaded the South.[464]

The rationale for the U.S. military presence being despised was not just the occasional bad behavior of our military, but rather the dependency it implied. A basic need for everyone is the ability to be independent. When we are dependent on another nation for a basic need like security, it sends a subtle but powerful pejorative message that I am not able to satisfy my basic needs and therefore I am inferior. The relationship is not between equals, but rather places one group in a position where it is dependent on another. Imagine how you would feel if a foreign military had been present in your hometown for the last 50 years.

The definition of dependence begins with "subordination to someone or something"[465] and can be illustrated by the stages of human development. Babies are certainly dependent. Countries are sometimes initially dependent. Healthy teenagers leave the dependent stage and become independent. A healthy teenager will grow beyond independence and form interdependent relationships as an adult. The same is true regarding our relationships with other nations. While the starting point is sometimes dependence, we benefit when we work with the others to help them become independent and ultimately interdependent.

When we develop the highest level of relationships and interdependence, we are interacting as equals and benefiting from the synergy. You may think this just another way of saying it is better to teach a person how to fish than to simply give a person a fish. While this is partly true, interdependence is when the person you taught to fish is now teaching you new skills so that your combined effectiveness exceeds your individual effectiveness. To make this concept more concrete, consider two fishermen unable to cross a waist-high river because the current is too strong. They decide to cross the river as a single unit or interdependent team. They become interdependent by locking their arms together. One man takes the brunt of the river's current and the man on the downstream side provides the needed stability as he is freed from the majority of the force of the current. Together, as an interdependent team, both are able to cross a river that is otherwise unsurpassable by a single or independent person.

My experience in South Korea did not benefit from knowledge of Korean history prior to the 1950 invasion by North Korea. Without understanding the relationship between the United States and Korea prior to the Korean War in 1950, I lacked the information to appreciate the perspective of South Koreans. I highlight a few key facts to reinforce this point and further illustrate how my support for the U.S. presence in South Korea changed.

In 1905, Secretary of War and future president William Howard Taft met secretly with Japan's foreign minister. The United States agreed to Japan's occupation of Korea in return for Tokyo's support for colonial domination of the Philippines by the United States. Japan immediately occupied Korea in 1905 and claimed it as a Japanese possession in 1910. At the end of World War II, the United States failed to support Korean independence. During the 1945 Yalta Conference, President Franklin D. Roosevelt proposed a U.S., Soviet and Chinese trusteeship. The actual division of the country at the 38th parallel was created by two lieutenant colonels during a White House strategy meeting on August 10, 1945.[466]

The betrayal felt by Koreans for both the Japanese occupation and the division of North and South are foundational for understanding modern-day feelings. When you combine these factors with the behavior of our troops and the unavoidable message of inferiority from our sustained military presence, the demand by South Koreans to send American soldiers home is not surprising.

With hundreds of thousands of soldiers constantly deployed in other countries, understanding this love-hate dynamic is critical. Over time it becomes a hate-hate and terrorist creating dynamic. This is certainly one of the reasons empires throughout history have always collapsed.

In 1985 I was shocked when I met South Koreans who believed that the likelihood of war with North Korea would decrease if the United States military left South Korea. I now share this belief and support the removal of all United States forces from the Korean peninsula. Our presence – and the growing discontent in South Korea for our military presence – actually helps North Korea maintain the fear that the United States will invade North Korea. Fear has always been instrumental for dictators and governments to maintain control of the people. The fear of invasion by the United States is a key reason why Kim Il Sung, now his son Kim Jong Il, and other dictators like Fidel Castro have been able to stay in power.

You might think that withdrawing forces from South Korea will increase the likelihood of North Korea invading South Korea. However, the United States has consistently made it clear since 1953 that the United States will not allow South Korea to fall. In addition, the South Korean military has weapons and resources that far surpass North Korea's antiquated arsenal. As I see it, the United States military presence in South Korea costs billions of dollars each year and only creates a public relations nightmare for peace-building efforts across Southeast Asia.

One lesson that is applicable from this experience for today's young soldiers is that, as a soldier myself in South Korea, I had no knowledge of any of this history leading up to the North Korean invasion in 1950. As a result, I did not appreciate the feelings of betrayal that many Koreans held. I highlight this because I can understand how a soldier is likely to overly rely on his or her elders and superiors for guidance on the worthiness of the cause. I feel for soldiers serving in the latest Iraq war because I know many are confident that they are fighting to avenge the 9/11 attacks. For me, the fact I was prepared to kill North Koreans with such a limited perspective of what was really going on is scary. Perhaps this is why most of the fighting in wars is performed by people under 30. Learning about the history before what appears to be the starting point for the conflict is an important lesson I took away from my experience in Korea.

There are several other noteworthy lessons from Korea. We should not make agreements as we did in 1905, giving Korea to Japan and control of the Philippines to the United States, because these agreements are inconsistent with the principles of democracy – regardless of the opportunities for the corporations of the time to profit.[467] A second learning point is that if you artificially create borders, you are likely to plant the seeds for a future war. Korea should never have been split and the United States and the former Soviet Union share the responsibility for this mistake that resulted in the Korean War. The third learning point, a strategic mistake we are currently making in many countries across the globe, is that we must be careful not to deploy troops for long periods of time so that we avoid creating dependency and hostility. We are currently in the process of making this mistake as permanent military bases are being constructed in Iraq.

In addition to the permanent military bases and pressing need for soldiers in Iraq, one very real reason the May 2004 U.S. troop reductions in South Korea were announced is anti-U.S. sentiment is spreading like a wildfire throughout South Korea. The U.S. decision to invade Iraq has added fuel to the fire of anti-U.S. sentiment in both South and North Korea. Another noteworthy reason for the May 2004 U.S. troop reductions is North Korea's announcement that it has nuclear weapons. In direct response to this development, in June 2003 the United States initiated a major redistribution of forces in South Korea.[468]

Today, only a fraction of the 2nd Infantry Division force that was within 20 miles of the DMZ remains. This is logical as in the event of war, nuclear weapons would likely be used to help clear the DMZ.

Serving in the military has helped me see the world from a perspective that would otherwise have been unlikely to develop. For example, soldiers in Iraq are being harmed by roadside attacks against their Humvee jeeps. I have spent a lot of time in the thin-skinned Humvee and can tell you that even the armored version of this vehicle provides far less protection than the M113 armored personnel carriers. During the first two years of the Iraq war I frequently asked why the ample M113 supply available and many thousands more that could be quickly returned to duty were not being deployed. This obvious way to lessen the harm done by roadside bombs was finally acknowledged by the Pentagon in 2005.[469] Donald Rumsfeld, clearly aware of this option (as he has been the Secretary of Defense before), complained of Humvee production issues. Humvees must be extremely profitable for friends of the Bush administration to manufacture as there is no logical reason for their continued use as the preferred armored transport vehicle.[470] If there was freedom of speech in the military, the calls for the M113s to the Humvees would have been numerous. To illustrate this point, one officer who asked not be identified, said Rumsfeld "didn't even let us go to war with the Army we had; he made us leave half our armored vehicles at home in pursuit of lighter, faster and cheaper."[471]

I left the military and joined corporate America in 1989. The people I served with in the military were some of the best and most honorable I have ever met. My departure from the military was primarily because of the woman I ended up marrying. I had a very positive experience in the military and would only years later question the value of my service. When I did question the value of my service, my assignments in Turkey and South Korea prompted me to learn more about why people in other countries are angry at the United States.

When I left the military I worked so hard as a businessman that I lost touch with what was going on in the world. I can appreciate the blank stare so many hard-working business people have when the subject of U.S. foreign policy, nuclear weapons, or other world events is discussed. I remained in this "heads down" mode advancing from one position to the next.

In 1995, I served as a senior officer with New England Financial.[472] A bad day for me then was no longer worrying about someone getting killed, but losing money rather than making money. I have been fortunate to work in large and small companies. The big company and small company experiences also gave me a strong appreciation for their differences. I share my New England Financial experience because it is my experience that most corporations are led and staffed by good people pursuing worthy objectives. I am someone who is grateful to my country for the amazing experiences I have had both in the military and in the business world.

As a businessman, I have seen how corporations are very skilled at forming Political Action Committees (PACs) to further their interests. The Congressional Research Service conducted a study because of a growing concern that PACs were undermining America's democracy by encouraging candidates to represent the most affluent and narrowly interested sectors. PACs grew in number from 608 in 1974 to 4,268 by 1988. In constant dollars the contribution to Senate and House candidates increased from $12.5 million to $147.8 million in this same period which is an increase of approximately 400%. In 2000, House incumbents received 42% of their campaign funding from PACs.[473] Without serious campaign finance reform, this will continue to be a distortion of power from the definition of democracy.[474] History and common sense tells us that when corporations play the leading role in formulating United States policy, the will of the people can take a back seat.

In my experience, when money is involved, people manage to convince themselves that what they are doing is what God would want, or else is good for the country. If the first two are not part of the equation, then it is good for business. To expect corporations to self-impose restrictions, like refraining from selling weapons to non-democratic governments or even pursuing international agreements with an eye to helping their country of origin, is simply unrealistic. Corporations are increasingly multinational and hold allegiance to only one flag – their corporate flag. While many corporations provide fantastic services and products, we should not forget that these entities cannot go to jail and are motivated by profitability, growth and their ongoing survival.

My efforts to strengthen America's democracy and promote peace as a businessman were exclusively outside of my work for corporations. As a result, this book may be surprising to many of the wonderful people I have worked with. One notable example to promote peace as a businessman occurred in September 2002. I rode my bicycle with the World Team Sports organization to remember the people who died in the 9/11 attacks.[475] I also rode my bike to raise awareness that an invasion of Iraq is what al Qaeda needs to unite the divisions in the Islamic world. I had previously read every word of the Koran and this background knowledge taught me that many Muslims believe that only one of the communities of Islam will go to heaven. The other followers of Islam are infidels and will go to hell. Studying Islam has helped me understand why the different Islamic communities have often been at war.

What Osama bin Laden needed was an outside enemy who would incite such anger that followers of Islam would set aside potentially divisive teachings (e.g., only one sect of Islam will go to heaven). Osama bin Laden and his followers needed the U.S. to invade a nation that was clearly not involved in the 9/11 attacks. A U.S. invasion in Iraq was thought, and correctly, to trap the U.S. in a situation that would result in a defeat similar to the Soviets' defeat in Afghanistan.

On the ride from Ground Zero in Manhattan to the Pentagon, I wore a shirt that said, "America Should Not Start Wars: Peace In Iraq." The majority of the riders, many having lost a loved one in the 9/11 attacks, thought wearing this shirt and opposing the anticipated invasion was wrong. I felt that a few people, especially the disabled riders on the joint Israeli and Palestinian team, were more likely to understand the logic in my opposition to starting a war. I remember riding my bike into the Pentagon and thinking about the Americans who would be killed and others coming home without limbs from a war that would only help create more terrorists.

American Hiroshima is materially influenced by my experiences as a volunteer in Asia, Central America and Africa. I have observed that Americans and American charities are increasingly absent from many of the world's disasters. This plays into the hands of people who wish to recruit terrorists and promote anti-American attitudes. I will illustrate this observation with just one experience in Liberia, Africa.

Liberia was created when the American Colonization Society (ACS) founded a colony for freed American slaves in 1822. The United States Congress appropriated $100,000 to the ACS to buy land in West Africa. Approximately 23,000 freed slaves were sent to Liberia between 1822 and 1867.[476] Liberia is Africa's first independent black republic. The official language is English and the people are among the friendliest on earth. The country experienced 133 years of peace and prosperity preceding the 1989 to 2003 civil war. Liberia is a land with abundant natural resources and a promising future as long as war does not resume.

The Liberian capital, Monrovia, was named in honor of President James Monroe. Visitors from the United States will be surprised to see a flag almost identical to that of the United States and pieces of America's culture mixed into the tribal cultures. For example, the Liberian pledge of the allegiance is the same as in the United States, with only the name of the country being different.

Liberia has a long history of aiding the United States in times of need. The best-known examples include assistance in both World Wars and throughout the Cold War. A lesser known fact is that Liberia was the deciding vote to create the nation of Israel. Liberia is also the African headquarters for the Central Intelligence Agency. Liberia has turned over its airports and seaports whenever the United States has asked for assistance, including resupply missions during the Gulf War.[477] Liberia has been a very good friend to America and was once one of the more prosperous nations in Africa.

And then, in 2003, the Economist magazine's Intelligence Unit selected Liberia as the worst place in the world to live. Why? This horrific selection was earned because of fourteen years of civil war and the subsequent total destruction of the country's infrastructure. In August 2003, one-third of the country's population was roaming the land, homeless, with no hope for electricity, clean water or medical care. Liberia had a total of twenty-five doctors for over three million people. With tens of thousands of doped-up child soldiers ransacking the country, the people suffered through rapes, murders and starvation. The best way for an American to relate to this is to imagine a nuclear bomb blast so severe that over twenty million Americans are killed and it is unsafe for the surviving millions of Americans to return to their homes.

In September 2003, the United Nations approved 15,000 peacekeepers for Liberia. The interim government was established in October. I was in Liberia on November second when the first 5,000 peacekeepers were preparing for the larger force to arrive. The purpose of my trip to Liberia was to start a program to assist orphans, replicating the success of a program my wife and I support in Honduras. The approximately thirty mile trip from the airport to the capital, Monrovia, took about an hour. That hour went by quickly because of the appreciative Liberians who stood on the side of the road crying with joy because peacekeepers had arrived.

I will never forget seeing the crowds of very hungry people with tears in their eyes as the United Nations convoy passed small villages along the road. I had never before witnessed the welcome of a foreign peacekeeping force following the end of a war. For the Liberian people along the road, this convoy meant that the gang rapes, the theft of what little food they had, the kidnapping of their children, and the years of unimaginable suffering were all coming to an end. While the situation started to improve in late 2003, thousands of rebels, many under the age of twelve, still roamed the countryside. Pockets of fighting continued in the areas outside Monrovia until the rebel forces were officially disarmed in November of 2004.

What was amazing and sad is that I met with the senior ranking U.S. military officer in Liberia and learned that the U.S. did not have a single peacekeeper on the ground as part of the 15,000-person U.N. peacekeeping effort. The vast majority of aid workers were from Europe. Americans in the country were often employees of DynCorp or other mercenary corporations. In the fourteen years of civil war, the United States is remembered in Liberia as not lifting a finger to help alleviate the suffering. Some believe this is because the U.S. feared another Somalia even though Liberia is primarily a Christian country. Others believe the United States did not help because it would aid Charles Taylor's efforts to continue leading the country.

In late 2004, I witnessed the first signs that the United States is helping the Liberian people. I am proud of my country when I see active involvement to promote peace; and I pray that it continues. I also wish to mention that embassy personnel have helped both Liberian and American people on many occasions. One event that is noteworthy is the U.N. peacekeepers that were sent in November 2004 to the Our Lady Of Fatima Rehabilitation Center. Sister Beltran stopped the initial attack with her prayer described in this book's dedication. The peacekeepers, including helicopter patrols, continued to keep the children safe by protecting the compound after the initial attack was pacified by her prayer. I hope to someday meet and thank the U.S. officer in Washington that approved this action and the U.S. embassy personnel in Monrovia that coordinated the operation.

I hope to have more success stories to share in the years to come. For now, I can't help but observe that poverty and hopelessness are fertile soil for terrorism – and the United States has not made addressing these problems a priority. It is sad but true: the amount the United States spends in less than one month in Iraq is enough to feed and educate all 11 million orphans in Africa for an entire year. I know this is true from my volunteer work with orphans in Liberia. With less money and people resources than we expended in Iraq in the first 20 months following the invasion, we could feed and educate the poorest of the poor, in not only Liberia, but in the entire continent of Africa for the next 20 years.

In my life experiences with soldiers, business people and aid workers, I often find the most innovative and exciting ideas on how to improve our world come from aid workers. In Liberia, the majority of international aid workers I met were from Germany, Belgium, the Netherlands, Ireland and England. In general they are a highly-educated and extremely well-traveled group of people.

Unfortunately, these same aid workers have a common problem. They struggle to operate on budgets that would be nothing more than a rounding error in the military or business worlds. I often wonder, why not have a country where we spend as much on peace development as we do on war preparation?

I have exercised care not to disclose classified information that comes from my experience as an intelligence officer. I stress this because readers should know that I have not compromised my agreement with the United States government. I believe the book achieves the goal of presenting ideas to strengthen America's democracy and make the world a safer place without my revealing information that is still classified. I find it odd that the information I am charged to protect is well known by America's enemies and is clearly only classified to keep this information from U.S. citizens. Unfortunately, America's democracy has far too many secrets and this threatens a democracy. After my 25-year free speech restriction passes, I'll have an opportunity to share some interesting facts that will only further strengthen the ideas expressed in this book.

This book is, finally, influenced by belief in Jesus and his message that we should love even our enemies. I believe we all have a purpose or path that our Creator wants us to follow. We know we are on the right path when the decisions we make bring us closer to God. Speaking the truth has never been the path to earthly acceptance and acclaim. I know that, even within the circle of my family and close friends, this book presents ideas that are hard for the people I love to accept. I hope that understanding my motivations for writing American Hiroshima will help you appreciate the ideas presented and see a clearer path for the future.

Your feedback is welcome and my contact information is provided at www. americanhiroshima.info.

APPENDIX B

IPB FRAMEWORK FOR FOREIGN POLICY ANALYSIS

INTELLIGENCE PREPARATION OF THE BATTLEFIELD or IPB was defined and explained in Appendix A. The following categories are suggested to organize the pieces of the available information and thereby connect the dots needed to establish what is going on with respect to America's foreign policy. Unfortunately, what is really going on is often classified for 20 or more years. This lack of transparency does more to hurt America's democracy than it does to protect it. In any event, figuring out what is really going on is like building a picture without all the puzzle pieces.

Start with a world, country or region map of the area you are trying to learn about. Organize the information available into the below 20 categories. You may want to document the pieces of information on layers of plastic that you can overlay on the map you have selected. The next step is to make the best attempt based on that information to answer each of the 20 questions. The summary conclusion for each category is written under the category title graphic. A review of the summary conclusions for each of the 20 answers tells a story that aids decision-making.

1. What information do we have that a threat exists?
2. What are the resources that the country possesses (with a special emphasis on oil and water)?
3. What business opportunities are influencing the situation?
4. What were the other wars and why were they war fought?
5. Who previously occupied the land?
6. Where are the people and how has the population distribution changed?
7. What are the religions of the people?
8. What are the political groups?
9. What are the weapons of mass destruction capabilities?
10. Where are the military forces and weapons systems?
11. What is the unemployment rate?
12. What is the foreign debt and who is it owed to?

13. Do alliances exist and are foreign troops present?
14. What are the major infrastructure points (i.e., clean water plants, hospitals, etc.)
15. When and where have genocides occurred in the past?
16. Who is selling and buying weapons in the region?
17. What are the weather patterns in the region?
18. What acts of terror have occurred in the past?
19. What other nations will aid or oppose the country/force?
20. What economic agreements with other nations influence the situation?

APPENDIX C

15 DEMOCRACY STRENGTHENING &
PEACE PROMOTING ACTIONS

THE MILITARY HAS MILLIONS FOR its public relations efforts; peace activists often have pennies.[478] Nonetheless, there are encouraging examples of overcoming insurmountable challenges.

Freedom of religion was won because of people such as Ann Hutchinson, who believed that conscience has a higher authority than law. Henry David Thoreau spent only one night in jail for refusing to pay taxes for the Mexican-American War, but his essay "On the Duty of Civil Disobedience" is part of the common heritage of the human race – reaching Tolstoy in Russia, and Gandhi in India. A young pastor in Alabama, Martin Luther King, Jr., began the Civil Rights revolution with a few people defying racial barriers. Ordinary people, successfully protesting in the 1960s and 70s, brought an end to the illegal war in Vietnam. History confirms that we can overcome the challenges of our time.

15 DEMOCRACY STRENGTHENING & PEACE PROMOTING ACTIONS

1. Make a real effort to be an informed citizen.
2. Promote non-violent democratic changes by voting.
3. Talk, with love in your heart, to your family, friends and other people.
4. Help the peace message get out by contacting newspapers and radio shows requesting they make time to interview peace speakers.
5. Ask a peace speaker to speak to your friends and local schools.
6. Join or start a peace organization and assist with a specific program to promote peace. (e.g., to join the Nuclear Age Peace Foundation visit www.wagingpeace.org).
7. Organize and demonstrate (e.g., be present for peace marches).
8. Call talk shows to communicate your views.
9. Share literature (e.g., give American Hiroshima, Confessions of an Economic Hitman or Empire of Sorrows to a friend).
10. Write to the editor to promote the peace and counter myths that support killing.

11. Contribute money to organizations promoting peace.
12. Lobby for peace (e.g., urging Congress to withdraw all U.S. forces from Iraq).
13. Invest and spend your money responsibly (e.g., don't invest in companies that make weapons and boycott consumer goods made by military contractors).
14. Wear a peace symbol or clothing with peace messages (and keep war toys away from your children).
15. Travel to obtain first-hand experiences.

Choose hope and make peace possible by accepting your share of the responsibility for a better world. Your daily acts of peace can inspire others and create a groundswell for peace too powerful to be set aside.

APPENDIX D

UNITED STATES INTERVENTIONS SINCE 1945

T HE UNITED STATES HAS FOUGHT in more than 65 countries since 1945. Blinded by oil and other corporate interests, U.S. foreign policy has at times resulted in assassinations, human rights abuses, and the overthrow of democratically elected leaders. The American public needs to understand these U.S. intervention in order to have an appreciation for why much of the world views America with suspicion and hatred. A selection of two dozen of the 65 interventions are summarized in this Appendix.[479] To learn about all of the interventions, William Blum's book Rogue State, provides an excellent analysis.

China, 1945-49: Intervened in a civil war, taking the side of Chiang Kaishek against the communists. The U.S. used defeated Japanese soldiers to fight for its side. The communists forced Chiang to flee to Taiwan in 1949.

Philippines, 1945-53 and to present: U.S. military fought against leftist forces (Huks) even while the Huks were still fighting against the Japanese invaders. After the war, the U.S. continued its fight against the Huks, defeating them, and then installing a series of puppets as president, culminating in the dictatorship of Ferdinand Marcos.

South Korea, 1945-53 and 1980: After World War II, the United States suppressed the popular progressive forces in favor of the conservatives who had collaborated with the Japanese. This led to a long era of corrupt, reactionary, and brutal governments. In 1980, the United States assisted the South Korean leader Chun Doo Hwan in suppressing an uprising of students and workers in the city of Kwangju. The government crackdown resulted in a death toll ranging between several hundred and 2,000 people. In 1996, a Korean court convicted Chun Doo Hwan of treason and murder. He was sentenced to death for his role in the Kwangju massacre.

Greece, 1947-49 and 1964-74: Intervened in a civil war, taking the side of the neo-fascists against the Greek left that had fought the Nazis courageously. The neo-fascists won and instituted a highly brutal regime, for which the CIA created a new internal security agency, KYP. Before long, KYP was carrying out all the practices of secret police everywhere, including systematic torture.

George Papandreou had been elected in February 1964. The military coup took place in April of 1967, just two days before the campaign for national elections was to begin, elections which appeared certain to bring the veteran liberal leader George Papandreou back as prime minister. The successful machinations to unseat him had begun immediately, a joint effort of the Royal Court, the Greek military, the American military, and CIA stationed in Greece. The 1967 coup was followed immediately by the traditional martial law, censorship, arrests, beatings, torture, and killings. The victims totaled some 8,000 in the first month. It was torture, however, which most indelibly marked the seven-year Greek nightmare. James Becket, an American attorney sent to Greece by Amnesty International, wrote in December 1969 that "a conservative estimate would place at not less than two thousand" the number of people tortured, usually in the most gruesome of ways, often with equipment supplied by the United States.

Iran, 1953: Prime Minister Mossadegh was overthrown in a joint U.S. and British operation. Mossadegh had been elected to his position by a large majority of parliament, but he had made the fateful mistake of spearheading the movement to nationalize the sole and British owned oil company operating in Iran. The coup restored the Shah to absolute power and began a period of 25 years of repression and torture, with the oil industry being restored to foreign ownership, as follows: Britain and the U.S., each 40 percent, other nations 20 percent.

Guatemala, 1953-1990s: A CIA-organized coup overthrew the democratically-elected and progressive government of Jacobo Arbenz, initiating 40 years of death-squads, torture, disappearances, mass executions, and unimaginable cruelty, totaling well over 100,000 victims. Arbenz had nationalized the U.S. firm, United Fruit Company, which had extremely close ties to the American power elite. As justification for the coup, Washington declared that Guatemala had been on the verge of a Soviet takeover, when in fact the Russians had so little interest in the country that it didn't even maintain diplomatic relations.

British Guiana/Guyana, 1953-64: For 11 years, two of the oldest democracies in the world, Great Britain and the United States, went to great lengths to prevent a democratically elected leader from occupying his office. Cheddi Jagan was elected three times. Although a leftist (more so than Sukarno or Arbenz) his policies in office were not revolutionary. Using a wide variety of tactics, from general strikes and disinformation to terrorism and British legalisms, the U.S. and Britain finally forced Jagan out in 1964.

Cambodia, 1955-73: Prince Sihanouk was yet another leader who did not fancy being an American client. After many years of hostility towards his regime, including assassination plots and the infamous Nixon/Kissinger secret "carpet bombings" of 1969-70, Washington finally overthrew Sihanouk in a coup in 1970. This was all that was needed to impel Pol Pot and his Khmer Rouge forces to enter the fray. Five years later, they took power. But five years of American bombing had caused Cambodia's traditional economy to vanish. The old Cambodia had been destroyed forever. Incredibly, the Khmer Rouge were to inflict even greater misery on this unhappy land.

Middle East, 1956-58: The United States twice attempted to overthrow the Syrian government. The U.S. staged several shows-of-force in the Mediterranean to intimidate movements opposed to U.S.-supported governments in Jordan and Lebanon, landed 14,000 troops in Lebanon, and conspired to overthrow Nasser of Egypt.

Indonesia, 1957-58 and 1965: Sukarno, like Nasser, was the kind of Third World leader the United States could not abide. He took neutralism in the Cold War seriously, making trips to the Soviet Union, China and the White House. He nationalized many private holdings of the Dutch, the former colonial power. The CIA began throwing money into the elections, plotted Sukarno's assassination, tried to blackmail him with a phony sex film, and joined forces with dissident military officers to wage a full-scale war against the government. Sukarno survived it all.

In 1965 a complex series of events took place involving a supposed coup attempt, a counter-coup, and perhaps a counter-counter-coup. American fingerprints were apparent at various points and the result was the ouster from power of Sukarno and his replacement by a military coup led by General Suharto. The massacre that began immediately of communists, communist sympathizers, suspected communists, suspected communist sympathizers, and others was called by the New York Times "one of the most savage mass slayings of modern political history." The estimates of the number killed in the course of a few years begin at half a million and go above a million. It was later learned that the U.S. embassy had compiled lists of "communist" operatives, from top echelons down to village cadres, as many as 5,000 names, and turned them over to the army, which then hunted those persons down and killed them.

Iraq, 1958-63, 1972-75 and 1990s to the present: A comprehensive understanding of interventions in Iraq requires going back in time to when the British occupied Iraq. The British invaded Iraq in World War I and again during World War II. In 1920 the Treaty of Sèvres established the British mandate of Iraq. An "elected" Iraqi assembly agreed in 1924 to a treaty with Great Britain. Britain established British military bases and held the true keys of power with a British right of veto over Iraqi legislation. The anger of the local population toward British imperialism grew and the British mandate was terminated in 1932. British military also fought during World War II when Rashid Ali al-Gaylani, leader of an anti-British and pro-Axis military group, seized power in April 1941. The British intervened and Rashid Ali al-Gaylani was defeated. The anger toward Britain and foreign occupiers in general continued to grow and influences how the American and British occupation is viewed today.[480]

In July 1958, Gen. Abdul Karim Kassem overthrew the monarchy and established a republic. Though somewhat of a reformist, he was by no means any kind of a radical. CIA Director Allen Dulles led a secret plan for a joint U.S.-Turkish invasion of Iraq. Soviet threats to intercede on Iraq's side forced Washington to hold back. In the 1960s, the United States began to fund the Kurdish guerrillas in Iraq and the CIA unsuccessfully attempted to assassinate Kassem. In 1963 Kassem told the French daily, Le Monde, that he had received threats from the United States for expressing Iraq's legitimate rights to Kuwait. A few days after his remarks were published, he was overthrown in a coup and executed. Papers of the British cabinet of 1963, later declassified, disclose that the coup had been backed by the British and the CIA.

In 1972-75, President Nixon and National Security Adviser Henry Kissinger provided military aid to the Kurds fighting for their autonomy in Iraq. Though the military aid was to total some $16 million, the object—unknown to the Kurds—was not to win their autonomy, but to sap the Iraqi resources and distract them from Iran. In 1975, oil politics brought Iraq and Iran together, and the latter, along with the United States, abandoned the Kurds to a terrible fate. At a crucial point, the Kurds were begging Kissinger for help, but he completely ignored their pleas. Kurd forces were decimated; several hundred of their leaders were executed. Later, when questioned about this by the Pike Committee, Kissinger responded: "Covert action should not be confused with missionary work."

On August 2, 1990, Iraq invaded Kuwait with the green light from the United States.[481] The United States expresses surprise when Saddam Hussein takes all of Kuwait instead of adjusting the northern border. Saddam Hussein makes the mistake of not listening to Washington and refuses to withdraw. Operation Desert Storm goes into action and the United States intervenes. Iraq was the strongest military power among the Arab states. This may have been its greatest crime.

The Gulf War starts on January 17, 1991. Relentless bombing for more than 40 days and nights, against one of the most advanced nations in the Middle East, devastated its ancient and modern capital city. Over 177 million pounds of bombs are dropped on the people of Iraq. This bombing is one of the most concentrated aerial onslaughts in the history of the world. Depleted uranium weapons are used to incinerate people and continue to cause cancer. The infrastructure is destroyed with a terrible effect on the populations' health. Economic sanctions are enforced that multiply the health problems. The United Nations estimated over 500,000 children were killed because of the sanctions and far more when adult deaths are added.

The 2003 invasion, discussed in detail in Chapter Five of this book, is in many respects a continuation of the Gulf War.

The Congo/Zaire, 1960-65: In June of 1960, Patrice Lumumba became the Congo's first prime minister after the country gained its independence from Belgium. But Belgium retained its vast mineral wealth in Katanga province, prominent Eisenhower administration officials had financial ties to the same wealth, and Lumumba, at Independence Day ceremonies before a host of foreign dignitaries, called for the nation's economic as well as its political liberation. Eleven days later, Katanga province seceded. In September, Lumumba was dismissed by the president at the instigation of the United States, and in January 1961 he was assassinated at the express request of Dwight Eisenhower. There followed several years of civil conflict and chaos and the rise to power of Mobutu Sese Seko, a man not a stranger to the CIA. Mobutu went on to rule the country for more than 30 years, with a level of corruption and cruelty that shocked even his CIA handlers. The Zairian people lived in abject poverty despite the plentiful natural wealth, while Mobutu became a multibillionaire.

Brazil, 1961-64: President Joao Goulart was guilty of the usual crimes: He took an independent stand in foreign policy, resuming relations with socialist countries and opposing sanctions against Cuba; his administration passed a law limiting the amount of profits multinationals could transmit outside the country; a subsidiary of ITT was nationalized; he promoted economic and social reforms. In 1964, he was overthrown in a military coup that had deep, covert American involvement. The official Washington line was...yes, it's unfortunate that democracy has been overthrown in Brazil...but, still, the country has been saved from communism.

Dominican Republic, 1963-65: In February 1963, Juan Bosch took office as the first democratically elected President of the Dominican Republic since 1924. In September, the military boots marched. Bosch was out. The United States, which could discourage a military coup in Latin America with a frown, did nothing. Nineteen months later, a revolt broke out which promised to put the exiled Bosch back into power. The United States sent 23,000 troops to help crush it.

Chile, 1964-73: Salvador Allende was the worst possible scenario for a Washington imperialist who could imagine only one thing worse than a Marxist in power – an elected Marxist in power. After sabotaging Allende's electoral endeavor in 1964, and failing to do so in 1970, the CIA and the rest of the American foreign policy machine left no stone unturned in their attempt to destabilize the Allende government over the next three years, paying particular attention to building up military hostility. Finally, in September 1973, the military with CIA support overthrew the government with human rights abuses and Allende dying in the process.

East Timor, 1975 to present: In December 1975, Indonesia invaded East Timor, which had proclaimed its independence after Portugal had relinquished control of it. The invasion was launched the day after U. S. President Gerald Ford and Secretary of State Henry Kissinger had left Indonesia after giving Suharto permission to use American arms. Under U.S. law these weapons could not be used for aggression. Indonesia was Washington's most valuable tool in Southeast Asia. Amnesty International estimated that by 1989, Indonesian troops, with the aim of forcibly annexing East Timor, had killed 200,000 people out of a population of between 600,000 and 700,000. The United States consistently supported Indonesia's claim to East Timor (unlike the United Nations and the European Union), and downplayed the slaughter to a remarkable degree. At the same time the U.S. supplied Indonesia with all the military hardware and training it needed for this massacre.

Nicaragua, 1978-90: When the Sandinistas overthrew the Somoza dictatorship in 1978, it was clear to Washington that they might well be that long-dreaded beast, "another Cuba." Under President Carter, attempts to sabotage the revolution took diplomatic and economic forms. Under Reagan, violence was the method of choice. For eight terribly long years, the people of Nicaragua were under attack by Washington's proxy army, the Contras. The Contras were formed from Somoza's vicious National Guard and other supporters of the dictator. It was all-out war, aiming to destroy the progressive social and economic programs of the government, burning down schools and medical clinics, raping, torturing, mining harbors, bombing and strafing. The Contras were President Ronald Reagan's "freedom fighters."

Grenada, 1979-84: What would drive the most powerful nation in the world to invade a country of 110,000? Maurice Bishop and his followers had taken power in a 1979 coup, and though their actual policies were not as revolutionary as Castro's, Washington was again driven by its fear of "another Cuba," particularly when public appearances by the Grenadian leaders in other countries of the region met with great enthusiasm. U. S. destabilization tactics against the Bishop government began soon after the coup and continued until 1983, featuring numerous acts of disinformation and dirty tricks. The American invasion in October 1983 met minimal resistance, although the U.S. suffered 135 killed or wounded; there were also some 400 Grenadian casualties, and 84 Cubans, mainly construction workers. At the end of 1984, a questionable election was held which was won by a man supported by the Reagan administration. One year later, the human rights organization, Council on Hemispheric Affairs, reported that Grenada's new U.S.-trained police force and counter-insurgency forces had acquired a reputation for brutality, arbitrary arrest, abuse of authority, and were eroding civil rights.

Afghanistan, 1979-92 and 2001 to the present: Everyone knows of the unbelievable repression of women in Afghanistan, carried out by Islamic fundamentalists, even before the Taliban. But how many people know that during the late 1970s and most of the 1980s, Afghanistan had a government committed to bringing the incredibly backward nation into the 20th century, including giving women equal rights? What happened, however, is that the United States poured billions of dollars into waging a terrible war against this government. On December 24, 1979 the former Soviet Union invaded Afghanistan. In the end, the Soviet Union left, and the people of Afghanistan, paid the highest price. More than a million dead, three million disabled, five million refugees, in total about half the population.

Afghanistan was a key host country for al Qaeda in 2001. On October 7, 2001, the attacks against the ruling Taliban were in response to the September 11, 2001 terrorist attacks that destroyed the World Trade Center in New York and heavily damaged the Pentagon.[482] Fighting continues in Afghanistan and is likely to continue as long as the United States occupies the country.

El Salvador, 1980-92: El Salvador's dissidents tried to work within the system. But with U.S. support, the government made that impossible, using repeated electoral fraud and murdering hundreds of protesters and strikers. In 1980, the dissidents started a civil war. Officially, the U.S. military presence in El Salvador was limited to an advisory capacity. In actuality, military and CIA personnel played a more active role. Considerable evidence surfaced of a U.S. role in the ground fighting. The war came to an official end in 1992 with 75,000 civilians killed.

Panama, 1989: In December of 1989, the U.S. Air Force bombed a large tenement barrio in Panama City, killing many and leaving 15,000 people homeless. Counting several days of ground fighting against Panamanian forces, 500-something dead was the official body count offered by the new U.S.-installed Panamanian government. Other sources, with no less evidence, insisted that thousands had died; 3,000-something wounded. Twenty-three Americans died, 324 were wounded. Manuel Noriega had been an American ally and informant for years until he outlived his usefulness. But getting him was not the only motive for the attack. President George H. W. Bush wanted to send a clear message to the people of Nicaragua, who had an election scheduled in two months, that the use of force in Panama might be their fate if Nicaragua's people reelected the Sandinistas. The official explanation for the American ouster was Noriega's drug trafficking, which Washington had known about for years and had ignored and condoned.

Haiti, 1987-94 and 2004: The U.S. supported the Duvalier family dictatorship for 30 years, then opposed the reformist priest, Jean-Bertrand Aristide. Meanwhile, the CIA was working intimately with death squads, torturers, and drug traffickers. With this as background, the Clinton White House found itself in the awkward position of having to pretend, because of all its rhetoric about democracy, that it supported Aristide's return to power in Haiti after he had been ousted in a 1991 military coup. After delaying his return for more than two years, Washington finally had the military restore Aristide to office, but only after obliging the priest to guarantee that he would not help the poor at the expense of the rich, and that he would stick closely to free-market economics. This meant that Haiti would continue to be the assembly plant of the Western Hemisphere, with its workers receiving literally starvation wages. Aristide was eventually removed from power by the U.S. on February 29, 2004. He was flown from Port-au-Prince by United States soldiers to the Central African Republic. Aristide stated he was "duped" by U.S. officials into being taken to the airport, then promptly removed from the country.[483]

Yugoslavia, 1995-99: The United States and the North Atlantic Treaty Organization (NATO) bombed the country back to a pre-industrial era. The term Kosovo War describes two sequential but different conflicts. The first was a civil war from 1996-1999 between Albanian separatists and the Serbian and Yugoslav security forces. The second war in 1999 was an international war between Yugoslavia and NATO. This war started on March 24, 1999 and ended on June 10, 1999.[484]

Venezuela, 2002-2005: President George W. Bush instructed the CIA to overthrow the democratic government of President Hugo Chavez. Leaked classified documents show that the U.S. government had advance knowledge of the military coup. Ari Fleischer's short-lived attempt on April 12, 2002 to convince the media that this incident was not a coup failed.[485] Not surprisingly, and reinforcing this book's chapter on An Uninformed Electorate, President Bush's fiasco did not even rate as an election issue in 2004. On March 5, 2005, President Hugo Chavez said he had evidence that the United States was planning to assassinate him. "We have enough evidence(...) If anything happens to me, the person responsible will be the president of the United States." [486]

To learn more about the two dozen post World War II interventions summarized in this Appendix and the many other U.S. interventions listed in Chapter Four, the reader is encouraged to read William Blum's Rogue State.

APPENDIX E

LIFE AFTER AN AMERICAN HIROSHIMA

IMAGINE THAT A NUCLEAR ACT of terror has happened. Now what can you do? What would the U.S. government likely do to retaliate? How can you help yourself and others as well as help protect America's democracy?

To begin to answer these questions, we need only think about what happened after 9/11 to get a glimpse into some of the likely reactions and new questions that would confront society. Without question, hostility toward Muslims in America will increase. Radio and television broadcasters will be demanding revenge and retaliation with nuclear weapons. Nationalism will increase with the visible sign of more American flags on cars, homes and clothing. The president will move quickly to pass the Patriot Act III and further strip away liberties. The government will be especially threatened by opponents calling for solutions other than the use of additional military force. Lists of people with opposing views, already maintained by the government, could result in people disappearing in a way that could make the current extraordinary renditions program look rather ordinary. The shift of power from the people to a few people is more likely in this situation than many Americans realize. To highlight this point, in January 2005, Doomsday legislation was passed that allows only 12 members of the House of Representatives to make vital decisions for the country, such as declaring war.[487]

Your immediate concern would likely not be the immediate threats to America's democracy but the threat to you and your family. To know how to react to a nuclear disaster you need to know the effects of nuclear weapons[488] and how to survive a disaster. Refer to the notes section in the back of this book to learn how to create a "Go Kit."[489] The U.S. Department of Homeland Security also has good disaster education and preparation information at www.ready.gov.[490]

The product of a nuclear explosion creates both an initial and residual danger. Initial effects are blast, burn, and radiation resulting in the death, destruction and injuries within the first minute after the explosion. There is not much you can do about this except choose not to live in the cities on the American Hiroshima target list. For most people, reducing the danger means reducing the residual effects in the following minutes, days and even years after the nuclear explosion. Your radio may be your best source of information and it may be smart to stay in your home to minimize exposure to radioactive fallout unless emergency broadcast messages instruct you to leave.

The key residual danger is fallout. Fallout occurs when soil, water and other particles are vaporized into the sky. As the vaporized radioactive particles cool, they are carried by the wind and fall back to earth as radioactive dust. Time, distance, and shielding are critical variables to protect you from fallout. Specifically this means minimizing the duration of the exposure, moving away from the radiation, and having a barrier between you and the radiation. The three variables are critical because the radiation received or avoided in this first week from a nuclear bomb may exceed the dosage accumulated during the rest of a lifetime spent in the same contaminated area. When a nuclear storage, power plant or research facility is blown up, the danger of the residual fallout increases dramatically and can make large areas of the United States uninhabitable for months to years to centuries.

During the initial chaos, people will flee the major cities.[491] After an American Hiroshima, the largest cities in America will become increasingly childless with the exception of the very poor. The dangers of radioactive fallout and resulting health issues in the days, weeks, months and years to follow will terrorize Americans. Will many Americans decide to leave the country to live in places like Canada? Will the very rich move to their west coast homes to avoid downwind radiation hazards? Will many people elect to build underground homes with radiation air filtration systems. The "Survival City" fears during the Cold War will take on a new meaning influencing numerous dimensions of everyday life.[492] For example, building glass-covered skyscrapers will no longer be an attractive architectural design. People will understand that following a nuclear explosion the blast would produce millions of flying object dangers to people inside the building and the far more outside of these buildings.

The financial ramifications are also tremendous. Real estate values downwind of a nuclear detonation will plummet.[493] For decades after an American Hiroshima, people will want to know the downwind ramifications when purchasing property. Given the increasing U.S. deficit and the declining U.S. dollar, a nuclear disaster could accelerate the Euro becoming the world's currency, especially as the U.S. economy absorbs the additional costs of decontamination and rebuilding. The change to the Euro will raise interest rates in the United States. Due to the decline in real estate values and higher interest rates, millions of highly leveraged Americans will be unable to pay their debts and will fall into bankruptcy. When real estate values plummet, many consumers will fall into bankruptcy as the bulk of their net worth is often in their home. Americans should expect to see corporations protect their profits by influencing government leaders to weaken consumer bankruptcy protections. In addition, insurance protection as a result of catastrophic terrorist damage to property will increasingly be limited as the insurance industry strengthens exclusions for acts of terror.

What will be the economic costs of having to abandon large regions of the United States until the radioactivity subsides? In the case of the ultimate dirty bomb, the destruction of a nuclear power plant or nuclear storage facility, would the area be "left as is" or abandoned for years, decades, or even centuries?[494] Where would the millions of "cleaners" or as called in the former Soviet Union, "liquidators" (the liquidators in the former Soviet Union are described in Chapter Two) come from? Are the potential costs to America being considered by the Bush Administration in their quest for global domination? What will be the health costs if the U.S. government fails to clean up the radioactive contamination? The Department of Homeland Security is already seeking to change existing standards so that the public could be exposed to what was previously considered unsafe levels of radioactivity.[495]

As soon as one nuclear weapon is used every nation in the world will go on high alert status. With ready to launch missiles already in several countries, could a scenario that results in the U.S., Russia, Israel, Pakistan, India, China, or another nation exchanging nuclear weapons result? Projecting events is always difficult but each use of a nuclear weapon brings the world closer to the chain of events that could produce a nuclear winter and end our world. When it comes to nuclear weapons, the best scenario is preventing their use. Americans need to consider the potential long term consequences of a foreign policy based on military domination versus on cooperation.

The greatest danger of an American Hiroshima may not come from the attack on the United States but from the counter-retaliation to the U.S. retaliation. Unless the forces of peace step forward to demand an end to this insanity, the cycle of destruction would likely result in many more people being killed in the retaliation and counter-retaliations. This would in turn produce in time another attack against the United States. The invasion of Iraq following the 9/11 attacks highlights how crazy and dangerous this escalating violence would become. Consider a few basic questions: Would America attack the correct country or group that sponsored the explosion? Would the American people be told the truth? Would the Bush administration claim "collaboration evidence" by other unaffiliated countries like it did with the 9/11 attack and also launch a nuclear attack against other countries deemed a threat?

While this book seeks to educate so what has been described never happens, an American Hiroshima will wake up a large number of people who support the current insanity of possessing nuclear weapons and U.S. efforts to dominate the world with weapons. History provides a noteworthy post-disaster possibility when we consider that the 800,000 liquidators of the Chernobyl nuclear plant in the former Soviet Union helped change their government for the better. To imagine this force for peace, think about how passionate the 9/11 families were when they demanded the U.S. government produce the 9/11 Report. Imagine not a few thousand, but a few million people with this passion for the truth. The American people may demand an end to U.S. imperialism and exceptionalism. A nuclear disaster may help the world see that until possession of weapons of mass destruction by any individual nation is eliminated, the incredible price in death and suffering paid by civilian populations will only intensify. Let us all work for justice and choose the only real solution, prevention of war.

APPENDIX F

TRANSFORMATIONAL "WHY NOTS"
FOR CONSIDERATION

WHY IS THE WORLD "SUDDENLY" opposed to the foreign policies of the United States? Is this jealously for the prosperous American way of life and freedoms as President Bush suggests, or is the anger a product of policies that hurt people outside the United States? This list is provided to facilitate reflection and promote group discussion.

Why not:

- end exceptionalist policies like possessing nuclear weapons and dominating space with weapons?
- demand free speech and freedom of religion from any country that receives most favored nation trading status?
- recognize that addressing human suffering is in our best interest?
- stop artificially splitting countries at the expense of the native people?
- stop supporting the seizure of one country by another?
- prevent long-term dependence and the hate-hate dynamic by withdrawing United States soldiers from South Korea and other countries around the world?
- direct savings from nuclear weapons development to help end worldwide hunger?
- support non-violent democratic movements across the globe and pursue non-violent means to oppose behaviors that suppress democracy?
- stop labeling to disable and focus on the idea presented?
- seek out thoughtful and well-informed people that may disagree with us so that we may enhance our understanding?
- challenge counter-intuitive myths like starting wars brings peaceful outcomes?
- seek sources of information beyond one country's television, radio and newspapers to obtain a more balanced understanding?
- make eliminating America's dependence on oil a national priority?

- understand the importance of key resources like water in regional conflicts?
- stop funding foreign militias?
- look at history, and not just the initial act of aggression, to give a more comprehensive context for today's appropriate solutions?
- stop the illegal war in Iraq?
- stop seeding nations like Iraq with weapons as the Reagan administration did by sending anthrax, the bacteria for botulinum toxin, and the germs to create gas gangrene?
- impeach and prosecute as a war criminal President George W. Bush for lying to the American people, starting an illegal war, betraying American soldiers, and the deaths of thousands of people?[496]
- outlaw unilateral preemptive wars as part of the U.S. Constitution?
- stop being the leader of developed and deployed weapons of mass destruction?
- restrict deployment of United States nuclear weapons to America's borders?[497]
- reduce the U.S. arsenal of thousands of nuclear weapons to 384?
- renounce the first use and testing of nuclear weapons?[498]
- strengthen U.S. commitment to international treaties like the Biological Weapons Convention and the Chemical Weapons Convention?[499]
- add the safeguards discussed in this book that would prevent a single person from having the power to destroy the planet?
- stop being the initial source for worldwide proliferation of weapons of mass destruction information?
- stop leading the world in international weapon sales?
- recognize that the foreign policy interests of corporations can conflict with the interests of the electorate?
- stop conflicts of interest between businesses and policymakers?
- make the true costs of war known?
- keep space free of weapons? [500]
- balance what we spend on war preparation with peace programs to alleviate suffering and promote justice?
- be perceived as the greatest worldwide source of peace instead of being perceived as the leading threat to world peace?
- make our world free of nuclear weapons?

If the citizens of the United States seriously debate these transformational ideas, a more peaceful world is possible now. Failing to wage peace now and act on these ideas will eventually result in an American Hiroshima.

NOTES

Additional notes and lesson plans for teachers are available at www.american-hiroshima.info.

[1] David Krieger is a founder of the Nuclear Age Peace Foundation (www.wagingpeace.org) and has served as its president since 1982. He is a leader in the global movement for a world free of nuclear weapons and is the author of many books and articles on peace in the Nuclear Age.

[2] In general, the author has observed the vast majority of soldiers, spies and mercenaries are Republicans. On a related note, the vast majority of U.S. aid workers tend to be Democrats. A scientific study of this dynamic would likely yield interesting findings.

[3] Noam Chomsky, Hegemony Or Survival (New York, New York: Henry Holt and Company, 2004), 10.

[4] Duncan Campbell, "NSA Builds Security Access Into Windows," TechWeb.com, 3 September 1999 or access this information on the Internet at www.techweb.com/wire/story/TWB19990903S0014. The U.S. government's ability to defeat Microsoft's security, and specifically the "_NSAKEY" is a key reason why Microsoft has fought European demands to open up the source code.

[5] Export and reexport controls on commercial encryption products are administered by the Bureau of Industry and Security (BIS) of the U.S. Department of Commerce. Rules governing exports and reexports of encryption items are found in the Export Administration Regulations (EAR), 15 C.F.R. Parts 730-774. Sections 740.13, 740.17 and 742.15 of the EAR. Encryption export control jurisdiction was transferred from the State Department to the Commerce Department in 1996.

[6] Howard Kurtz, "Administration Paid Commentator: Education Dept. Used Williams to Promote 'No Child' Law," The Washington Post, 8 January 2005, A01. One of these rare views into secret funding of propaganda messages was the disclosure that the Bush administration paid Armstrong Williams at least $240,000 to promote the No Child Left Behind law on his nationally syndicated television show. This unusually sloppy secret operation leveraged the Education Department who then used the Ketchum public relations firm to manage the program with Williams. One may wish to consider the extremely close presidential 2004 race to better understand this specific propaganda effort.

[7] The Church Committee of the Senate disclosed in 1976 that "well over a thousand books" had been produced or subsidized by the CIA. A few CIA sponsored books include "The New Class" by Milovan Djilàs; "In Pursuit of World Order" by Richard N. Gardner; "The Yenan Way" by Eudocio Ravines"; "The Anthill" by Suzanne Labin; "Why Viet Nam?" by Frank Trager; and "Terror in Vietnam" by Jay Mallin. For more information visit www.killinghope.org.

[8] Michael Scheuer, Imperial Hubris (Dulles, VA: Brassey's, Inc., 2004), 241.

[9] Bill Gertz, "CIA funds liberal efforts," The Washington Times, 7 September 2004. The CIA's Counterterrorist Center has spent more than $15 million since 2000 funding studies, reports and conferences.

[10] Liberia Mission is an orphanage in Liberia, Africa that works to break the cycle of violence and poverty. For more information on how you can help an orphan, visit www.liberiamission.org.

Book profits will also be used to support the Nuclear Age Peace Foundation (www.wagingpeace.org) and other programs working to make our world a better one.

[11] David Alan Rosenberg, "A Historian's Assessment of Atomic Audit," speech given at The Brookings Institution, 30 June 1998.

[12] Wikipedia, s.v. "Israel," a free-content encyclopedia in many languages. The English edition started in January 2001 and supporting information can be found on the Internet at http://en.wikipedia.org/wiki/Israel#History. In 1947, fulfillment of the 1947 U.N. Partition Plan would have divided the mandated territory roughly in half between the Jewish and Arab people. This plan was rejected by Arab leaders and a guerilla war was launched using many of the same tactics the Jewish fighters had previously used against the British. On May 14, 1948, the nation of Israel was created.

[13] Over 178,000 members of the U.S. Peace Corps have been welcomed by 138 countries to work on issues ranging from AIDS education, information technology, and environmental preservation. Source: About The Peace Corps, 4 April 2005. Available on the Internet at www.peacecorps.gov/index.cfm?shell=learn.whatispc.

[14] Perry-Castañeda Library Map Collection, modified CIA produced map, 2004. Permission notification received on 6 April 2005. Internet addresses are www.lib.utexas.edu/maps/middle_east_and_asia/middle_east_ref04.jpg and www.lib.utexas.edu/maps/middle_east_and_asia/korean_peninsula.gif.

[15] General Omar N. Bradley, Chief of Staff, United States Army. Speech in Boston on November 10th, 1948.

[16] When biological, chemical and nuclear weapons of mass destruction (WMD) are considered, most industrialized nations possess or can manufacture WMD. The Natural Resources Defense Council Nuclear Program's Archive of Nuclear Data at www.nrdc.org/nuclear/nudb/datab19.asp provides an estimate of nuclear arsenals.

[17] "Israel approves plan to attack Iran," London Sunday Times, 13 March 2005. London's Sunday Times published a report saying that Prime Minister Ariel Sharon's security cabinet gave "initial authorization" to attack Iran if negotiations failed to persuade the Islamic republic to halt its nuclear program.

Seymour M. Hersh, "The Coming Wars: What the Pentagon can now do in secret," The New Yorker, posted on 17 January 2005. Available on the Internet at www.newyorker.com/fact/content/?050124fa_fact.

The "packaging of an attack on Iran" for the American public would likely have the following four key messages. Eliminating a rogue state's weapons of mass destruction, promoting democracy in the Middle East by using force to make a regime change in Iran, aiding Israel, and promoting peace through war. Of the four messages for American consumption, only aiding Israel would be accurate. Iran has weapons of mass destruction that will survive any Israeli or U.S. attack. Using force helps those who wish to suppress democracy in Iran and the Middle East. Promoting peace through war is the equivalent of raping a person to protect their virginity.

[18] In 2005, the nuclear club includes the United States, the Russian Federation, Great Britain, France, China, Israel, India, Pakistan and North Korea. While nuclear weapons deployed by the United States outside its borders is classified, the United States is likely to have nuclear weapons in Great Britain, Turkey, Germany, Belgium, Italy and the Netherlands. Iran's nuclear program, clearly not needed to produce electricity, is expected to increase the number of countries to 15.

[19] David Albright, Frans Berkhout, and William Walker, "Global Fissile Material Inventories," The Institute for Science and International Security, June 2004.

[20] Robert S. McNamara and James G. Blight, Wilson's Ghost: Reducing The Risk Of Conflict, Killing,

And Catastrophe In The 21st Century (New York, New York: Public Affairs, 2001), 26.

[21] Albert Einstein, quote from January 22, 1947.

[22] Graham Allison, Nuclear Terrorism: The Ultimate Preventable Catastrophe (New York, New York: Time Books, Henry Holt & Company, LLC, 2004), 3. Graham Allison cites: David Johnston and James Risen, "Traces of Terrorism: The Intelligence Reports; Series of Warnings," New York Times, 17 May 2002.

Paul Hughes, "Iran Says It Has Military Might to Deter Any Attack," Reuters, 18 January 2005. Iran's Defense Minister, Ali Shamkhani has suggested Iran already has a nuclear deterrent. His quote in January 2005 is "We can claim that we have rapidly produced equipment that has resulted in the greatest deterrent." It is the responsibility of the Qods Force to create and execute the plan to deliver the greatest deterrent in the United States.

Also see, Federation of American Scientist, Qods (Jerusalem) Force: Iranian Revolutionary Guard Corps (IRGC-Pasdaran-e Inqilab), access at http://fas.org/irp/world/iran/qods/, 13 February 2005.

[23] Bill Keller, "Nuclear Nightmares," New York Times Magazine, 26 May 2002. General Habiger, the retired four-star general who ran the anti-terror program until 2001, stated "it is not a matter of if; it's a matter of when." Keller noted "that, may explain why he now lives in San Antonio."

[24] Nicholas D. Kristof, "An American Hiroshima," New York Times, 11 August 2004. Available on the Internet at www.nytimes.com/2004/08/11/opinion/11kris.html?ex=1249963200&en=81ff0a19e 469c48a&ei=5090&partner=rssuserland.

[25] Graham Allison, Nuclear Terrorism: The Ultimate Preventable Catastrophe (New York, New York: Time Books, Henry Holt & Company, LLC, 2004), 1-2.

Graham Allison is the founding dean of Harvard's John F. Kennedy School of Government. He cites: Massimo Calabresi and Romesh Ratnesar, "Can We Stop the Next Attack?," Time, 11 March 2002.

[26] David Ray Griffin, The New Pearl Harbor (Northampton, MA: Olive Branch Press, 2004).

[27] Daniel Benjamin and Steven Simon, The Next Attack (London: Hodder and Stoughton, 2005) 18-19.

[28] Congressman Curt Weldon, Countdown To Terror (Washington, DC: Regnery Publishing, Inc., 2005), 9 and 83. Terrorists seeking to fly a plane from Canada into the Seabrook Nuclear Reactor were arrested in August 2003. This nuclear facility is 40 miles north of Boston.

[29] Graham Allison, Nuclear Terrorism: The Ultimate Preventable Catastrophe (New York, New York: Time Books, Henry Holt & Company, LLC, 2004), 19. Graham Allison notes that Khalid Sheikh Mohammed was interviewed by Al Jazerra about his leadership role in the 9/11 attacks. He revealed that nuclear facilities were removed by Osama bin Laden "for now" against the wishes of other al Qaeda leaders.

[30] Ibid.

[31] Last Best Chance produced by Aaron Goddard and directed by Ben Goddard, 2005. The Nuclear Threat Institute is distributing The Last Best Chance video. The video is based on intelligence collected by the U.S. government and specifically warns of al Qaeda's American Hiroshima plan. To obtain the video, visit www.lastbestchance.org.

[32] Shankar Vedantam, "Nuclear Plants Are Still Vulnerable, Panel Says," Washington Post, 7 April 2005, A12. The Bush administration is failing to harden nuclear power plants for the same reason it consciously failed to harden airplane cockpits. Specifically, the cost to business is deemed excessive and only after a disaster will Americans demand of the government a complete rethinking of exposed nuclear facilities.

[33] Graham Allison, Nuclear Terrorism: The Ultimate Preventable Catastrophe (New York, New York: Time Books, Henry Holt & Company, LLC, 2004), 12. Osama bin Laden's official spokesman, Suleiman Abu Gheith, announced on a now-defunct Web site, www.alneda.com, "We have the right to

kill four million Americans–two million of them children–and to exile twice as many and wound and cripple hundreds of thousands."

The announcement, especially the reference to children, can be better understood by adding the number of Muslim children killed since the Gulf War. Abu Gheith calculates economic sanctions and American bombings have killed over a million Muslim children. While the exact number is unknown and is continuing to increase with the war in Iraq, the United Nations has acknowledged the deaths of over 500,000 children from economic sanctions.

[34] Wikipedia, s.v. "Little Boy," a free-content encyclopedia in many languages. The English edition started in January 2001 and supporting information can be found on the Internet at http://en.wikipedia.org/wiki/Little_Boy. The Little Boy bomb was dropped by pilot Lt. Col. Paul Tibbets from a B-29 called the Enola Gay. The explosive yield was between twelve and a half and thirteen kilotons.

The Nagasaki bomb, called Fat Man, had a yield of twenty kilotons. The pilot, Major Charles Sweeney, dropped the Fat Man bomb from a B-29 called Bockscar.

[35] William J. Broad and David E. Sanger, "As Nuclear Secrets Emerge in Khan Inquiry, More are Suspected," New York Times, 26 December 2004.

[36] Even a conventional bomb detonated at a nuclear facility could disperse, for many miles, the highly radioactive material at the nuclear facility.

[37] The Manhattan Project, the name for the project that created the atomic bomb, may, in one of history's tragic ironies, result in a future terrorist atomic explosion in Manhattan.

Additional target list key supporting facts, assumptions and rationale for the American Hiroshima conclusions above are described in detail on the Internet at www.americanhiroshima.info.

[38] Multiple sources including the Koran, Islamic terrorist debriefings, official al Qaeda announcements, statements by Osama bin Laden, mathematics, historical events like the bombing date for Hiroshima and the birthday of a 12th century Imam called the Mahdi. The most likely detonation dates are August 6 and November 23-26 (the year is dependent on when the weapon or weapons can be obtained). Beyond New York City and Washington, al Qaeda seeks the destruction of Miami, Los Angeles, Philadelphia, Chicago, San Francisco, Las Vegas and Boston. The destruction that can be delivered downwind is a variable in determining targets. For example, a nuclear bomb detonated at a nuclear power plant near Chicago could produce downwind damage all the way to the Atlantic Ocean. A nuclear bomb detonated in downtown Boston or Miami would be less valuable relative to an attack on a nearby nuclear facility or one further west for this reason.

[39] Mike Nartker, "Missing Russian Nuclear Material Could be Used to Produce Weapon, CIA Chief Warns," Global Security Newswire, 17 February 2005.

[40] Graham Allison, Nuclear Terrorism: The Ultimate Preventable Catastrophe (New York, New York: Time Books, Henry Holt & Company, LLC, 2004), 23.

[41] Neil Doyle, Terror Tracker (Edinburgh, London: Mainstream Publishing, 2004), 87. Osama bin Laden was interviewed by Pakistani journalist Hamid Mir at a secret location believed to be near Kabul on November 8, 2001.

[42] Daniel Benjamin and Steven Simon, The Next Attack (London: Hodder and Stoughton, 2005) 71. On a related note, al Qaeda documents are often available online. This enables a person to walk into an Internet café in most cities in the Muslim world and participate in a virtual jihad training course.

[43] "Nuclear Terrorism Greatest Threat," Associated Press, 28 January 2005. Ashcroft also noted, "If you were to have nuclear proliferation find its way into the hands of terrorists, the entire world might be very seriously disrupted by a few individuals who sought to impose their will, their arcane philosophy, on the rest of mankind."

[44] William Werfelman, "New York Life On Schedule To Occupy Westchester Campus In Late Spring,"

New York Life, 18 May 2004. Another noticeable trend is CEOs are also less interested in having offices not easily reachable by firefighters.

[45] "Urgent Action Needed to Protect Reactors from Terrorist Attack. NRC Comment Period Ends Monday, January 24," Nuclear Information and Resource Service, 19 January 2005. The proposal recommends construction of "Beamhenge" shields, constructed of steel I-beams, with cabling between them, at stand-off distances from sensitive reactor structures, so that an incoming plane crashes into the shield rather than the reactor, spent fuel pool, or critical support facilities, preventing massive radioactive release.

[46] The Design Basis Threat regulations for the nuclear industry only require nuclear facilities be protected against three attackers on foot, acting as a single team, with weapons no greater than hand-carried automatic weapons, plus the possible assistance of one insider. In 2003, the Nuclear Regulatory Commission issued secret "Orders" that marginally increased the Design Basis Threat. The Nuclear Regulatory Commission has conceded that the strengthened Design Basis Threat still falls short of protecting nuclear facilities from a terrorist attack with a force the size of the nineteen 9/11 highjackers.

[47] The Project for the New American Century, available on the Internet at www.newamericancentury.org.

[48] "Israel approves plan to attack Iran," London Sunday Times, 13 March 2005. London's Sunday Times published a report saying that Prime Minister Ariel Sharon's security cabinet gave "initial authorization" to attack Iran if negotiations failed to persuade the Islamic republic to halt its nuclear program.

Steven R. Weisman, "Sharon says Israel has no plan to attack Iran ," The New York Times, 15 April 2005. Ariel Sharon has said no immediate attack is planned. Referring to his April three day meeting with President Bush, he provided insights on if Israel would attack Iran, "We exchange views, we discuss these issues, but it's not that we are planning any military attack on Iran." He also indicated the trigger point for an attack when he said, "I would say the point of no return depends upon the ability of the Iranians to solve some technical issues."

[49] "Arms Control Association Vows to Oppose Renewal of New Nuclear Weapons Research," Arms Control Association, 7 February 2004.

[50] In President Bush's second term, the Deputy Defense Secretary was rewarded with a new position as the World Bank President. "Paul Wolfowitz Approved as World Bank President," Reuters, 31 March 2005. Unlike Donald Rumsfeld, who was deemed essential as remaining as the Secretary of Defense, Wolfowitz's was assigned a new role. This significant leadership change during a time of war is because Wolfowitz is the recognized architect for the U.S. invasion of Iraq. In addition, his close ties with Israel were potentially damaging in light of the fact that Americans are discovering the real reasons for the invasion of Iraq.

On a related note, another key leadership change in President Bush's second term is Condoleezza Rice's promotion to Secretary of State following Colin Powell's departure.

[51] Robert Burns, "Pentagon Tries to Explain Spy Unit," Associated Press, 24 January 2005. See the section in Chapter 4, Sowing The Seeds To Create Terrorists, for information on why the SAPs that bypass Congress are illegal.

[52] Seymour M. Hersh, "The Coming Wars: What the Pentagon can now do in secret," The New Yorker, posted on 17 January 2005. Available on the Internet at www.newyorker.com/fact/content/?050124fa_fact.

[53] Ibid.

[54] Nazila Fathi, "Iran Says Pilotless U.S. Jets Are Spying on Nuclear Sites," New York Times, 17 Feburary 2005. Iran said that American pilotless spy planes had been seen over its nuclear sites and threatened to shoot them down if they came within range.

[55] Seymour M. Hersh, "The Coming Wars: What the Pentagon can now do in secret," The New Yorker, posted on 17 January 2005. Available on the Internet at www.newyorker.com/fact/content/?050124fa_fact.

[56] Laurie Copans, "U.S. to send 4,500 smart bombs to Israel in arms deal," Associated Press, 22 September 2004. The "sale" of the weapons, worth $319 million, was reported by the Israeli newspaper Haaretz as costing Israel nothing because the funding for the sale comes from U.S. military aid. The military aid also includes an additional 3,000 1-ton bombs, 1,000 half-ton bombs and 500 quarter-ton bombs.

"US Building Army Base Near Iran Border," Pajhwok News Agency, 29 November 2004. A 300-hectare airbase in the desert area of Holang, in Ghorian district of Herat province, was under construction. just 27 miles the Iranian border.

[57] "Israel approves plan to attack Iran," London Sunday Times, 13 March 2005.

Seymour M. Hersh, "The Coming Wars: What the Pentagon can now do in secret," The New Yorker, posted on 17 January 2005. Available on the Internet at www.newyorker.com/fact/content/?050124fa_fact. Mr. Hersh notes Iran is anywhere from months to a few years away from developing a nuclear bomb. An Israeli attack appears extremely likely in this same time period as Silvan Shalom, Israel's Foreign Minister, has said "Israel cannot live with Iran having a nuclear bomb."

[58] Amir Paivar, "Reporters Visit Underground Iran Nuclear Plant," Reuters, 30 March 2005. Iran's President Mohammad Khatami took a group of journalists deep underground into the heart of a key nuclear plant in Natanz which Washington wants dismantled and whose existence was kept secret until 2002.

[59] "The Qods Force," National Council of the Resistance of Iran, accessed at www.iranncrfac.org/Pages/Dossiers/Mullahs%27%20Terrorism/the%20Qods%20force.htm, 25 March 2005.

[60] Federation of American Scientist, Qods (Jerusalem) Force: Iranian Revolutionary Guard Corps (IRGC-Pasdaran-e Inqilab), access at http://fas.org/irp/world/iran/qods/, 13 February 2005.

[61] "The Qods Force," National Council of the Resistance of Iran, accessed at www.iranncrfac.org/Pages/Dossiers/Mullahs%27%20Terrorism/the%20Qods%20force.htm, 25 March 2005.

[62] Mohammad Mohaddessin, Islamic Fundamentalism: The New Global Threat, Chapter 9 - An International Islamic Army, 1993. Available on the Internet at www.iranncrfac.org/Pages/Publications/BOOKS/Islamic-Fundamentalism/index.htm.

[63] "Iranian Revolutionary Guards occupy Iraqi soil," IranFocus.com, 8 October 2004.

[64] Federation of American Scientist, Qods (Jerusalem) Force: Iranian Revolutionary Guard Corps (IRGC-Pasdaran-e Inqilab), access at http://fas.org/irp/world/iran/qods/, 13 February 2005.

[65] Paul Hughes, "Iran Says It Has Military Might to Deter Any Attack," Reuters, 18 January 2005.

[66] Seymour M. Hersh, "The Coming Wars: What the Pentagon can now do in secret," The New Yorker, posted on 17 January 2005. Available on the Internet at www.newyorker.com/fact/content/?050124fa_fact. Mr. Hersh notes Iran is widely believed by Western intelligence agencies to have serious technical problems with its weapons system, most notably in the production of the hexafluoride gas needed to fabricate nuclear warheads.

[67] "Pakistan mulls nuclear handover," BBC News, 25 March 2005. Pakistan's President Pervez Musharraf said he would consider sending nuclear parts to the United Nations to help determine if Iran is building a nuclear bomb. The previously delivered centrifuges from Pakistan to Iran are essential to produce enriched uranium for nuclear weapons.

[68] Josh Meyer, Illegal Nuclear Deals Alleged, Los Angeles Times, 26 March 2005. Officials say Pakistan secretly bought high-tech components for its weapons program from U.S. companies. The acquisition of 200 U.S.-made precision electronic switches designed to detonate nuclear weapons may have also been distributed by Abdul Qadeer Khan, the father of the Pakistani nuclear bomb, to

Iran, North Korea and Libya.

[69] Douglas Farah and Dana Priest, "Bin Laden Son Plays Key Role in Al Qaeda," The Washington Post, 13 October 2003.

[70] Neil Doyle, Terror Tracker (Edinburgh, London: Mainstream Publishing, 2004), 100. When Operations Northwoods was finally made public, the U.S. government knew that America was in the countdown phase for the 9/11 attacks. For more information to reinforce what was known by the U.S. government prior to 9/11, read Paul Thompson's, The Terror Timeline, published by Harper-Collins Publishers Inc. in 2004.

[71] James Bamford, "Operation Northwoods plan," National Security Archive, 30 April 2001.Available on the Internet at www.gwu.edu/~nsarchiv/news/20010430/doc1.pdf.

[72] Walter Cronkite, comments in Santa Barbara at a Nuclear Age Peace Foundation dinner, 23 October 2004.

[73] Encyclopædia Britannica Premium Service, s.v. "democracy," (Chicago, Illinois: Encyclopædia Britannica, 20 September 2004). Internet address is www.britannica.com/eb/article?tocld=9029895.

[74] The American Heritage Dictionary of the English Language, 4th ed., s.v. "democracy," (Boston, MA: Houghton Mifflin Company, 2000).

[75] From the American Revolution to recent times, history teaches us that the concepts of freedom, justice, peace and prosperity can take root around the world. One only need reflect on the influence of the U.S. democracy on western Europe and the resulting prosperity for an example of this point.

[76] The "Declaration of Sentiments" was created at the first voting equality convention in 1848. The convention took place at Seneca Falls in New York. In 1852, at the Woman's Rights Convention in Syracuse, Susan B. Anthony called for the right to vote for women. The Nineteenth Amendment was passed by Congress on June 4, 1919 and ratified on August 18, 1920.

David A. Strother (1843-1905) was the first African-American in the United States to vote as a result of the 15th Amendment.

[77] Ursula Weiss, "Malaria," Nature Insight, 7 February 2002. Available on the Internet at www.nature.com/nature/insights/6872.html. Nearly ten per cent of the global population, 500 million people, becomes ill from malaria each year.

"U.S. $1.5 Billion To U.S. $2.5 Billion Needed Annually To Prevent And Control Malaria In Africa," World Health Organization, 2 November 2004. Malaria prevention and treatment consumes 40% of all health care spending in Africa. Available on the Internet at www.afro.who.int/press/2004/pr20041102.html.

[78] "United Against Hunger Facts," United Nations World Food Programme, 2004. Established in 1963, the World Food Programme is the United Nations frontline agency in the fight against global hunger. In 2003, WFP fed 104 million people in 81 countries, including most of the world's refugees and internally displaced people. Internet address is www.unitedagainsthunger.org/facts/facts.htm.

[79] George F. Kennan, "Policy Planning Study 23", written as a classified document for the State Department in 1948. Kennan died on March 17, 2005 at the age of 101. The original context of this quote was for the U.S. to leave Asia to the Asians and base its security on the Philippines and Japan.

[80] World Watch Institute, State of the World 2004: Consumption By the Numbers, 7 January 2004. On the Internet at www.worldwatch.org/press/news/2004/01/07/.

[81] Ibid.

[82] Ibid.

[83] William F. Schulz, In Our Own Best Interest: How Defending Human Rights Benefits Us All (Boston, MA: Beacon Press, 2001), preface xviii.

[84] The Soviet Union collapsed primarily because it was an inefficient economy and could not contain internal pressures. Many factors put pressure on the inefficient economy including the Soviet invasion of Afghanistan, the workers rising against the state in Poland, an increasing awareness that life was better outside their borders, and internal disgust over the Chernobyl lies just to name a few. An inefficient economy and internal demands for something better than communism deserve the credit, not the fact that Ronald Reagan wasted billions on weapons the United States did not need.

The author believes the largest single external blow that was dealt to communism was President Truman's Marshall plan of economic development. The success of the Marshall plan highlighted the economic inefficiencies more than any other single external event. The Marshall Plan is decisive proof that sharing, caring and nonviolence eliminates more terrorists than policies that end up killing innocent bystanders.

[85] William Blum, "The Myth of the Gipper: Reagan Didn't End the Cold War," Counterpunch, 7 June 2004. Internet site is www.counterpunch.org/blum06072004.html

Georgi Arbatov, head of the Moscow-based Institute for the Study of the U.S.A. and Canada, insists in his 1992 memoirs that the U.S. military buildup during the Reagan years actually delayed the breakup of the Soviet Union.

George F. Kennan, the former US ambassador to the Soviet Union, and father of the theory of "containment" of the same country, asserts that "the suggestion that any United States administration had the power to influence decisively the course of a tremendous domestic political upheaval in another great country on another side of the globe is simply childish." He contends that the extreme militarization of American policy strengthened hard-liners in the Soviet Union. "Thus the general effect of Cold War extremism was to delay rather than hasten the great change that overtook the Soviet Union."

Aleksandr Yakovle, Gorbachev's close adviser, when asked whether the Reagan administration's higher military spending, combined with its "Evil Empire" rhetoric, forced the Soviet Union into a more conciliatory position, responded: "It played no role. None. I can tell you that with the fullest responsibility. Gorbachev and I were ready for changes in our policy regardless of whether the American president was Reagan, or Kennedy, or someone even more liberal."

[86] Mike Hersh, "The Real Reagan Legacy: Debunking Myths About Reagan," American Politics Journal, 19 March 2002. When President Reagan took office the CIA briefed him that the Soviet Union was collapsing from within. A Ronald Reagan fact that many wish was a myth is, as President, he believed submarine launched nuclear missiles could be recalled. The Internet address is www.americanpolitics.com/20020319Hersh.html.

[87] Harvey Wasserman, "Rock & radiation, not Ronald Reagan, brought down the Kremlin," The Free Press, 10 June 2004. Internet address is www.freepress.org/columns/display/7/2004/909/columns/display/7>Harvey.

[88] Wikipedia, s.v. "1991," a free-content encyclopedia in many languages. The English edition started in January 2001 and supporting information can be found on the Internet at http://en.wikipedia.org/wiki/1991. On 31 December 1991, The Union of Soviet Socialist Republics officially ceases to exist.

[89] David Corn, "Loyal Opposition: Clinton Allowed Genocide, New Report Says," AlterNet, 25 July 2000. Available on the Internet at http://www.alternet.org/story/9494/.

[90] Robert S. Norris and Hans M. Kristensen, "What's Behind Bush's Nuclear Cuts," Arms Control Today, October 2004, Volume 34, Number 8, 6. On June 1, 2004, Linton F. Brooks, head of the National Security Administration, announced that by 2012 the United States would reduce the number of nuclear weapons in the stockpile by "about half." The Bush administration did not highlight this announcement because the Bush administration was simultaneously pursuing developing additional new nuclear weapons.

"Arms Control Association Vows to Oppose Renewal of New Nuclear Weapons Research," Arms Control Association Media Advisory, 7 February 2004. The Arms Control Association and other leading nuclear security experts criticized the Bush administration's decision to renew its funding request for research on new, earth penetrating nuclear weapons, which Congress denied last year. The Department of Energy's fiscal year 2006 budget request includes $4 million for research on the Robust Nuclear Earth Penetrator. It also envisions spending $14 million on the project in fiscal year 2007. The Department of Defense's fiscal year 2006 budget request also includes $4.5 million for work on the project, and it foresees spending $3.5 million in fiscal year 2007.

[91] E-Update, "Arming Dictators, Rewarding Proliferators," Arms Control Association, 1 April 2005. The F-16 fighter jet is capable of delivering nuclear bombs and this fact escalates the South Asian nuclear and missile arms race. To alleviate India's fear that it will now be even easier for Pakistan to use nuclear weapons, President George W. Bush also offered to sell India advanced combat aircraft and missile defenses. Regardless of how you look at it, the people of Pakistan and India are less safe from the presence of one of the world's most advance nuclear weapon delivery systems.

[92] Jonathan S. Landay, "Bush administration eliminating 19-year-old international terrorism report," Knight Ridder Newspapers, 15 April 2005. According to U.S. intelligence officials, the Patterns of Global Terrorism report is being eliminated because it contradicts President George W. Bush's claims that progress is being made in the war on terror. Statistics that the National Counterterrorism Center provided to the State Department reported 625 "significant" terrorist attacks in 2004. That compared with 175 such incidents in 2003, the highest number in two decades. The statistics didn't include attacks on American troops in Iraq, which President Bush as recently April 12, 2005 called "a central front in the war on terror." To read past "Patterns of Global Terrorism" reports online, go to www.mipt.org/Patterns-of-Global-Terrorism.asp.

[93] Associated Press, "Census: More Americans living in poverty and number of insured also rises," CNN.com, 31 August 2004. Approximately 45 million people lacked health insurance (15.6 percent of the population). A total of 35.8 million people lived below the poverty line in 2003 (12.5 percent of the population). The Census Bureau's definition of poverty varies by the size of the household. For instance, the poverty threshold for a family of four was $18,810, while for two people it was $12,015.

[94] Bob Schildgen, "Bush's 7 Deadly Sins: Sierra's staff curmudgeon tallies the president's environmental crimes," Sierra Club Magazine, September/October 2004.

One has to wonder if President George W. Bush and the Republican party allowed the anti abortion legislation to move forward without a clause for the health and welfare of the woman so that this subject would be a key issue in the 2004 presidential elections.

[95] Michael Dobbs, "Education 'Miracle' Has a Math Problem: Bush Critics Cite Disputed Houston Data," Washington Post, 8 November 2003, A01. "It is all phony; it's just like Enron," said Linda McNeil, a professor of education at Houston's Rice University, referring to the bankrupt Houston-based energy services company that boosted its stock price by covering up losses. "Enron was concerned about appearances, not real economic results. That pretty much describes what we have been doing to our children in Houston."

[96] "The Texas Miracle," 60 Minutes, Aug. 25, 2004. Robert Kimball, assistant principal at Sharpstown High School in Houston said, "I was shocked." His school claimed that no students – not a single one – had dropped out in 2001-2002. But that's not what Kimball saw: "I had been at the high school for three years, and I had seen many, many students, several hundred a year, go out the door."

Houston School Superintendent Rod Paige was given credit for the schools' success, by making principals and administrators accountable for how well their students did. Once he was elected president, Mr. Bush named Paige as secretary of education. Houston became the model for the "No Child Left Behind" education reform act.

Rick Casey, "HISD plan: Fight fraud on the cheap," Houston Chronicle, 8 January 2005.

[97] Michael Moore, Fahrenheit 9/11 (New York, NY: Simon & Schuster, 2004). The Inauguration Day video is included in documentary version of the book.

[98] Lawrence "Jeff" Johnson, "Key Indicators of the Labor Market 2001-2002: U.S. Leads Industrialized World in Hours Worked, Productivity," International Labor Organization, Accessed 5 April 2005. Available on the Internet at www.us.ilo.org/archive/ilofocus/2001/fall/0110focus_6.cfm.

[99] James F. Hoge, Jr., "Foreign News: Who Gives a Damn?" Columbia Journalism Review, November/December 1997.

[100] Walter Cronkite, comments in Santa Barbara at a Nuclear Age Peace Foundation dinner, 23 October 2004.

[101] Noam Chomsky and Edward S. Herman, Manufacturing Consent (New York, NY: Pantheon Books, 1988). The five filters are called the propaganda model.

[102] 95Eric Alterman, What Liberal Media? The Truth About Bias and the News (New York, New York: Basic Books, 2003).

[103] Robert Greenwald director, Outfoxed: Rupert Murdoch's War On News (New York, New York: The Disinformation Company, 2004).

Michael & Me, LP and narrated by Dick Morris, Fahrenhype 9/11 (Westlake Village, CA: Trinity Home Entertainment, 2004).

Michael Moore, Fahrenheit 9/11 (New York, NY: Simon & Schuster, 2004). Readers are encouraged to view this film as well as Michael Moore's Bowling for Columbine film.

[104] The American Heritage Dictionary of the English Language, 4th ed., s.v. "propaganda," (Boston, MA: Houghton Mifflin Company, 2000). Propaganda is defined as the systematic propagation of a doctrine or cause or of information reflecting the views and interests of those advocating such a doctrine or cause.

[105] Robert Greenwald director, Outfoxed: Rupert Murdoch's War On News (New York, New York: The Disinformation Company, 2004).

[106] "The Commission on the Intelligence Capabilities of the United States Regarding Weapons of Mass Destruction," the Commission's report submitted to the president on March 31, 2005. Available on the Internet at www.wmd.gov/report/index.html. The findings of the Commission concluded that Iraq did not have nuclear, biological, or chemical weapons and CIA officers who tried to make the truth known were reassigned enabling the Bush administration to continue to maintain in 2003 that Iraq did have weapons of mass destruction. This information is buried about 200 pages in the report and is also summarized in the following article: "CIA Analysts Concerned About Faulty Iraq WMD Source Were 'Forced to Leave,' Report Says," Global Security Newswire, 1 April 2005.

A single binary weapon was discovered after the PIPA/Knowledge Networks poll in May 2004. "U.S. Army Says It Finds Shell with Sarin Agent in Iraq," Reuters, 17 May 2004. Brigadier General Mark Kimmitt told a news conference the substance had been found by a U.S. convoy in an artillery shell inside a bag. He said the round had exploded, causing a small release of the substance but no one was killed. This artillery shell was either a left over weapon from the previous program the United States aided Saddam Hussein in developing or a plant by U.S. or British intelligence agents so that WMD could be proclaimed as found in Iraq. In any event, Saddam Hussein's claim to have destroyed his WMD arsenal was brought to final closure on January 12, 2005 when it was announced that the 1,700 members of the Iraq Survey Group had left Iraq without finding WMD.

[107] David Barstow and Robin Stein, "Under Bush, a New Age of Prepackaged TV News," New York Times, 13 March 2005.

[108] Ibid., To the viewer, the reports appear like any other 90-second segment on the local news. For example, a State Department camera crew in Kansas City provided the following "news segment" from a jubilant Iraqi-American about the reaction to the fall of Baghdad. "Thank you, Bush. Thank

you, U.S.A." Viewers did not know that this was not real time news but a covert government orchestrated propaganda broadcast.

[109] "Exiled rebel set for lead role," The Guardian, 8 April 2003.

[110] Deema Khatib in the documentary Control Room, directed by Jehane Noujaim and released by Magnolia Pictures in 2004. Her statements regarding the deception in Firdus Square can be heard on the Internet at www.controlroommovie.com.

[111] Ibid.

[112] "U.S troops topple Saddam statue," CNN.com, 9 April 2003. "We thought we were going to get a lot of resistance but we never did, so we just kept pushing and pushing until we got here," said Cpl. Steven Harris with the Marines in the square.

[113] Vice President Dick Cheney, remarks at the American Society of Newspaper Editors, 9 April 2003. His statement was "With every day, with every advance of our coalition forces, the wisdom of that plan becomes more apparent."

[114] "Bombing of journalists may have been a war crime," Reporters Without Borders, 9 April 2003.

[115] Robert Fisk, "Is there some element in the US military that wants to take out journalists,"RobertFisk.com, 9 April 2003.

[116] Saddam Hussein's statue was brought down by a M-88 armored recovery vehicle. All armor units are supported by recovery vehicles that are equipped with chains and wire cables.

[117] Robert Greenwald director, Outfoxed: Rupert Murdoch's War On News (New York, New York: The Disinformation Company, 2004).

[118] Edward N. Wolff, "Recent Trends in Wealth Ownership, 1983-1998: Working Paper No. 300," The Levy Economics Institute of Bard College, May 2000. Bill Gates net worth is approximately $43 billion. Internet address for the working paper is www.levy.org/2/index.asp?interface=standard&screen=publications_preview&datasrc=f73a204517.

[119] Andrew Kohut, "Anti-Americanism: Causes and Characteristics," The Pew Research Center for the People and the Press, 10 December 2003. Internet address is http://people-press.org/commentary/display.php3?AnalysisID=77.

[120] Donald Rumsfeld, "Rumsfeld's war-on-terror memo," USATODAY.com, 16 October 2003. Internet address for the full memo is www.usatoday.com/news/washington/executive/rumsfeld-memo.htm.

[121] "America's Image Further Erodes, Europeans Want Weaker Ties: But Post-War Iraq Will Be Better Off, Most Say ," The Pew Research Center for the People and the Press, 18 March 2003. Internet address is http://people-press.org/reports/display.php3?ReportID=175.

[122] Jules Witcover, "Resolute speech shows caliber not seen in 8 months," Baltimore Sun National Staff, 21 September 2001. President George W. Bush said, "They hate what we see right here in this chamber—a democratically elected government…They hate our freedoms—our freedom of religion, our freedom of speech, our freedom to vote and assemble and disagree with each other." Another variation of this statement in 2002 was, "They hate us for who we are" and "They hate us because we are free."

"Views of a Changing World 2003: War With Iraq Further Divides Global Publics," The Pew Research Center for the People and the Press, 3 June 2003. Internet address is http://people-press.org/reports/display.php3?ReportID=185.

[123] James Fallows, "Bush's Lost Year," The Atlantic Monthly, October 2004, 82.

[124] Ibid., on a related note CIA officer, Michael Scheuer is the author of the book Imperial Hubris.

[125] Michael Scheuer, discussion prior and presentation during the World Affairs Council in San Francisco, 28 February 2005.

[126] Howard Zinn, A People's History of the United States 1492 – Present (New York, NY: Harper-

Collins Publishers Inc., Twentieth anniversary edition published 1999), 62 and 96.

[127] Ibid., 85.

[128] On a related note, John Quincy Adams and George W. Bush are the only two presidents that are sons of former presidents. The United States has never had a son of a president elected in a first term by a majority of the people. In President George W. Bush's first presidency, he was the fourth person to attain the highest office in the U.S. without the backing of the majority of the people. The other three presidents were John Quincy Adams (1825-29), Rutherford B. Hayes (1877-81), and Benjamin Harrison (1889-93).

[129] Associated Press, "Colo. weighs proportional electoral votes," USATODAY.com, 16 August 2004, www.usatoday.com/news/politicselections/state/colorado/2004-08-16-colo-electoral_x.htm.

Two other states do not have winner-take-all systems of casting Electoral College votes. These states are Nebraska and Maine. Both give two votes to the winner of each state with the remaining votes cast to show who won each congressional district.

[130] Howard Zinn, On War (New York, NY: Seven Stories Press, 2001), 167-170.

[131] U.S., Department of State, Publication 1983, Peace and War: United States Foreign Policy, 1931-1941, Washington, D.C.: U.S. Government Printing Office, 1943, pp. 656-61. On May 12, 1941, the Japanese Ambassador handed to the Secretary of State, a proposal for the Japanese Government's terms for an agreement to the prior disputes over resources. The letter stated "American cooperation shall be given in the production and procurement of natural resources (such as oil, rubber, tin, nickel) which Japan needs."

[132] Dafna Lizer, A year later, the 19 hijackers are still a tangle of mystery, Associated Press, 8 September 2002. Wail Alshehri, Waleed M. Alshehri, Abdulaziz Alomari, Satam M.A. Al Suqami, Mohald al-Shehri, Hamza Alghamdi, Ahmed Alghamdi, Hani Hanjour, Nawaf Alhazmi, Khalid Almihdhar, Majed Moqed, Salem Alhazmi, Saeed Alghamdi, and Ahmed Alnami were from Saudi Arabia.

[133] George Gedda, "U.S. Criticizes Saudi Arabia for Lack of Religious Freedom," The Associated Press, 15 September 2004.

[134] John J. Adams, "The View From NRDC: Oil-Fueled Foreign Policy," On Earth (Spring 2003). Excerpt from Natural Resources Defense Council.

[135] Fareed Zakaria, "Imagine: 500 miles per gallon," Newsweek, 7 March 2005, 27.

[136] Diane Raines Ward, Water Wars: Drought, Flood, Folly and the Politics of Thirst (New York, New York: Riverhead Books, June 2003), 188.

[137] Arab Human Development Report 2004: Towards Freedom in the Arab World, United Nations Development Programme Regional Bureau for Arab States, 2005.

[138] "Rumsfeld braces for more violence in Iraq: Says insurgency could endure 'for any number of years,' perhaps until 2017," Associated Press, 26 June 2005.

[139] Marq De Villers, Water: The Fate Of Our Most Precious Resource (New York, New York: First Mariner Books, 2001), 286.

[140] Ibid., 297.

[141] Ibid., 189.

[142] Peter Gleick, The Worlds Water 2002-2003: The Biennial Report on Freshwater Resources (Washington, DC: Island Press, 2002), 198-205.

[143] Diane Raines Ward, Water Wars: Drought, Flood, Folly and the Politics of Thirst (New York, New York: Riverhead Books, June 2003), 188.

[144] Wikipedia, a free-content encyclopedia in many languages. The English edition started in January 2001 and supporting information can be found on the Internet at http://en.wikipedia.org/wiki/Sinai_Peninsula. In 1979 Israel and Egypt signed a Peace Treaty transferring control over Sinai to

Egypt. Israel pulled out of Sinai in several stages with the final pull out in 1982.

[145] Marq De Villers, Water: The Fate Of Our Most Precious Resource (New York, New York: First Mariner Books, 2001), 202.

[146] Diane Raines Ward, Water Wars: Drought, Flood, Folly and the Politics of Thirst (New York, New York: Riverhead Books, June 2003), 205.

[147] Ibid., 269.

[148] Yedidya Atlas, "Israel's Water Basics," commentator for Arutz-7 Israel National Radio, article online on 20 September 2004. Internet address is www.freeman.org/m_online/nov99/atlas.htm. The West Bank provides 25% of Israel's water. The water supply is stored in three main sources (i.e., Lake Kinneret, the Coastal Aquifer, and the Mountain or Yarkon-Taninim Aquifer).

Marq De Villers, Water: The Fate Of Our Most Precious Resource (New York, New York: First Mariner Books, 2001), 200. In 1997, Minister of Agriculture Refael Eitan said that Israel would be in mortal danger if it lost control of the Mountain Aquifer.

Diane Raines Ward, Water Wars: Drought, Flood, Folly and the Politics of Thirst (New York, New York: Riverhead Books, June 2003), 194. Bechtel Corporation is working with Israel on the feasibility of building water and oil pipelines from Turkey. The water under the future Bechtel plan is then distributed to the places it is needed in Israel.

[149] David Chazan, "Turkey and Israel seal water deal," BBC News, 6 August, 2002. Available on the Internet at http://news.bbc.co.uk/1/hi/world/europe/2177295.stm.

[150] Peter Gleick, The Worlds Water 2002-2003: The Biennial Report on Freshwater Resources (Washington, DC: Island Press, 2002), 47.

[151] Stephen C. Pelletiere, "A War Crime or an Act of War?," The New York Times, 31 January 2003.

[152] The American Heritage Dictionary, 2nd College ed., s.v. "terrorism," (Boston, MA: Houghton Miffin Company, 1985), 1255-1256.

[153] "Kings and Queens of the United Kingdom: George III," The Official Website Of The British Monarchy, accessed 5 December 2004. Internet address is www.royal.gov.uk/output/page111.asp. George III was born on 4 June 1738 in London. He became heir to the throne on the death of his father in 1751, succeeding his grandfather, George II, in 1760. He died at Windsor Castle on 29 January 1820, after a reign of almost 60 years - the second longest in British history.

[154] William Blum, "A Brief History Of U.S. Interventions 1945 To The Present," Z Magazine, June 1999. Permission for inclusion of text obtained on 16 September 2004. A more comprehensive listing of U.S. interventions is available in Chapter 17 of his book, Rogue State: A Guide to the World's Only Superpower, published in 2000.

[155] Ibid.

[156] Noam Chomsky and Edward Herman, The Washington Connection and Third World Fascism (New York, NY: South End Press, 1979).

[157] RFE/FL Iran Report Volume 3, Number 13, "Hostile Official Reaction To Albright Speech," Radio Free Europe/Radio Liberty, 27 March 2000. Available on the Internet at www.globalsecurity.org/wmd/library/news/iran/2000/13-270300.html.

[158] James Risen, "Secrets of History: The C.I.A. In Iran," The New York Times, 16 April 2000. Available on the Internet at www.nytimes.com/library/world/mideast/041600iran-cia-index.html.

[159] Ibid.

[160] Wikipedia, s.v. "Mohammed Mossadegh," a free-content encyclopedia in many languages. The English edition started in January 2001 and supporting information can be found on the Internet at http://en.wikipedia.org/wiki/Mohammed_Mossadeq.

[161] Ibid. After the coup Mossadegh was sentenced to three years in prison. Following his release he

spent the rest of his life under house arrest. Mossadegh died in 1967.

[162] James Risen, "Secrets of History: The C.I.A. In Iran," The New York Times, 16 April 2000. Available on the Internet at www.nytimes.com/library/world/mideast/041600iran-cia-index.html.

[163] Ibid.

[164] David Farber, Taken Hostage: The Iran Hostage Crisis and America's First Encounter With Radical Islam (Princeton, New Jersey: Princeton University Press), 2005, 13.

Other good resources for additional information are: David Harris, The Crisis: The President, the Prophet, and the Shah – 1979 and the Coming of Militant Islam (New York, New York: Little, Brown and Company), 2004.

Wikipedia, s.v. "Iranian hostage crisis," a free-content encyclopedia in many languages. The English edition started in January 2001 and supporting information can be found on the Internet at http://en.wikipedia.org/wiki/Iranian_hostage_crisis.

Like most historical events, there were numerous motivations for the Iranian hostage crisis. Certainly the hostages were held in part an act of retaliation against the United States' support for the Shah and to demonstrate that the new Iranian government was capable of opposing the United States. Reza Aslan in "Days of Rage" published in the December 13, 2004 issue of The Nation, has noted that the crisis was also very much about an internal struggle between Iran's religious and secular forces.

[165] National Commission on Terrorist Attacks upon the United States, "The 9-11 Commission Report, Final Report of the National Commission on Terrorist Attacks Upon the United States," Official Government Edition, 24 July 2004, 362.

[166] "Target America," Frontline, timeline aired October 2001.

[167] "The Man Who Knew: Al Qaeda's Global Context," Frontline, 3 October 2002 and updated in 2004.

[168] President George W. Bush, statement on 27 May, 2002. "It is fitting that we remember those who sacrificed," he said, "because today we defend our freedoms. We defend our freedoms against people who can't stand freedom."

[169] Neil Doyle, Terror Tracker, Mainstream Publishing Company LTD, Edinburgh, 2004.

[170] "September 11 in History," September 11 News.com. The World Trade Center attacks on September 11, 2001 killed 2,792 people. The Pentagon attacks killed 124 people on the ground and 64 people who were on American Airlines Flight 77. The United Airlines Flight 93 highjacking killed 40. Total deaths from all attacks is 3,020. The Internet address is www.september11news.com/Sept11History.htm and www.september11news.com/911Art.htm.

[171] Jonathan S. Landay, "Bush administration eliminating 19-year-old international terrorism report," Knight Ridder Newspapers, 15 April 2005. Available on the Internet at http://www.realcities.com/mld/krwashington/11407689.htm.

[172] Editorial, "Washington should promote the rule of law, not lawless militias," The Daily Star in Beirut, Lebanon, 13 August 2004.

[173] Richard Clarke, statement on National Public Radio, 22 September 2004.

[174] Scott Lindlaw, "Bush Suggests War on Terror Cannot Be Won," Associated Press, 30 August 2004.

[175] To help downplay the slaughter and torture of innocent people from graduates of the U.S. Army's School of the Americas, the program was renamed the Western Hemisphere Institute for Security Cooperation. The Fort Benning, Georgia program continues to produce graduates with deadly skills. These graduates are ultimately outside the U.S. system of justice and military command structure.

[176] Gary Cohn and Ginger Thompson, "Unearthed: Fatal Secrets," The Baltimore Sun, 11 June 1995.

Internet site for article is www.baltimoresun.com/news/local/bal-negroponte1a%2C0%2C3704648. story.

[177] Seymour M. Hersh, "The Gray Zone: How a secret Pentagon program came to Abu Ghraib," The New Yorker, 15 May 2005. Available on the Internet at www.newyorker.com/fact/content/ ?040524fa_fact.

[178] Ibid.

[179] Brian Dominick, "Opposition Builds Against 'Torture Apologist' Gonzales," The New Standard, 5 January 2005.

[180] Seymour M. Hersh, "The Gray Zone: How a secret Pentagon program came to Abu Ghraib," The New Yorker, 15 May 2005. Available on the Internet at www.newyorker.com/fact/content/ ?040524fa_fact

[181] Jane Mayer, "Outsourcing Torture," The New Yorker, February 14 and 21, 2005 80th Anniversary Issue, 106. Also Michael Scheuer responded to a question at the February 28, 2005 World Affairs Council meeting in San Francisco confirming his role as one of the authors of the extraordinary renditions program.

[182] Ibid. Mayer reported that the most common destinations for rendered suspects are Egypt, Morocco, Syria, and Jordan, each of which is known to use torture in interrogations. People have also been sent to Uzbekistan.

[183] Tim Reid, "Flight to torture: where abuse is contracted out," Times Online, 26 March 2005.

[184] Jane Mayer, "Outsourcing Torture," The New Yorker, February 14 and 21, 2005 80th Anniversary Issue. Mayer also writes that William Howard Taft IV, the State Department's counsel, sent a memo to Alberto Gonzales and John Yoo in January 2002, warning them that their legal advice to the president—that he had almost unfettered latitude in his prosecution of the war on terror—was "untenable," "incorrect," and "confused."

[185] Robert Burns, "Pentagon Tries to Explain Spy Unit," Associated Press, 24 January 2005. Also, William Arkin, a former Army intelligence officer and author of the book, "Code Names: Deciphering U.S. Military Plans, Programs and Operations in the 9-11 World," noted that the DIA unit may be a permutation of a secret intelligence unit known as Gray Fox.

[186] Barton Gellma, "New Espionage Branch Delving Into CIA Territory," Washington Post, 23 January 2005, A01.

[187] Gary Cohn and Ginger Thompson, "Unearthed: Fatal Secrets," The Baltimore Sun, 11 June 1995.

[188] Christopher Dickey, With the Contras: A Reporter in the Wilds of Nicaragua (New York, NY: Simon & Schuster, A Touchstone Book, 1 May 1987).

The situation in the Middle East deteriorated because President Reagan's illegal weapon transfers to Iran increased the anger of Iraq toward the United States. Other Arab nations also viewed this event as another example of the United States selling weapons of death in the Middle East.

[189] 189Dr. Joy Gordon, "Cool War: Economic Sanctions as Weapons of Mass Destruction," Harper's Magazine, November 2002. The United Nations Children's Fund (UNICEF) reported the half-million children and toddlers killed were a direct result of the sanctions. Richard Garfield, a critic of the 500,000 number, concluded the rise in the mortality rate was between a minimum of 100,000 and a more likely estimate of 227,000 excess deaths among young children from August 1991 through March 1998. He attributed one-quarter of the deaths to the Gulf war and the remaining excess deaths as primarily associated with economic sanctions. His work is available at www.cam. ac.uk/societies/casi/info/garfield/dr-garfield.html.

[190] Arundhati Roy, "The Algebra of Infinite Justice," The Guardian, 29 September 2001. On the Internet at http://humanrightsonline.net/algebra.html.

[191] Economist Magazine, "Toward a more relevant United Nations," Economist.com, 1 December

2004. Benon Sevan, the former head of the Oil for Food Program, allegedly took oil vouchers from Saddam. The Secretary-General's son, Kojo Annan, received payments as recently as 2004 from one of the firms that won an Oil for Food Program contract from the United Nations. Kojo Annan worked for this Swiss firm until December 1998. The Swiss firm, Cotecna, inspected goods at border-crossings. The fact that Kojo Annan continued to receive payments until 2004 surprised and embarrassed his father.

[192] Dr. Joy Gordon, "Cool War: Economic Sanctions as Weapons of Mass Destruction," Harper's Magazine, November 2002.

[193] "The Health Conditions Of The Population In Iraq Since The Gulf Crisis," World Health Organization, March 1996. Available on the Internet at www.who.int/disasters/repo/5249.html.

[194] Dr. Joy Gordon, "Cool War: Economic Sanctions as Weapons of Mass Destruction," Harper's Magazine, November 2002.

[195] Ibid.

[196] Ibid.

[197] Ibid.

[198] "The Health Conditions Of The Population In Iraq Since The Gulf Crisis," World Health Organization, March 1996. Available on the Internet at www.who.int/disasters/repo/5249.html.

[199] Dr. Joy Gordon, "Cool War: Economic Sanctions as Weapons of Mass Destruction," Harper's Magazine, November 2002.

[200] Ibid.

[201] Ibid.

[202] Hassan Ibrahim in the documentary Control Room, directed by Jehane Noujaim and released by Magnolia Pictures in 2004.

[203] U.S. Secretary of Defense Donald H. Rumsfeld, Rumsfeld gave a briefing on situation in Iraq, 11 April 2003. He said, "And I think it's increasingly clear that most welcome coalition forces and see them not as invaders or occupiers, but as liberators. The images of thousands of cheering Iraqis, celebrating and embracing coalition forces, are being broadcast throughout the world, including the Arab world."

[204] "The West: New Perspectives On The West," PBS, September 1996. This documentary is an eight-part series on the genocide of native Americans. Available on the Internet at www.pbs.org/weta/thewest/places/states/montana/mt_littlebighorn.htm.

[205] Jonathan Granoff, "Nuclear Weapons, Ethics, Morals, and Law," Brigham Young University Law Review, 2000, 1413-1442.

[206] Holy Bible: New American Standard Bible (Grand Rapids, Michigan: Zondervan, 2002), 790. Matthew, 5:43 to 5:44. The quotation sentence comes to an end in Matthew 5:45. The complete text in Matthew is: 5:43 You have heard that it was said, 'YOU SHALL LOVE YOUR NEIGHBOR and hate your enemy.' 5:44 But I say to you, love your enemies and pray for those who persecute you, 5:45 so that you may be sons of your Father who is in heaven; for He causes His sun to rise on the evil and the good, and sends rain on the righteous and the unrighteous.

[207] "Kuwait History," Arabic German Consulting, 17 September 2004. Internet address is www.arab.de/arabinfo/kuwaithis.htm.

[208] Secretary of Defense Donald H. Rumsfeld, "Secretary Rumsfeld Remarks on ABC "This Week with George Stephanopoulos," United States Department of Defense News Transcript, 30 March 2003. Secretary of Defense Donald Rumsfeld said, "We know where they are. They're in the area around Tikrit and Baghdad and east, west, south and north somewhat."

[209] Matt Kelly, "U.S. Supplied Germs to Iraq in '80s," Associated Press, 30 September 2002. The

deadly exports by the Centers for Disease Control and the American Type Culture Collection were cleared by the Reagan Administration Commerce Department and are detailed in a 1994 Senate Banking Committee report.

"U.S. Chemical and Biological Warfare-Related Dual Use Exports to Iraq and their Possible Impact on the Health Consequences of the Persian Gulf War, Senate Committee on Banking, Housing and Urban Affairs with Respect to Export Administration," report of May 25, 1994, page 11 in stand-alone report or page 239 in Senate publication S. Hrg. 103-900.

[210] Ibid. Also, "Report of the Secretary-General on the activities of the Special Commission established by the Secretary-General pursuant to paragraph 9 (b) (i) of resolution 687 (1991)," United Nations, 6 October 1997.

[211] Wikipedia, s.v. "Iran-Iraq War," a free-content encyclopedia in many languages. The English edition started in January 2001 and supporting information can be found on the Internet at http://en.wikipedia.org/wiki/Iran-Iraq_War.

[212] "The Long Road To War: To The Brink Of War," Frontline, 17 March 2003.

[213] "Excerpts From Iraqi Document on Meeting With U.S. Envoy," The New York Times, 23 September 1990, 19.

[214] Ibid.

[215] "The Long Road To War: To The Brink Of War," Frontline, 17 March 2003. Testimony in the Hearing before the Subcommittee on Europe and the Middle East of the House Committee on Foreign Affairs, "Developments in the Middle East," 31 July 1990.

[216] Edited by Douglas Harrecht, "Toting the Casualties of War," Business Week Online, 6 February 2003.

[217] "Gunning For Saddam: Interview James Baker," Frontline, mid October 2001. Internet site for quote is www.pbs.org/wgbh/pages/frontline/shows/gunning/interviews/baker.html.

[218] "History News Network: History Q & A," History News Network, 30 September 2002. The assassination was to take place between April 14 and April 16, 1993. The Kuwaiti authorities arrested 17 persons suspected in the plot to kill Present George H. W. Bush using explosives hidden in a Toyota Landcruiser. On June 26, 1993, the United States launched a cruise missile attack in Baghdad in retaliation for the assassination attempt on former President George H. W. Bush. The attack is believed have killed between six and eight persons and injured approximately 12 others. On June 27, 1993, Madeleine Albright, U.S. Ambassador to the United Nations, addressed an emergency session of the Security Council to provide evidence for the attack. The Internet site for the full text is www.hnn.us/articles/1000.html.

[219] Katharine Q. Seelye, "Guantánamo Bay Faces Sentence of Life as Permanent U.S. Prison," The New York Times, 16 September 2002.

[220] "Countries Where Al Qaeda Has Operated," U.S. Department of State's Bureau of International Information Programs, posted on November 10, 2001. Was on the USINFO.STATE.GOV Internet site but now the message at http://usinfo.state.gov/products/pubs/terrornet/homepage.htm informs visitors "The Network of Terrorism is no longer available on the web." The information was still available in September 2004 although the actual date for its removal is unknown.

[221] National Commission on Terrorist Attacks upon the United States, "The 9-11 Commission Report, Final Report of the National Commission on Terrorist Attacks Upon the United States," Official Government Edition, 24 July 2004, 334.

[222] Bob Woodward, Plan of Attack (New York, New York: Simon & Schuster 2004), 199.

[223] John Pilger, "Pilger claims White House knew Saddam was no threat," The Sydney Morning Herald, 23 September 2003. Colin Powell in Cairo on February 24, 2001 said, "He (Saddam Hussein) has not developed any significant capability with respect to weapons of mass destruction. He is un-

able to project conventional power against his neighbors." Two months later, Condoleeza Rice said, "We are able to keep his arms from him. His military forces have not been rebuilt."

[224] Katherine Pfleger Shrader, U.S. Weapons Inspector: Iraq Had No WMD, Associated Press, September 16, 2004.

[225] "Bush: Don't wait for mushroom cloud," CNN.com, 8 October 2002. President George W. Bush and his administration did not want to talk about the true threat of a mushroom cloud from terrorists because it would reveal how little was really being done to protect America. Internet address for the complete text is www.cnn.com/2002/ALLPOLITICS/10/07/bush.transcript/.

[226] Ari Fleischer, "Press Briefing by Ari Fleischer," Office of the Press Secretary, 9 January 2003. Internet address with complete text is www.whitehouse.gov/news/releases/2003/01/20030109-8.html.

[227] President George W. Bush, "State of the Union," The White House, 28 January 2003. Internet address with complete text is www.whitehouse.gov/news/releases/2003/01/20030128-19.html.

[228] Dana Priest and Karen DeYoung, "CIA Questioned Documents Linking Iraq, Uranium Ore," Washington Post, 22 March 2003, A30.

[229] Bill Gertz, "FBI probing forged papers on Niger uranium," The Washington Times, 19 July 2003. Available on the Internet at http://www.washtimes.com/national/20030719-120154-5384r.htm.

[230] Colin L. Powell, "Remarks to the United Nations Security Council," U.S. Department of State, 5 February 2003. Internet address with complete text is www.state.gov/secretary/rm/2003/17300.htm.

[231] Peter Beaumont, Antony Barnett and Gaby Hinsliff, "Iraqi mobile labs nothing to do with germ warfare, report finds," Guardian Unlimited: The Observer, 15 June 2003.

[232] Glenn Frankel, "Blair Acknowledges Flaws in Iraq Dossier," Washington Post Foreign Service, 8 February 2003, A15.

[233] Tom Happold and agencies, "Official explodes key WMD claim," Guardian Unlimited, 29 May 2003.

[234] The American people deserve to know who fabricated the forged documents. Israel and the United States were also working hard to build a case to invade Iraq. The Israeli government has acknowledged providing the U.S. with incorrect intelligence. See Offer Shelah, "Israeli Intelligence Probe Asks: What Did We Know and When?," The Forward Newspaper, The Situation, 13 February 2004. Former CIA intelligence analyst Larry C. Johnson has written that Italy's SISME intelligence service had a hand in creating the forged documents. See "Dick Cheney's Covert Action," TomPaine.com, 19 October 2005. Available on the Internet at http://www.tompaine.com/articles/20051019/dick_cheneys_covert_action.php.

[235] President George W. Bush, "President Says Saddam Must Leave Iraq Within 48 Hours," Office of the Press Secretary, 17 March 2003. Internet address for the complete text www.whitehouse.gov/news/releases/2003/03/20030317-7.html.

[236] "Duelfer Report Further Disproves U.S. Claims on Iraq WMD," Arms Control Association, 15 October 2004.

[237] Richard Morin and Claudia Deane, "71% of Americans Support War, Poll Shows," Washington Post, 19 March 2003, A14. Also Gallup/USA Today poll on 21 March 2003 that showed 76 percent of Americans supported the decision to launch the war.

[238] David Manning, "The secret Downing Street memo," The Sunday Times – Britain, 1 May 2005. The memo was written by Matthew Rycroft on 23 July 2002. Available on the Internet at http://www.timesonline.co.uk/article/0,,2087-1593607,00.html.

[239] Stephen C. Pelletiere, "A War Crime or an Act of War?," The New York Times, 31 January 2003.

[240] President George W. Bush, "State of the Union," The White House, 28 January 2003. President Bush said "The dictator who is assembling the world's most dangerous weapons has already used them on whole villages -- leaving thousands of his own citizens dead, blind, or disfigured." Internet

address for the complete text www.whitehouse.gov/news/releases/2003/01/20030128-19.html.

[241] Walter Cronkite, comments in Santa Barbara at the Nuclear Age Peace Foundation, 23 October 2004. Also Thomas Schultz, "Cronkite: U.S. 'excited the Arab world' by waging war on Iraq," Nuclear Age Peace Foundation Press Release, 24 October 2004.

[242] Israel is the only country that benefits tremendously from the 2003 Iraq war. Saddam is no longer able to fund Palestinian suicide bombers, Israel's traditional enemies are now the United States' enemies, and the United States is now the primary focus of Muslim anger and violence. In addition, a United States controlled Iraq can solve Israel's water shortage. In short, from one vantage point the United States is paying for Israel's war as no Israeli soldiers or civilians are caught in the crossfire.

"Israel ready to bomb Iran N-plant," Rediff.com, 29 August 2003. Internet site is www.rediff.com/us/2003/aug/29iran.htm. Article discusses prior attack on Iraq and a likely future attack on Iran.

[243] Stephen C. Pelletiere, "A War Crime or an Act of War?," The New York Times, 31 January 2003. In this article the author describes how control of Iraq's Tigris, Euphrates, the Greater Zab and Lesser Zab rivers could alter the destiny of the Middle East for decades. The strategic value of Iraq's water is not a new development. In the 1990's, a "Peace Pipeline" was proposed to bring the waters of the Tigris and Euphrates south to the Gulf states and Israel.

[244] Christine Spolar, "14 `enduring bases' set in Iraq," Chicago Tribune, 23 March 2004.

[245] Richard Clarke, Against All Enemies (New York, NY: Free Press, 2004), 265 Richard Clarke provides an insider perspective that the five real Bush Administration reasons for starting the 2003 Iraq war are: to clean up the mess left by the first Bush administration; improve Israel's strategic position by eliminating a large, hostile army; to create an Arab democracy that could serve as a model to other Arab states; to permit the withdrawal of U.S. forces from Saudi Arabia; and to create another friendly source of oil for the United States.

[246] Wikipedia, s.v. "invasion of Afghanistan," a free-content encyclopedia in many languages. The English edition started in January 2001 and supporting information can be found on the Internet at http://en.wikipedia.org/wiki/Soviet_invasion_of_Afghanistan.

[247] Richard Clarke, Against All Enemies (New York, NY: Free Press, 2004), 49-51.

[248] Comedian George Carlin was born 1937 and is currently performing in the United States.

[249] Richard Clarke, Against All Enemies (New York, NY: Free Press, 2004), 52-53.

[250] "Looking For Answers: Prince Bandar bin Sultan," Frontline, interview conducted in late September 2001.

[251] Richard Clarke, Against All Enemies (New York, NY: Free Press, 2004), 59.

[252] Ibid., 71.

[253] Maggie Michael, "Television Networks Air Tape of bin Laden," Associated Press, 29 October 2004.

[254] Samia Nakhoul, "Bin Laden Labels Saddam an Infidel – Jazeera TV," Reuters, 11 February 2003.

[255] Michael Dobbs, "Inside the Mind of Osama Bin Laden: Strategy Mixes Long Preparation, Powerful Message Aimed at Dispossessed," The Washington Post, 20 September 2001, A01.

[256] Ibid.

[257] Maggie Michael, "Television Networks Air Tape of bin Laden," Associated Press, 29 October 2004.

[258] Offer Shelah, "Israeli Intelligence Probe Asks: What Did We Know and When?," The Forward Newspaper, The Situation, 13 February 2004. Israel provided the United States and Britain with incorrect intelligence. Israel's security benefits by the U.S. invasion as Saddam Hussein was a very real threat to Israel. In addition, the U.S. became the number one focus of Muslim anger in the world and future access to Iraq's water becomes possible.

[259] Richard Clark, "Clarke's Take On Terror," CBS, 3/21/04. Internet address is www.cbsnews.com/

stories/2004/03/19/60minutes/main607356.shtml.

[260] "700 named in Iraq's death toll after a year of slaughter," The Iraq Body Count Project, 19 March 2004. The latest count of civilian deaths is available at www.iraqbodycount.net/.

[261] "Iraq war illegal, says Annan," BBC News, 16 September, 2004.

Matthew Rycroft, "The secret Downing Street memo," The Sunday Times, 1 May 2005. This UK Eyes Only document was written on July 23, 2002. The Downing Street memo confirms that the Blair and Bush governments knew invading Iraq would be illegal and if the truth of the operation became known, the Blair and Bush leadership could be convicted of war crimes. Furthermore, the document confirms that the Bush administration was lying to the American people. The memo states that Iraq is not a threat, contrary to public no war decision communications by the Bush administration that the decision to go to war was already made, and the intelligence would be "fixed" to sell the war to the American people. The Downing Street memo is available at www.timesonline. co.uk/article/0,,2087-1593607,00.html.

[262] George Bernard Shaw, Man and Superman: Maxims for Revolutionists, 1903 Play. Shaw was an Irish dramatist & socialist (1856 - 1950). "The golden rule is that there are no golden rules."

[263] Robert S. McNamara and James G. Blight, Wilson's Ghost: Reducing The Risk Of Conflict, Killing, And Catastrophe In The 21st Century (New York, New York: Public Affairs, 2001), 5.

[264] Ibid., 26.

[265] Ibid., 26.

[266] The United States House of Representatives Select Committee on U.S. National Security and Military/Commercial Concerns with the People's Republic of China declassified report issued on 3 January 1999.

[267] Ibid.

[268] Mary Perea, "4 Workers Fired in Los Alamos Lab Scandal," Associated Press, 16 September 2004.

[269] Japan is a nuclear weapon free country. The adoption of policies prohibiting weapons of mass destruction were a direct result of the suffering experienced following the atomic bombs at Hiroshima and Nagasaki in August 1945.

[270] Special Report, "Fighting For Survival," The Economist, 20 November 2004, 26. Kofi Annan is seeking to make the United Nations more relevant. The organization of the United Nations was established by the allied powers during the World War II. The main victors in the war were—America, Russia, Great Britain and China—plus France. These five nations have permanent membership and veto power. The ten non-permanent regional members (serving renewable two-year terms) do not have veto power. This undemocratic system undermines the United Nations. To illustrate this point, Britain, with its 60 million people, has a permanent seat. India has a billion people and does not have a permanent seat. Another example cited in the Special Report is Japan, the world's second biggest economy, also does not have a permanent seat.

[271] "Toward a more relevant United Nations," Economist Magazine, 1 December 2004.

[272] Anup Shah, High Military Expenditure in Some Places, 16 June 2004. He includes information from the article "U.N. Financial Crisis," Global Policy Forum available at www.globalpolicy.org/finance/. Anup Shah's article is available on the Internet at www.globalissues.org/Geopolitics/ArmsTrade/Spending.asp#InContextUSMilitarySpendingVersusRestoftheWorld.

[273] Imagine the active peacekeeping that the United Nations could implement if members allocated 5% of their unilateral military budgets to multilateral peacekeeping led by the United Nations. Based on projected 2006 worldwide military spending, 5% would exceed $50 billion dollars. The additional $35 billion plus that would be generated is more than the amount needed to end world hunger ($19 billion) and provide clean water for the world ($10 billion) as explained in Chapter 2.

[274] Errol Morris director, Fog Of War (The studio is Columbia Tristar Hom and the release date

was 19 December 2003). Robert McNamara shares insights on lessons learned from the Vietnam War.

[275] Robert S. McNamara and James G. Blight, Wilson's Ghost: Reducing The Risk Of Conflict, Killing, And Catastrophe In The 21st Century (New York, New York: Public Affairs, 2001), 53.

[276] Law Reports of Trials of War Criminals. Selected and Prepared by the United Nations War Crimes Commission,Volume IV, London: HMSO, 1948. General Tomoyuki Yamashita, formerly Commanding General of the Fourteenth Army Group of the Imperial Japanese Army in the Philippine Islands, was tried and condemned by a United States Military Commission in Manila. His crime was unlawfully disregarding and failing to discharge his duty as commander to control the acts of members of his command by permitting them to commit war crimes. Judgment was delivered on February 4, 1946.

[277] Christopher Hitchens, The Trial (New York, NY: Verso, 2001), 25.

[278] Praful Bidwai and Achin Vanaik, New Nukes: India, Pakistan and Global Nuclear Disarmament (Interlink Books, New York, 2000), preface xxix.

On a related note, on July 16, 1945, the first atomic bomb was detonated at a site in New Mexico named "Trinity." The source for the selection of the Trinity site name is unknown. Major W. A. (Lex) Stevens and J. Robert Oppenheimer are two of the possible sources for the Trinity name. The name Trinity (i.e., Father, Son and Holy Spirit) or "power of all life" for a weapon site with "the power to destroy everything" is another example of history being stranger than fiction.

[279] History and experiences like Albert Speer's, as described in his book Inside The Third Reich (New York, NY: Simon & Schuster, 1970), guide us on what can happen when the checks and balances of power have been removed. For example, Speer concludes that when good people fail to speak up against injustice evil people can seize control of a government. To protect ourselves and other people in the world, adding checks and balances to safeguard the use of weapons of mass destruction would likely have a domino effect, influencing other nations, like Israel, to do the same with their nuclear arsenals.

[280] For more information on the explosive power of nuclear weapons, visit the Federation of American Scientist Web site at www.fas.org/nuke.

[281] Carl Sagan, "The Nuclear Winter," Council for a Livable World, speech given in Boston, MA, 1983.

[282] Robock, Alan. "New models confirm nuclear winter," Bulletin of the Atomic Scientist, September 1989, 32-35.

[283] Non-profit organizations like the Natural Resources Defense Council or NRDC have acquired information on the killing power of modern nuclear weapons because of nuclear non-proliferation agreements and the openness in Russia following the end of the Cold War. The NRDC has created a sophisticated software simulation to approximate the effects on likely nuclear, military, and industrial targets. To learn more about the NRDC, visit www.nrdc.org on the Internet.

[284] National Intelligence Council, "China and Weapons of Mass Destruction: Implications for the United States," Central Intelligence Agency site, 5 November 1999. The report notes Dr. Paul Godwin, "China's Nuclear Forces," and "A senior U.S. intelligence official has confirmed that Chinese missiles are usually unfueled and unmated to their warheads." Internet address is www.cia.gov/nic/confreports_chinawmd.html#rft95.

John J. Lumpkin, "China launches new class of nuclear submarine designed to fire ICBMs," Associated Press, 3 December 2004. Internet address is www.signonsandiego.com/news/world/20041203-1838-us-china-submarine.html. United States defense officials announced on that China has launched the first submarine capable of launching nuclear weapons that could reach the U.S. from the country's home waters. In the last few years China did not have a submarine capable of launching nuclear missiles. China had previously developed a missile capable submarine called the Type

092, or Xia class. A 2001 Pentagon report said the Xia missiles could fly 600 miles but the submarine was not operational. The significance of this development is China will likely have mated warheads on this subset of its nuclear arsenal.

[285] Stephen I. Schwartz, Atomic Audit, The Costs and Consequences of U.S. Nuclear Weapons Since 1940 (Washington, D.C.: Brookings Institution Press, 1998).

[286] In time the world may have the courage to eliminate all weapons of mass destruction. While the author presents ideas to reduce world arsenals because these steps are more likely to be taken, individual nations would be best served by rapidly eliminating their weapons of mass destruction.

[287] President Theodore Roosevelt (1858 - 1919), "Crucible of Empire," Public Broadcasting Station, 1999. President McKinley appointed Theodore Roosevelt in 1897 as the Assistant Secretary of the Navy. Roosevelt's once said, "I should welcome almost any war, for I think this country needs one."

[288] Martin Luther King, Jr., "The Casualties of the War in Vietnam," speech in Los Angeles, California, 25 February 1967. In contrast to Martin Luther King, Jr.'s insights, the majority of the American people thought prior to the 2003 Iraq war that starting a war was the path to peace. Richard Morin and Claudia Deane, "71% of Americans Support War, Poll Shows," The Washington Post, 19 March 2003, 14.

[289] If you replace the word terror with murder you can see how sustainable this war can be. A war to end murder will never end, and so it is true when terror is not understood to be a response to imperialism. Abstract nouns like murder and terror are hard to bring to a surrender-signing ceremony. For the war on terror against the U.S. to be won, terrorism by groups like al Qaeda need to be understood as acts of terror in response to a previous and usually ongoing injustice.

[290] Joseph K. Leach, Smedley Butler: Marine Corps Legend, accessed site on 19 September 2004. Internet address for the complete text www.grunts.net/legends/butler.html.

[291] Smedley Butler with introduction by Adam Parfrey, War Is a Racket (Los Angeles, CA: Feral House, 1935, reprint edition April 2003), 16-17. The Facist Plot Officially Confirmed, 74th Congress, 1st Session, House of Representatives Report No. 153, February 15, 1935.

[292] Ibid., 12-17. The Great Depression produced a movement among World War I soldiers to demand their "war bonus" of approximately $1,000. Smedley supported the Bonus Marchers' cause. Due to his integrity and leadership, Smedley had the loyalty of 500,000 veterans in 1934. When companies like J.P. Morgan stood to lose money by the elimination of the gold standard, senior business leaders started a plot to overthrow President Franklin Delano Roosevelt. President Roosevelt's New Deal had to be stopped and the plotters approached Smedley and asked him to lead the veterans in a coup.

Coup attempt leaders included Gerald G. MacGuire of the brokerage firm Grayson M.P. Murphy, John W. Davis of J.P. Morgan, and Company, founders of the American Liberty League, heads of the American Legion, with the National City Bank for financing, Remington Arms Company for weapons and a loan for the weapons from the DuPont family.

[293] Ibid., 23.

[294] Smedley Butler with introduction by Adam Parfrey, War Is a Racket (Los Angeles, CA: Feral House, 1935, reprint edition April 2003), 1.

The oil companies and war profiteers Butler refers to are the Halliburton's of today. Neil King, Jr., "Army Plan Lets Halliburton Keep Disputed Payments," The Wall Street Journal, October 22, 2004. Halliburton's Kellogg Brown & Root unit, which performs much of the company's Iraq work, has billed about $12 billion in Iraq. Approximately $3 billion remains in dispute. Pentagon records show that $650 million in Halliburton billings is deemed "questionable," a term government auditors use when they see strong evidence of overcharges or contracting irregularities. Another $2 billion is considered "unsupported," meaning that KBR remains unable to provide sufficient paperwork. Army, Brig. Gen. Jerome Johnson, head of the Army's Field Support Command, called the move to hire the consultants the only way to resolve the dispute between Pentagon auditors and the Halliburton unit. Brig. Gen. Johnson wrote "If supporting documentation just does not exist, we must have an equitable solution to declaring an acceptable cost level and moving forward...It would be totally inappropriate and unfair of us to disallow all costs when, in the fog of the contingency, KBR did not obtain sufficient supporting documentation."

[295] Kevin Phillips, "Bush Family Values: War, Wealth, Oil: Four generations have created an unsavory web of links that could prove an election-year Achilles' heel for the president," The Los Angeles Times, 8 February 2004.

[296] "Office of Alien Property Custodian, Vesting Order No. 248," Signed by Leo T. Crowley, 20 October 1942. Prescott Bush was a director of Union Banking Corporation from 1934 to 1943.

[297] "Exposed: The Carlyle Group," Information Clearing House, accessed on 19 September 2004 at www.informationclearinghouse.info/article3995.htm.

[298] United Defense 2001 Press Release, "United Defense Industries Commences Initial Public Offering Today," United Defense Public Relations, 14 December 2001.

[299] Mark Fineman, "Arms Buildup Enriches Firm Staffed by Big Guns, Ex-president and other elites are behind weapon-boosting Carlyle Group," Los Angeles Times, 10 January 2002.

[300] President Dwight D. Eisenhower, "Farewell Address," Our Documents initiative, 17 January 1961. Internet address is www.ourdocuments.gov.

[301] Smedley Butler with introduction by Adam Parfrey, War Is a Racket (Los Angeles, CA: Feral House, 1935, reprint edition April 2003), 42.

[302] Thomas B. Cochran, Matthew G. McKinzie, Robert S. Norris, William M. Arkin, Co-authors in the National Resources Defense Council Nuclear Program, The U.S. Nuclear War Plan: A Time For Change, (National Resources Defense Council, June 2001), 130. Also, Frances Fitzgerald, Way out There in the Blue: Reagan, Star Wars, and the End of the Cold War (New York, New York: Touchstone, Simon and Schuster, April 2001), 85. Fitzgerald references McGeorge Bundy, Danger and Survival: Choices About the Bomb in the First Fifty Years (New York: Random House, 1988), 565. The United States and Russia maintain nuclear arsenals that are capable of destroying civilization on the planet. One U.S. nuclear submarine can carry 192 warheads and is capable by itself of destroying every large and medium-sized city in Russia and over one-third of Russia's citizenry.

[303] Robert S. McNamara and James G. Blight, Wilson's Ghost: Reducing The Risk Of Conflict, Killing, And Catastrophe In The 21st Century (New York, New York: Public Affairs, 2001), 174.

Jon Brook Wolfsthal, Cristina-Astrid Chuen, Emily Ewell Daughtry, Editors, Nuclear Status Report: Nuclear Weapons, Fissile Material, And Export Controls In The Former Soviet Union, Number 6, (Carnegie Endowment for International Peace and the Monterey Institute of International Studies, June 2001), 2. Also, Thomas B. Cochran, Matthew G. McKinzie, Robert S. Norris, William M. Arkin, Co-authors in the National Resources Defense Council Nuclear Program, The U.S. Nuclear War Plan: A Time For Change, (National Resources Defense Council, June 2001), 18.

[304] Bruce G. Blair, "America Doesn't Need All These Warheads," International Herald Tribune, 14 June 2000, 6.

[305] Stephen I. Schwartz, Atomic Audit, The Costs and Consequences of U.S. Nuclear Weapons Since 1940 (Washington, D.C.: Brookings Institution Press, 1998).

[306] John Barry and Evan Thomas, "Dropping the Bomb," Newsweek, 25 June 2001.

[307] Ken Silverstein, Private Warriors (New York, NY: Verso, October 2000), Page viii.

[308] Carl Kaysen and others, "War With Iraq: Costs, Consequences and Alternatives," The American Academy of Arts and Sciences, December 2002, 59. Internet address for this information is www.amacad.org/publications/monographs/War_with_Iraq.pdf).

[309] Senator Hiram Johnson (1866-1945), a progressive Republican Senator in California, his state-

ment to the United States Senate in 1917. "The first casualty when war comes is truth."

[310] Arthur Okun, The Political Economy of Prosperity (Washington, D.C.: Brookings, 1970), Chapter 3.

[311] Donald H. Rumsfeld, "Secretary Rumsfeld Media Stakeout," United States Department of Defense, 19 January 2003.

[312] James Fallows, "Bush's Lost Year," The Atlantic Monthly, October 2004, 70. A guaranteed way to be forced out of the Bush administration is to offer a realistic estimate for the cost of a war. Lawrence Lindsey, President George W. Bush's chief economic adviser, learned this when he was fired in December 2002 for calculating the cost of the invading Iraq at $100 billion to $200 billion. This was a direct contradiction of the statements by Donald Rumsfeld and Paul Wolfowitz that the U.S. costs would be offset by Iraq's oil revenues and contributions from allies.

[313] "Bush Seeks More Than $80 Billion for Iraq, Afghan," Reuters, 25 January 2005.

Carl Kaysen and others, "War With Iraq: Costs, Consequences and Alternatives," The American Academy of Arts and Sciences, December 2002, 82. Internet address for this information is www. amacad.org/publications/monographs/War_with_Iraq.pdf).

P.J. Crowley and Sonal Shah, "The WMD Sequel: Iraq, Afghanistan and Deficit Reduction," Center for American Progress, 30 March 2004. The U.S. is spending over $4.7 billion a month fighting in Iraq and Afghanistan.

[314] Audrey McAvoy, "Japan pledges $500 million in tsunami aid," Associated Press, 1 January 2005. Article is on the Internet at www.boston.com/news/world/asia/articles/2005/01/01/japan_pledges_500_million_in_tsunami_aid?mode=PF.

The December 26, 2004 tsunami killed over 226,000 people. On January 1, 2005, Japan's Prime Minister Junichiro Koizumi pledged $500 million in grant aid for tsunami disaster relief. This announcement made Japan the largest single donor to victims of the catastrophe. The Japanese origin of the word "tsunami" notes Japan's long history with deadly quake-triggered waves. The United States following Japan's announcement, increased its pledge from $35 million to $350 million.

[315] Elisabeth Sköns, Catalina Perdomo, Sam Perlo-Freeman and Petter Stålenheim of the Stockholm International Peace Research Institute, SIPRI Yearbook 2004: Armaments, Disarmament And International Security (Oxford: Oxford University Press), 2004, Chapter 10.

[316] Anup Shah, "High Military Expenditure in Some Places," Global Issues, 16 June 2004. He compiles his information from the Center for Arms Control and Non-Proliferation's World Military Spending project, February 2004. The Center for Arms Control and Non-Proliferation compiled information from multiple sources including the International Institute for Strategic Studies and the U.S. Department of Defense. The U.S. military spending figure is the 2005 annual budget request. Other figures are current as of 2003 with the exception of those noted with an asterisk signifying that they are current as of 2002.

[317] Friends Committee on National Legislation Newsletter, March 2005, 5. Available on the Internet at www.fcnl.org/now/pdf/mar05.pdf.

[318] Anup Shah, "High Military Expenditure in Some Places," Global Issues, 16 June 2004.

[319] Martin Luther King, Jr., statement at Riverside Church, 4 April 1967.

[320] "Unmet Human Needs At Home and Abroad," Friends Committee on National Legislation, September 2004. The U.S. spent 42 cents of every income tax dollar on war, preparing for war, and obligations from past wars in 2004.

[321] Ibid., The Kaiser Commission on Medicaid and the Uninsured study in 2003 report is the source for the 44 million uninsured information.

[322] Ibid., According to the U.S. Census Bureau, 17.6% or nearly one in five children live in poverty.

[323] George W. Bush, as a candidate for President, statement on 23 May 2000 regarding national

security issues and the prospect of a brighter future.

[324] Congress passed the Omnibus Appropriations Bill on November 20, 2004. This bill denied funding for new nuclear "bunker buster" weapons that President Bush promoted. The Bush administration request for funds to build a facility for plutonium pits for new nuclear weapons was approved but reduced from $29.8 million to $7 million.

[325] Wade Boese, "Global Arms Market Still U.S. Domain, Arms Control Today (October 2004, Volume 34, Number 8), 39.

[326] Holy Bible: New American Standard Bible (Grand Rapids, Michigan: Zondervan, 2002), 812. Matthew 26:52: "Put your sword back into its place; for all those who take up the sword shall perish by the sword." If the Bible is a source of guidance for you, does this mean that unless the United States changes the policy of being the number one sword wielder, the United States will someday perish by nuclear weapons?

[327] Robert S. McNamara and James G. Blight, Wilson's Ghost: Reducing The Risk Of Conflict, Killing, And Catastrophe In The 21st Century (New York, New York: Public Affairs, 2001), 93.

[328] Ibid., 39. Also, while Russia has been perceived by Americans as a country to be beware of, it is likely that Germany and France will assume a similar status. Could it be possible that if Germany and France were not significant weapons sellers that pejorative statements about "old Europe and new Europe" and jokes about "renaming french fries freedom fries" would not be played on the major media networks?

[329] Christopher Bodeen, China: Law Would Allow Action Vs. Taiwan, Associated Press, 8 March 2005. China unveiled a law authorizing military action to stop rival Taiwan from pursuing formal independence. Tension with the Bush administration increases as President Bush weapons sales and statements of support for Taiwan have contradicted the One China policy and prompted China to send this message that war is authorized. The Chinese government said an attack would be a last resort if peaceful means fail.

[330] Arsenal of Hypocrisy, The Space Program And The Military Industrial Complex, AOH Productions Inc., www.arsenalofhypocrisy.com, 2003.

[331] Ken Silverstein, Private Warriors (New York, NY: Verso, October 2000), 30. Raymond Mabus, a former ambassador to Saudi Arabia, interview with the Boston Globe in 1996.

[332] Ibid., 31.

[333] "Terrorism Questions & Answers: Foreign Aid," Council on Foreign Relations, August 2002. Available on the Internet at www.cfrterrorism.org/policy/foreignaid.html#Q4.

[334] Smedley Butler with introduction by Adam Parfrey, War Is a Racket (Los Angeles, CA: Feral House, 1935, reprint edition April 2003), 51.

[335] Ibid., 51.

[336] William Greider, Fortress America: The American Military and the Consequences of Peace (Public Affairs, New York, December 1999), 183.

[337] Ibid., 166-167.

[338] These private mercenary corporations tend to change their corporate ownership often; it is analogous to a soldier changing his or her camouflage.

[339] Vinnell Corporation, information on the corporate Web site, 22 September 2004. Internet address is www.vinnell.com/.

[340] Ken Silverstein, Private Warriors (New York, New York: Verso, October 2000), 180-182.

[341] Langley, Virginia is the headquarters for the Central Intelligence Agency. The headquarters compound was named the George H.W. Bush Center for Central Intelligence in 1998.

[342] Ken Silverstein, Private Warriors (New York, New York: Verso, October 2000), 191-193.

[343] Mark Bowden, Black Hawk Down: A Story of Modern War (New York, New York: Penguin Books, February 2000). To learn more, visit www.blackhawkdown.com.

[344] Ibid. About 120 U.S. soldiers attempted to capture two top lieutenants of Somalian warlord Mohamed Farrah Aidid.

[345] William Greider, Fortress America: The American Military and the Consequences of Peace (New York, New York: Public Affairs, December 1999), 147.

[346] On 07/15/2004, the United States House of Representatives passed H.AMDT.706 - H.R.4818: to prohibit Economic Support Funding assistance to the government of any country that is a party to the International Criminal Court and has not signed an Article 98 agreement to surrender U.S. nationals to the ICC by a vote of 241-166.

[347] Natural Resources Defense Council, The U.S. Nuclear War Plan: A Time For Change (NRDC, June 2001), preface x.

[348] Kelley Beaucar Vlahos, "Analysts Ponder U.S. Basing in Iraq," Fox News, 1 November 2004. Available on the Internet at http://www.foxnews.com/story/0,2933,137210,00.html.

Also, Arsenal of Hypocrisy, The Space Program And The Military Industrial Complex, AOH Productions Inc., www.arsenalofhypocrisy.com, 2003.

[349] Ibid., The nickname for the U.S. Air Force Space Command's Space-Based Laser is the Death Star.

[350] Dwight D. Eisenhower, April 16, 1953.

[351] Arsenal of Hypocrisy, The Space Program And The Military Industrial Complex, AOH Productions Inc., www.arsenalofhypocrisy.com, 2003. Also the article from Bruce K. Gagnon, "NAZI PAST OUR PRESENT...," Available on the Internet at http://www.arsenalofhypocrisy.com/article.asp#top.

Mr. Gagnon observes, "the Nazi rocket scientists brought to the U.S. after WWII in the secret military program called Operation Paperclip. Operation Paperclip is described in detail in Linda Hunt's book, Secret Agenda. Linda Hunt describes how 1,500 top Nazi scientists were smuggled into the U.S. through Boston and West Palm Beach, Florida. One hundred of them, along with 100 copies of Hitler's V-2 rocket, were brought to Huntsville, Alabama to create the U.S. space program.

In Germany, the Nazis had a concentration camp called Dora where 40,000 Jews, French resistance fighters, homosexuals, communists and other prisoners of war (including a black American GI) were brought to build the V-1 and V-2 inside a mountain tunnel called Mittelwerk. By the time the slaves were liberated by the allies, over 25,000 had perished at the hands of the Nazi rocketeers.

Hitler's military liaison to von Braun's rocket team was Maj. Gen. Walter Dornberger. Several times Dornberger and von Braun met with Hitler requesting more money and more slaves so they could step up the rocket production effort. Hitler was anxious to use the rockets to terrorize the cities of London, Paris and Brussels toward the end of the war as the Nazi army began to lose. Dornberger and von Braun showed Hitler moving pictures of the V-2 rocket launches to prove they were making significant progress.

According to author Jack Manno in his book Arming the Heavens: The Hidden Military Agenda for Space, 1945-1995, Dornberger was appointed as a vice-president at Bell Aviation Corporation and went on to serve on the first military oversight committee that ensured that NASA was controlled by the Pentagon from the first days.

Kurt Debus, the chief of V-2 launch operations in Hitler's Germany, later became Chief of Operations for NASA at Cape Canaveral. When tourists converge on the Kennedy Space Center they will pass by a portrait of the former German SS member that hangs in the entrance in honor of Debus's service as the center's first director.

In a book called The Hunt for Zero Point, Cook spent the last 10 years researching secret military programs in the U.S. and believes that over $20 billion a year is spent on these programs outside the purview of Congress. Cook traces the roots of the U.S.'s secret programs back to the Nazi scientists brought to the U.S. after WW II in Operation Paperclip. He states, "We know the size and scope of Operation Paperclip, which was huge. And we know that the U.S. operates a very deeply secret defense architecture for secret weapons programs...it is highly compartmentalized...and one of the things that's intrigued me over the years is, How did they develop it? What model did they base it on? It is remarkably similar to the system that was operated by the Germans - specifically the SS - for their top-secret weapons programs."

"What I do mean," says Cook, "is that if you follow the trail of Nazi scientists and engineers who were recruited by America at the end of the second world war, the unfortunate corollary is that by taking on the science, you take on - unwittingly - some of the ideology...What do you lose along the way?"

Could this be what former President Dwight Eisenhower was talking about just a few years later when in 1961 he warned the American people to "beware" of the power of the military industrial complex? Could Eisenhower's prophetic warning been that an ideological contamination had come from America's embracing of the Nazi operatives?"

[352] Ibid.

[353] Ibid.

[354] Ibid.

[355] The Arsenal of Hypocrisy documentary can be obtained at www.arsenalofhypocrisy.com. Another resource to learn more about the weaponization of space is the Global Network Against Weapons & Nuclear Power in Space. Their Web site address is www.space4peace.org.

[356] "Reagan Announces SDI," PBS, 23 March 1983. The video can be viewed at www.pbs.org/wgbh/amex/reagan/sfeature/sdi.html.

[357] Frances Fitzgerald, Way out There in the Blue: Reagan, Star Wars, and the End of the Cold War (New York, New York: Touchstone, Simon and Schuster, April 2001).

[358] Ken Silverstein, Private Warriors, (New York, New York: Verso, October 2000), 229.

[359] News Briefs, "Russia Re-Establishes Independent Space Forces," Arms Control Today, July/August 2001. "Space Forces chief Colonel General Anatoly Perminov has said the change indicates that Russia has recognized the increasing importance of space assets in conventional conflicts. At the same time, Perminov has emphasized in a recent series of press briefings and interviews that the increased prominence of the force should not be misinterpreted as evidence of a Russian intention to weaponize space." To read the complete News Brief go to www.armscontrol.org/act/2001_07-08/briefsjul_aug01.asp#russia.

The Russian Space Forces announcement may be a reaction to the May 2001 revelation by Defense Secretary Donald Rumsfeld that the Pentagon's space programs are being reorganized to better support "sustained offensive and defensive space operations." Rumsfeld's announcement is discussed by Paul B. Stares, "Making Enemies in Space," The New York Times, 15 May 2001.

[360] 360News Briefs, "CD Reconvenes, Stalemate Likely to Continue," Arms Control Today, June 2001. China and Russia are continuing to lead the charge for formal negotiations on the prevention of an arms race in outer space, an effort the United States staunchly opposes. To read the complete article go to www.armscontrol.org/act/2001_06/briefsjun01.asp#cd.

[361] "Treaty On Principles Governing The Activities Of States In The Exploration And Use Of Outerspace, Including The Moon And Other Celestial Bodies," Outer Space Treaty, 10 October 1967. The Arms Control Today makes the treaty available on the Internet at www.armscontrol.org/documents/outerspace.asp. The treaty was signed at Washington, London, and Moscow on 27 January 1967. Ratification advised by U.S. Senate 25 April 1967 and ratified by U.S. President 24 May 1967. U.S. ratification deposited at Washington, London, and Moscow 10 October 1967. Proclaimed by U.S. President 10 October 1967. Entered into force 10 October 1967.

[362] Arsenal of Hypocrisy, The Space Program And The Military Industrial Complex, AOH Produc-

tions Inc., www.arsenalofhypocrisy.com, 2003. The 34 nuclear reactor cores were launched by the United States and the former Soviet Union going back to the 1960s.

[363] Michael R. Gordon and Steven Lee Myers, "Bush Team Vows To Speed Up Work On Missile Shield," The New York Times, 30 April 2001. Gordon and Myers write, "American officials say the Pentagon is developing plans for a multilayered system that would involve ship-based radars and interceptors, in addition to land-based and space-based elements. A panel appointed by Defense Secretary Donald H. Rumsfeld has recommended vastly increased spending on the development of an airborne laser and, in the longer-term, a space-based laser."

[364] National Missile Defense is designed to protect against Intercontinental Ballistic Missiles and not shorter-range missiles. Even within the long-range class of missiles, the subset is further restricted to nuclear missiles and not biological or chemical missiles. The subset of missiles also excludes protection from large arsenals as best illustrated by the arsenal maintained by Russia.

[365] National Intelligence Council, "Foreign Missile Development and the Ballistic Missile Threat to the United States Through 2015," U.S. Central Intelligence Agency Unclassified Summary, September 1999.

[366] "Report on the Patriot missile failure at Dhahran, Saudi Arabia," General Accounting Office, 4 February 1992. The full report is available at www.fas.org/spp/starwars/gao/im92026.htm.

[367] "Raytheon's Response to WGBH Frontline Gulf War," Raytheon, 1996. Raytheon claims the overall failure rate was approximately 40%. The article by the Raytheon corporation can be found on the PBS site at www.pbs.org/wgbh/pages/frontline/gulf/weapons/raytheontext.html. The Frontline criticism of the Patriot is also found on the PBS site at www.pbs.org/wgbh/pages/frontline/gulf/weapons/patriot_old.html.

Frances Fitzgerald, Way out There in the Blue: Reagan, Star Wars, and the End of the Cold War, (New York, New York: Touchstone, Simon and Schuster, April 2001), 489. The 158 Patriot missiles hit no more than 4 of the 45 Scud missiles they were aimed at.

[368] Space-based weapons can reduce the "time on target" element although a submarine could conceivable launch a short range missile a few miles from the U.S. coastline and hit a nearby city in a time span of a few minutes. A surprise attack by a bomb in a delivery vehicle other than a missile, a moving truck for example, could be without warning.

[369] Joseph Cirincione, Editor, Repairing the Regime: Preventing the Spread of Weapons of Mass Destruction, (New York, New York: Routledge, April 2000), 58. Mr. Cirincione also notes that another version of this story is the Russian military provoked this incident to force Norway to halt the future launches that the Russian military believed were actually electronic reconnaissance missions.

[370] Peter J. Boyer, "When Missiles Collide," The New Yorker, 11 September 2000.

[371] Jim Geraghty, "Markey's N-alert: We could be toast," The Boston Globe, 7 September 2001, A15.

[372] Vladimir Putin, quoted in William Pfaff, "Nothing Very Romantic About Putin's Nationalism," International Herald Tribune, 28 February 2000, 10.

[373] David E. Sanger, "US to Tell China It Will Not Object to Missile Buildup," The New York Times, 2 September 2001. Mr. Sanger quotes Joseph R. Biden Jr., the Democrat of Delaware and chairman of the Senate Foreign Relations Committee. "This is absolutely absurd," he said today. "It shows that these guys will go to any length to build a national missile defense, even one they can't define. Their headlong, headstrong, irrational and theological desire to build a missile defense sends the wrong message to the Chinese and to the whole world." This is especially true, he said, regarding India, which would try to balance against any Chinese buildup.

[374] Patrick E. Tyler, "Russia and China Sign 'Friendship' Pact," The New York Times, 17 July 2001.

[375] President George H. W. Bush, State of the Union address, 29 January 1991. President Bush said "Now, with remarkable technological advances like the Patriot missile, we can defend the ballistic missile attacks aimed at innocent civilians."

[376] Michelle Ciarrocca, "Holes in the Coverage: What's left out of reporting on missile defense," Extra!, November/December 2000. For the complete article, go to www.fair.org/extra/0011/star-wars. html.

[377] Barton Gellman, "New Study Cuts Patriot Missile Success To 9 Percent," Washington Post, 30 September 1992, A4. Mr. Gellman noted, a study of the Patriot missile, apparently based on full access to classified Army records from the Persian Gulf War, said there is strong evidence to confirm that the Patriot destroyed incoming Iraqi Scud missile warheads in only 9 percent of all engagements. The study by the General Accounting Office was the latest in an embarrassing series of reassessments of what was once portrayed as the preeminent performer of the Gulf War's technology showcase.

[378] George Lardner Jr., "Missile Critic Says Article Was Classified After Fact: Army Bans Discussion Of Patriot, Panel Told," Washington Post, 19 March 1992, A7. Mr. Lardner wrote, MIT professor, Theodore A. Postol, protested to a House subcommittee yesterday that an article he wrote criticizing the Patriot missile's accuracy has been classified after the fact and he has been warned not even to talk about it. Postal said Defense Department officials told him the article, published in January in the Harvard quarterly International Security, contained classified information.

[379] Joseph Cirincione, Editor, Repairing the Regime: Preventing the Spread of Weapons of Mass Destruction (New York, New York: Routledge), April 2000, 4.

[380] Amy Goldstein and Alan Sipress, "ABM Withdrawal Likely, But Not Set, Bush Says," Washington Post, 24 August 2001, A01.

[381] To read the Anti-Ballistic Missile Treaty go to www.armscontrol.org/documents/abmtreaty.asp.

[382] To read the Intermediate-Range Nuclear Forces Treaty go to www.armscontrol.org/documents/inf. asp.

[383] To read the Nuclear Non-Proliferation Treaty go to www.armscontrol.org/documents/npt.asp. A total of 187 parties had signed the treaty as of March 2002.

[384] Joseph Cirincione, "Making Sense of Missile Defense," Foreign Service Journal, November 2000. The full report is available at www.carnegieendowment.org/npp/publications/index. cfm?fa=view&id=560.

[385] "Bush Administration's Missile Defense System Provides No Protection," Arms Control Association, 15 October 2004. This media advisory was received by the author who is a member of ACA.

[386] "Stop The World, I Want To Get Off: Has George Bush Ever Met A Treaty That He Liked?," The Economist, 28 July 2001, 35. "Unilateralist, moi? Bush administration actions: January 2nd—Announces it will not send the treaty establishing an International Criminal Court to the Senate for ratification; March 28th –Abandons the 1997 Kyoto Protocol; May 1st—Threatens to abrogate the 1972 Anti-Ballistic Missile Treaty;

July 21st – Threatens to withdraw from a United Nations conference to impose limits on illegal trafficking of small arms; and July 25th – Rejects proposed enforcement measures for the 1972 Biological Weapons Convention.

[387] Chomsky, Noam, American Power and the New Mandarins (New York, New York: Pantheon, 1969).

[388] Miles O'Brien and CNN senior White House correspondent John King, "Bush unveils vision for moon and beyond: President seeks $1 billion more in NASA funding," CNN.com, 15 January 2004.

[389] The U.S. Air Force Transformation Flight Plan, produced by HQ USAF/XPXC Future Concepts and Transformation Division, November 2003.

[390] Strategic Master Plan FY06 and Beyond, Air Force Space Command, HQ AFSPC/XPXP, 1 October 2003.

[391] Ibid., Foreword, i.

[392] Vision for 2020, U.S. Space Command, February 1997. Available online at the Federation of American Scientists site at http://fas.org/spp/military/docops/usspac/visbook.pdf.

[393] The Air Force Space Command Strategic Master Plan FY06 is available online from the Center For Defense Information at www.cdi.org/news/space-security/afspc-strategic-master-plan-06-beyond.pdf.

The Vision for 2020 is available online from the Federation of American Scientists at http://fas.org/spp/military/docops/usspac/visbook.pdf.

[394] Strategic Master Plan FY06 and Beyond, Air Force Space Command, HQ AFSPC/XPXP, 1 October 2003, 1.

[395] Air Force Historical Research Agency, "Major Commands." Maxwell Air Force Base repository for Air Force historical documents, obtained on 21 September 2004. Internet site is www.au.af.mil/au/afhra/wwwroot/rso/major_commands.html#top. The AFSC has its headquarters at Peterson Air Force Base in Colorado.

The AFSC was established originally as the Space Command on September 1, 1982, with President Reagan's aggressive promotion of what came to be known as Star Wars. The Space Command was renamed the AFSC on November 15, 1985. It was a component of the U.S. Space Command that was disbanded on October 1, 2002, and made a component of STRATCOM. Globalsecurity.org, United States Space Command, obtained on 21 September 2004.

STRATCOM was created on June 1, 1992, when the Strategic Air Command (SAC) ceased to exist. Maryann Mrowca, "Strategic Air Command is No More," Boston Globe, 26 May 1992, 3.

[396] Major Jon M. Fontenot, United States Air Force, "A New Era: From SAC to STRATCOM," Command Staff College, 1995.

[397] Dan Caterinicchia, "Stratcom acquires new IT missions," FCW Media Group, 6 February 2003.

[398] Ken Silverstein, Private Warriors, (New York, NY: Verso, October 2000), 144.

[399] Ibid., 166-167.

[400] Walter Pincus, "Satellite Agency Has Tradition of Secrecy," Washington Post, 25 August 2001, A10.

[401] Arsenal of Hypocrisy, The Space Program And The Military Industrial Complex, AOH Productions Inc., www.arsenalofhypocrisy.com, 2003.

[402] Stephen I. Schwartz, Atomic Audit, The Costs and Consequences of U.S. Nuclear Weapons Since 1940 (Washington, D.C.: Brookings Institution Press, 1998).

[403] President Dwight D. Eisenhower, "Farewell Address," Our Documents initiative, 17 January 1961. Internet address is www.ourdocuments.gov.1961. President Eisenhower can be heard making this warning in the documentary, Arsenal of Hypocrisy, The Space Program And The Military Industrial Complex, AOH Productions Inc., www.arsenalofhypocrisy.com, 2003.

[404] Abraham Johannes Muste, observation in 1941. J. Muste is the author of multiple essays and books. He was born in Zeeland of the Netherlands on January 8, 1885. His family brought him to the United States at the age of six and raised him in Michigan as a Calvinist.

[405] William Blum, "A Brief History Of U.S. Interventions 1945 To The Present," Z Magazine, June 1999. Also Chapter 17 of William Blum's book, Rogue State: A Guide to the World's Only Superpower, published in 2000. Permission for inclusion of text obtained on September 16, 2004. The list compiled by Mr. Blum is updated to the date American Hiroshima was published. For more information on U.S. interventions, see Chapter 17 of Rogue State.

[406] Ibid.

[407] Pema Chodron, The Places That Scare You: A Guide to Fearlessness in Difficult Times (Boston, MA: Shambhala Publications, Inc., 2001), 7.

[408] Edited by The Committee for the Compilation of Materials on Damage Caused by the Atomic Bombs in Hiroshima and Nagasaki, Translated by Eisei Ishikawa and David L. Swain, Hiroshima and Nagasaki: The Physical, Medical, and Social Effects of the Atomic Bombings (New York, New York, Basic Books, Inc., 1981), 115.

To obtain a better sense of the widespread devastation, pages 114 and 353 provide additional statistics. For example, Nagasaki's population was 270,000 people on August 6, 1945. In addition to the over 70,000 killed, 74,909 were injured and 120,820 were affected by radiation.

[409] James McClain, A Modern History of Japan (New York, New York: WW Norton and Company, 2002). Secretary of State Henry L. Stimson and General George Marshall pulled the number 1 million out of thin air to help justify the use of the bomb. As additional background, in June of 1945 President Truman ordered the US military to calculate the cost in American lives for a planned assault on Japan. On June 15, 1945 the Joint War Plans Committee prepared a report for the Chiefs of Staff providing an estimate of 40,000 U.S. soldiers killed, 150,000 wounded, and 3,500 missing.

[410] President Truman, in a radio speech to the nation on August 9, 1945. "Public Papers of the Presidents of the United States: Harry S. Truman, Containing the Public Messages, Speeches and Statements of the President April 12 to December 31, 1945," (Washington D.C.: United States Government Printing Office, 1961) 212. The full text also was published in the New York Times, August 10, 1945, page 12.

[411] It is noteworthy that Tibbets received the award from Robert Brown of Solider of Fortune magazine.

[412] United States Strategic Bombing Survey: Japan's Struggle to End the War, (Washington: Government Printing Office, 1946).

[413] Doug Long, "Hiroshima: Was It Necessary?," 1995-2000. Mr. Long notes: Foreign Minister Togo met with the Emperor on August 8, 1945 to tell him what he knew of the Hiroshima bombing. They agreed that the time had come to end the war at once (Pacific War Research Society, The Day Man Lost, 300; Pacific War Research Society, Japan's Longest Day, 21-22). The complete article is available on the Internet at www.doug-long.com/hiroshim.htm.

[414] Ibid., Japan's peace messages in 1945, read by the U.S. at the time, clearly indicated that Japan was seeking to end the war:

- July 11: "make clear to Russia... We have no intention of annexing or taking possession of the areas which we have been occupying as a result of the war; we hope to terminate the war".

- July 12: "it is His Majesty's heart's desire to see the swift termination of the war".

- July 13: "I sent Ando, Director of the Bureau of Political Affairs to communicate to the [Soviet] Ambassador that His Majesty desired to dispatch Prince Konoye as special envoy, carrying with him the personal letter of His Majesty stating the Imperial wish to end the war" (for above items, see: U.S. Dept. of State, Potsdam 1, pg. 873-879).

- July 18: "Negotiations... necessary... for soliciting Russia's good offices in concluding the war and also in improving the basis for negotiations with England and America." (Magic-Diplomatic Summary, 7/18/45, Records of the National Security Agency, Magic Files, RG 457, Box 18, National Archives).

- July 22: "Special Envoy Konoye's mission will be in obedience to the

Imperial Will. He will request assistance in bringing about an end to the war through the good offices of the Soviet Government." The July 21st communication from Togo also noted that a conference between the Emperor's emissary, Prince Konoye, and the Soviet Union, was sought, in preparation for contacting the U.S. and Great Britain (Magic-Diplomatic Summary, 7/22/45, Records of the National Security Agency, Magic Files, RG 457, Box 18, National Archives).

- July 25: "it is impossible to accept unconditional surrender under any circumstances, but we should like to communicate to the other party through appropriate channels that we have no objection to a peace based on the Atlantic Charter." (U.S. Dept. of State, Potsdam 2, pg. 1260 - 1261).

- July 26: Japan's Ambassador to Moscow, Sato, to the Soviet Acting Commissar for Foreign Affairs, Lozovsky: "The aim of the Japanese Government with regard to Prince Konoye's mission is to enlist the good offices of the Soviet Government in order to end the war." (Magic-Diplomatic Summary, 7/26/45, Records of the National Security Agency, Magic Files, RG 457, Box 18, National Archives).

Mr. Long observes that President Truman knew of the messages' content, noting, for instance, in his diary on July 18, "Stalin had told P.M. [Prime Minister Churchill] of telegram from Jap [sic] Emperor asking for peace" (Robert Ferrell, ed., Off the Record - the Private Papers of Harry S. Truman, 53). Mr. Long notes that President Truman likely authorized the use of the bomb because he did believe "We have used it in order to shorten the agony of war, in order to save the lives of thousands and thousands of young Americans" (Public Papers of the Presidents, Harry S. Truman, 1945, 212).

[415] Blackett, P.M.S. Fear, War and the Bomb: Military and Political Consequences of Atomic Energy (New York, New York: McGraw-Hill, 1948).

[416] Alperovitz, Gar, Atomic Diplomacy (New York, New York: Vintage, 1967).

[417] O.R. Frisch, Eyewitness Report by O.R Frisch, Nuclear Age Peace Foundation, 16 July 1945. Available on the Internet at www.nuclearfiles.org/redocuments/1945/450716-frisch.html.

[418] Michael Sherry, The Rise of American Air Power (New Haven: Yale University Press, 1987), 255. Also Tom Vanderbilt, Survival City: Adventures Among The Ruins Of Atomic America, (New York, New York: Princeton Architectural Press, 2002), 73.

Also in Sherry's book, pages 300 and 410. Air Force General Hap Arnold asked in June 1945 when the war was going to end. The commander of the B-29 raids, General Curtis LeMay, told him September or October 1945, because by then they would have run out of industrial targets to bomb.

[419] Doug Long, "Hiroshima: Was It Necessary?," 1995-2000. After the Hiroshima atomic bombing, the Japanese Army and Navy had sent separate teams of scientists to determine what type of bomb had destroyed the city. By August 11th, both teams had reported to Tokyo that the bomb was, indeed, atomic. Mr. Long cites Leon Sigal, Fighting To a Finish, 1988, 236.

[420] Ibid., The Nagasaki atomic bomb would have likely never happened if the U.S. Air Force scheduled the Nagasaki atomic bomb anytime after August 14, 1945. Japan's Emperor could not unilaterally end the war. He needed the Japanese Cabinet to authorize the surrender. Rumors in Tokyo that the next bomb would detonate in Tokyo inhibited the ability of the Emperor to influence the Japanese Cabinet prior to August 9, 1945.

The following is a condensed version of Mr. Long's summary of the key events leading to Japan's surrender: The Potsdam Proclamation authored by the United States, China, United Kingdom called for the Unconditional Surrender of Japan, July 26, 1945. On August 13, 1945, the Supreme Council For the Direction of the War met to address the Potsdam Proclamation's call for surrender. Three members of this group of six or "Big 6" favored immediate surrender. The War Minister Anami, Army Chief of Staff Umezu, and Navy Chief of Staff Toyoda refused to surrender. The meeting adjourned in a deadlock, with no decision to surrender (Robert Butow, Japan's Decision To Surrender, 1954, 200-202). Later that day the Japanese Cabinet met. It was only this body - not the Big 6, not even the Emperor - that could rule as to whether Japan would surrender. A unanimous decision was required (Robert Butow, Japan's Decision To Surrender, 176-177, 208(43n)). War Minister Anami led the opponents of surrender, resulting in a vote of 12 in favor of surrender, 3 against, and 1 undecided. The key concern for the Japanese military was loss of honor, not Japan's destruction. Having failed to reach a decision to surrender, the Cabinet adjourned (Leon Sigal, Fighting To a Finish, 1988, 265-267).

On the following day, August 14, Anami, Umezu, and Toyoda were still arguing that there was a chance for victory (John Toland, The Rising Sun, pg. 936). But then that same day, the Cabinet unanimously agreed to surrender (John Toland, The Rising Sun, pg. 936). Where none of the previous events had succeeded in bringing the Japanese military leaders to surrender, surrender came at Emperor Hirohito's request: "It is my desire that you, my Ministers of State, accede to my wishes and forthwith accept the Allied reply" (Robert Butow, Japan's Decision To Surrender, pg. 207-208).

What made the Emperor's "desire" more powerful than the revulsion the military leaders felt toward surrender? The Emperor was believed to be a god by the Japanese. The dean of historians on Japan's surrender, Robert Butow, notes in regard to the military leaders in Japan's government, "To have acted against the express wishes of an Emperor whom they had unceasingly extolled as sacred and inviolable and around whom they had woven a fabric of individual loyalty and national unity would have been to destroy the very polity in perpetuation of which they had persistently declared they were fighting" (Robert Butow, Japan's Decision To Surrender, pg. 224). Or as War Minister Anami said after he agreed to surrender, "As a Japanese soldier, I must obey my Emperor" (Pacific War Research Society, Japan's Longest Day, pg. 87-88).

Surrender was so repugnant to Anami that he committed hara-kiri the day after he signed the surrender document (Butow, pg. 219-220). Where fear and reason had failed, religious devotion to the Emperor enabled the military leaders to overcome their samurai resistance to surrender.

[421] Martin Sherwin, A World Destroyed: The Atom Bomb and the Grand Alliance. (New York, New York: Knopf, 1975).

[422] President Harry Truman, State of the Union Address, Washington, DC, 7 January 1953.

[423] President John F. Kennedy, Radio and Television Address to the American People on the Nuclear Test Ban Treaty, 26 July 1963.

[424] David Krieger, "From Hiroshima to Humanity," Nuclear Age Peace Foundation, August 2005. Available on the Internet at www.wagingpeace.org/articles/2005/08/00_krieger_from-hiroshima-to-humanity.htm.

[425] Ibid.

[426] Peter J. Kuznick, "A Tragic Life: Oppenheimer and the Bomb", Arms Control Association, July/August 2005. Available on the Internet at http://www.armscontrol.org/act/2005_07-08/Kuznick.asp.

[427] Martin Luther King, Jr., Strength To Love (New York, Harper & Row, 1963).

[428] Nuclear Age Peace Foundation, About Us available at www.wagingpeace.org/menu/about/index.htm, 22 September 2004.

[429] World Affairs Councils of America, Home page available at www.worldaffairscouncils.org/index.htm.

[430] World Affairs Council, About Us available at www.itsyourworld.org/general/, 22 January 2005.

[431] Arm Control Association, About Us available at www.armscontrol.org/about.asp, 22 September 2004.

[432] Natural Resources Defense Council, About Us at www.nrdc.org/about/, 22 September 2004.

[433] Carnegie Endowment for International Peace, About Us, available at www.carnegieendowment.org/about/, 22 September 2004.

[434] Physicians for Social Responsibility, SMART Security, available at www.psr.org/home.cfm?id=sm_sec_pg, 1 April 2005.

[435] Ibid., About Us, available at www.psr.org/home.cfm?id=about_security, 31 March 2005.

[436] The National Security Act of September 17, 1947, replaced the separate War and Navy departments with a unified military establishment called the Department of Defense.

[437] U.S. Department of Peace Coalition. Internet site and source of content at www.dopc.us/ and the Global Renaissance Alliance Department of Peace campaign at www.dopcampaign.org/, 23 September 2004.

[438] National Campaign for a Peace Tax Fund. H.R.2037 is to affirm the religious freedom of taxpayers who are conscientiously opposed to participation in war, to provide that the income, estate, or gift tax payments of such taxpayers be used for nonmilitary purposes. The bill is sponsored by Representative John Lewis and was introduced on 8 May 2003. On that same day the bill was referred to the House Committee on Ways and Means. The bill can be read on the Internet at www.peacetaxfund.org/index.html.

[439] "No nations should have nukes, most in USA say," AP-Ipsos poll, 31 March 2005. Two-thirds of respondents say no nation should have nuclear weapons, including the United States.

[440] The Writing of Thomas Jefferson: Memorial Edition (Washington, D.C.: Lipscomb and Bergh, editors, 1903-1904), 2:221. Thomas Jefferson: Notes on Virginia Q.XVII, 1782. Internet address for the quote is http://etext.lib.virginia.edu/jefferson/quotations/jeff1500.htm.

[441] Jimmy L. Spearow, Ph,D, "Factors Driving Nuclear and Conventional Arms Race," Physicians for Social Responsibility presentation, 7 April 2005.

[442] Albert Einstein, US (German-born) physicist (1879 - 1955). Available on the Internet at www.brainyquote.com/quotes/quotes/a/alberteins137744.html.

[443] James K. Galbraith, "Did the U.S. Military Plan a Nuclear First Strike for 1963?," The American Prospect, 21 September 1994, Volume 5, Issue 19. President Kennedy, after a briefing on the effects of nuclear weapons, in the summer of 1961. President Kennedy was briefed on the net assessment of a general nuclear war between the two superpowers. As he walked with Dean Rusk from the cabinet room to the Oval Office President Kennedy said: "And we call ourselves the human race."

During the Kennedy administration, children were taught to "duck and cover" under their desks at school. At the time, the only reason that was put forth was the government wanted citizens to be prepared for a communist attack. Like today's "terrorist state threat," there is some truth here. The "duck and cover" was primarily taught so that U.S. citizens would be protected from the Soviet response to a U.S. first strike.

[444] Errol Morris director, Fog Of War (The studio is Columbia Tristar Hom and the release date was 19 December 2003).

[445] Martin Luther King, Jr., sermon in Montgomery, Alabama, Nov.6, 1956.

[446] Jean Vanier, Becoming Human (Mahwah, New Jersey: Paulist Press, 1998), 34. On the notion of why underdogs are often supported, "Weakness carries within it a secret power. The cry and the trust that flow from weakness can open up hearts. The one who is weaker can call forth powers of love in the one who is stronger."

[447] Andrew Kohut, "Anti-Americanism: Causes and Characteristics," The Pew Research Center for the People and the Press, 10 December 2003. Internet address is http://people-press.org/commen-

tary/display.php3?AnalysisID=77.

[448] Martin Luther King, Jr., the night before he was assassinated, 3 April 1968, Dr. King told thousands of people at the Mason Temple in Memphis, Tennessee: "For years now, we have been talking about war and peace. But now, no longer can we just talk about it. It is no longer a choice between violence and nonviolence; it's nonviolence or nonexistence."

[449] Fareed Zakaria, "Imagine: 500 miles per gallon," Newsweek, 7 March 2005, 27.

[450] "Strategic Master Plan FY06 and Beyond: Case 1," Air Force Space Command, 1 October 2003, 13. The Air Force already lists over $456 billion in projects required to weaponize space. The updated and Top Secret plan would likely show a far higher estimate that would certainly in time exceed the five trillion dollars spent by the U.S. on nuclear weapons.

[451] Martin Luther King, Jr., statement at Riverside Church, 4 April 1967.

[452] The border countries to Turkey in 1982 were: Syria, Iraq, Iran, the Soviet Union, Bulgaria, Greece and Cyprus. With the fall of the Soviet Union, current border countries include Georgia, Russia, Ukraine and Romania.

[453] Many terrorist bombs have been exploded in Bursa, Turkey. A recent report of these incidents can be read at www.turkishpress.com/turkishpress/news.asp?ID=12540. Turkish Press.com, "Pipebomb Explodes In Bursa Injuring A Person," 18 August 2003.

[454] Visitors to South Korea can tour Panmunjom. Tours can be arranged by many major hotels in Seoul. Visitors are asked to sign a release that your trip will entail entry into a hostile area and possibility of injury or death as a direct result of enemy action. A visitor to Panmunjom is sure to experience the tension between the North and the South.

[455] "Timeline: N. Korea's Nuke Program," Fox News, 2 January 2004.

[456] 456Don Oberdorfer, The Two Koreas (United States and Canada: Basic Books, Revised Edition December 2001). He reported that in 1994 advisers to President Bill Clinton predicted 52,000 U.S. casualties in the first 90 days of combat alone.

[457] Joseph Coleman, "American accused of defecting to North Korea will receive treatment for ailments," The Associated Press, 19 July 2004. Also, Jim Frederick, "In From The Cold," Time, 13 December 2004. Articles note that Charles Jenkins, who vanished from his platoon in 1965, played devilish American characters in communist propaganda films. Jenkins reveals how he and other American defectors were used to create babies for North Koreas intelligence services.

[458] Marcus Warren in Moscow," Japan sinks 'North Korea spying ship," News.telegraph, 24 December 2001. This article is very similar to incidents that frequently occurred in 1986 but were not covered by the U.S. media.

[459] U.S. Army Field Manual 34-130 Intelligence Preparation of the Battlefield. See Appendix B for the Intelligence Preparation of the Battlefield framework used to help create American Hiroshima.

The basic approach of IPB is to define the major categories that would impact the outcome. Since pictures can communicate volumes, each IPB category that could have a material impact on the outcome is depicted graphically. In the 1980s we used sheets of clear plastic to overlay the map with each category of information. For example, we would create a summary of the weather at the time of the planned operation on a clear sheet. Another common graphic we put on top of the map was that of all enemy locations. Today, battlefield computers enable the same graphical depiction without the inconvenience of erasable markers drawings on clear sheets of plastic. You can also paint a mental picture, but this is challenging as the information inputs increase in number.

IPB is of high value in the military; and, if modified, is of extremely high value in business or anytime a person is confronted with information overload. People like to pick out information that supports current beliefs. As a result, we sometimes lose sight of important facts and overly emphasize pieces of misleading information. The structured format of IPB also improves communication with other people. A decision-maker trained in the skill can quickly obtain an executive summary or dive into a specific set of facts by directing the support team to brief him or her on one of the established categories of information.

[460] Jong-Heon Lee, "South Korea Facing Suit Over Prostitutes," United Press International, 16 October 2002. "There were 222 "clubs" in South Korea serving 37,000 U.S. soldiers in 2002."

[461] "Bush Apologizes Over South Korea Schoolgirl Deaths," Reuters, 27 November 2002, "President Bush apologized to the South Korean people on Wednesday over a road accident in which a U.S. Army vehicle crushed two schoolgirls to death, prompting anti-American protest. The accident in June, and the court martial acquittal of the vehicle's driver and navigator last week, sparked angry street demonstrations and calls for the withdrawal of 37,000 U.S. troops stationed in South Korea."

[462] 462Lee Wha Rang, "Anti-US Sentiment in South Korea: Root Causes," December 16, 2002. www.kimsoft.com/2002/anti-uslwr.htm.

[463] Patrick Goodenough, "Chilly Winter Looms For American Troops In Korea," CNSNews.com, 9 December 2002. "U.S. military personnel in Korea are reporting an increase in incidents of hostility and verbal abuse from locals, and some businesses have even shut their doors to Americans."

[464] The Korean War started when North Korea invaded South Korea on June 25, 1950 with a force of 135,000 men. The United States, North Korea and China signed an armistice, which ended the war but did not bring a permanent peace. No peace treaty has ever been signed. A total of 33,651 U.S. service members died in battle during the Korean War. Source for statistics is the United States of America Korean War Commemoration (http://korea50.army.mil/welcome.shtml).

[465] Editors of the American Heritage Dictionaries, The American Heritage® Dictionary of the English Language (Boston, MA: Houghton Mifflin Company Fourth Edition, 2000).

[466] Don Oberdorfer, The Two Koreas (United States and Canada: Basic Books, Revised Edition December 2001), 5-6.

[467] Ibid., 5. The 1905 agreement with Japan by William Howard Taft was codified in the Treaty of Portsmouth, New Hampshire which was signed by President Theodore Roosevelt that same year.

[468] Robert Burns, "U.S. military in South Korea to move farther south from border with North Korea," Associated Press, 5 June 2003. Internet site for article is www.sfgate.com/cgi-bin/article.cgi?f=/news/archive/2003/06/05/national1616EDT0678.DTL

[469] Joseph L. Galloway, "Army to Send Older Armored Personnel Carriers to Iraq After Upgrading Armor," Knight Ridder Stars and Stripes European edition, 4 January 2005.

[470] Donald Rumsfeld, "GIs pepper Rumsfeld with tough questions," The New York Times, 9 December 2004.
The original M113 Armored Personnel Carrier or APC helped to revolutionize mobile military operations. The M113 can transport 11 soldiers plus a driver and track commander. The armor protection far exceeds the Humvee. The modern versions are air transportable, air-droppable, and swimmable. The Pentagon announced in January 2005, almost two years after the invasion, that it would begin to deploy the M113 vehicles to Iraq to protect soldiers from roadside bombs.

[471] Joseph L. Galloway, "Army to Send Older Armored Personnel Carriers to Iraq After Upgrading Armor," Knight Ridder Stars and Stripes European edition, 4 January 2005.

[472] In 2001-2004, the author worked for MetLife, a financial service corporation. Prior to MetLife, the author worked for DirectAdvice which was a start-up technology company.

[473] Joseph E. Cantor, "Campaign Financing: CRS Issue Brief for Congress," Congressional Research Service, 15 December 2003. House candidates received 35%, slightly less than incumbents, of their total funding from PACs. Available on the Internet at www.fpc.state.gov/documents/organization/28105.pdf.

[474] The 2004-2005 edition of The Almanac of Federal PACs contains vital background and political finance information for every PAC - more than 1,300 of them. PAC contribution information is also

available at www.tray.com/.

475 World Team Sports organizes and hosts innovative and challenging sporting events that encourage all individuals, especially those with disabilities, to reach new levels of achievement. The organization is famous for bringing soldiers who fought in the Vietnam war together on a bike ride across Vietnam in 1998. The Internet address is www.worldteamsports.org/.

476 Lester S. Hyman, United States Policy Toward Liberia 1822 to 2003 (Cherry Hill, New Jersey: Africana Homestead Legacy Publishers, 2003), 2-5.

477 Ibid., xi.

478 Modified from the War Resistance League "Things You Can Do," on the Internet at www.warresisters.org/mosquito.htm.

479 William Blum, "A Brief History Of U.S. Interventions 1945 To The Present," Z Magazine, June 1999. Also Chapter 17 of William Blum's book, Rogue State: A Guide to the World's Only Superpower, published in 2000. Permission for inclusion of text obtained on September 16, 2004. The list compiled by Mr. Blum is updated to the date American Hiroshima was published. For more information on U.S. interventions, see Chapter 17 of Rogue State.

480 "Iraq: Early History through British Influence," Encyclopedia.com, 15 April 2005. Available on the Internet at www.encyclopedia.com/html/section/iraq_history.asp.

481 "Excerpts From Iraqi Document on Meeting with U.S. Envoy," The New York Times, 23 September 1990.

482 CNN.com, "Afghanistan wakes after night of intense bombings," 7 October 2004. Internet address is http://archives.cnn.com/2001/US/10/07/gen.america.under.attack/.

483 Carmen Gentile, "Can Aristide's Tale Be True," United Press International, 17 March 2004.

484 Wikipedia, s.v. "Kosovo War," a free-content encyclopedia in many languages. The English edition started in January 2001 and supporting information can be found on the Internet at http://en.wikipedia.org/wiki/Kosovo_War.

485 Mark Weisbrot, "CIA Documents Cast New Light on Washington's Role in Venezuela," Center for Economic and Policy Research, 10 December 2004.

On 12 April 2004, White House spokesman Ari Fleischer gave the coup leaders' version of events -- that violence at the demonstrations had led to Chavez' "resignation," and that the government was responsible for the violence. "The results of these events are now that President Chavez has resigned the presidency. Before resigning, he dismissed the vice president and the cabinet, and a transitional civilian government has been installed." The documents are available at www.venezuelafoia.info/CIA/CIA-index.htm and show that the White House knew that there were detailed plans for a coup in April.

486 ChinaDaily.com, "Chavez: Evidence proves Washington murder plot, US denies," 6 March 2005.

487 Noelle Straub, "Congress passes `doomsday' plan," Boston Herald, 9 January 2005.

Greg Szymanski, "DOOMSDAY' LEGISLATION: Handful of Congressmen Could Rule America in Event of Catastrophe," American Free Press, 5 January 2005. Available on the Internet at www.americanfreepress.net/html/doomsday.html. GOP House leaders pushed the controversial House Resolution 5 "doomsday legislation" through for passage as a part of a hefty and voluminous rules package. It drew little attention and was probably not even discovered by many who voted on it since the rules package centered on recent ethics violations. "I think the new rule is disgusting, terrible and unconstitutional," said Norm Ornstein, of an independent, bipartisan panel called the Continuity of Government Commission which is studying the issue. "The way it was passed was deceitful and the intent behind the legislation was very foolish." Rep. Brian Baird, (D-Wash.) agrees, arguing that the rule change violates the Constitution, which specifically states: "a majority of each Chamber shall constitute a quorum to do business." Rep. Baird emphasized, "Allowing for as few as 12 lawmakers to make vital decisions and to possibly declare war on another nation is not what this country is all about."

[488] Ira Helfand, M.D., "The Effects of a Nuclear Explosion on Medical Care," Physicians for Social Responsibility, accessed 31 March 2005. Available on the Internet at www.psr.org/home.cfm?id=di sarmament22#major. This article is based on the May 1962 Special Study Section of Physicians for Social Responsibility report.

[489] Go Kit Checklist. The Go Kit Checklist is modified from the "Disaster Supplies Kit" developed by the Federal Emergency Management Agency and the American Red Cross. Unfortunately, the EMP or electromagnetic pulse from a nuclear explosion may damage your computer and other electronic equipment. This checklist will help you assist your family and others following a nuclear attack or any other disaster. Have needed materials ready to go by establishing a family disaster plan to make an absolutely chaotic situation more manageable. The key items that you should have in your disaster kit are: water, food, first aid supplies, clothing and bedding, tools and emergency supplies, and special items. Keep the items that you would most likely need during an evacuation in an easy-to carry container.

GO KIT CHECKLIST

WATER

- Store one gallon of water per person per day.
- Keep at least a three-day supply of water per person (two quarts for drinking, two quarts for each person in your household for food preparation/sanitation).

FOOD
- Store at least a three-day supply of non-perishable food. Select foods that require no refrigeration, preparation or cooking, and little or no water.

FIRST AID SUPPLIES

- Assemble a first aid kit with the following non-prescription drugs: aspirin or nonaspirin pain reliever, anti-diarrhea medication, antacid (for stomach upset), syrup of Ipecac (use to induce vomiting if advised by the Poison Control Center), laxative, activated charcoal (use if advised by the Poison Control Center) and potassium iodide tablets also known as thyroid blocking agents. Include prescription drugs as applicable.

CLOTHING AND BEDDING

- Include at least one complete change of clothing and footwear per person
- Sturdy shoes or work boots
- Rain gear
- Blankets or sleeping bags
- Hat and gloves
- Thermal underwear
- Sunglasses

TOOLS AND EMERGENCY SUPPLIES

- Mess kits, or paper cups, plates, and plastic utensils
- Battery or hand crank powered radio with cell phone charger and extra batteries
- Flashlight and extra batteries
- Cash or traveler's checks
- Non-electric can opener, utility knife
- Fire extinguisher
- Tent

- Pliers
- Tape
- Compass
- Matches in a waterproof container
- Aluminum foil
- Plastic storage containers
- Signal flare
- Paper, pencil
- Needles, thread
- Medicine dropper
- Shut-off wrench, to turn off household gas and water
- Whistle
- Plastic sheeting
- Map of the area and route to alternate location

SPECIAL ITEMS

- Discuss a common meeting location and what your family would do if you needed to leave your home with only a few minutes' notice. Using a small adhesive label, put the phone number of a contact in another state on the back of the identification card for each member of your family.
- A breathing mask to protect against particles from radioactive fallout.
- A disaster preparation manual.
- Fill the gas tank in your vehicle when the U.S. government raises the terror alert above the yellow "elevated condition." If this does not help you in a disaster, you may thank yourself the first time you are stuck in a traffic jam.
- Have your important family documents organized and available should you need to travel or obtain medical assistance after you have left the area where you live.
- Bring needed sanitation items.

If you have a baby, bring formula, diapers, bottles, powdered milk, and medications

[490] Additional resources to learn more about surviving a nuclear disaster can be found in Cresson H. Kearny, Nuclear War Survival Skills (Aurora, Illinois: Caroline House Publishers, Inc., 1982 and updated in 1987).

Last Aid: The Medical Dimensions of Nuclear War (San Francisco, California: W.H. Freeman and Company, 1982), edited by Eric Chivian, M.D., Susanna Chivian, Robert Jay Lifton, M.D., and John E. Mack, M.D.

[491] Arthur M. Katz, Life After Nuclear War: The Economic And Social Impacts Of Nuclear Attacks On The United States (Cambridge, Massachusetts: Ballinger Publishing Company, 1982), 232.

[492] Tom Vanderbilt, Survival City: Adventures Among The Ruins Of Atomic America,(New York, New York: Princeton Architectural Press, 2002), 129.

[493] The financial services industry understands that millions of Americans would seek bankruptcy protection following a major nuclear catastrophe. In part for this reason, the credit card industry is very interested in doing everything possible to weaken bankruptcy protections so that their profit margins remain protected.

[494] The "leave as is" decision is often made when contaminated military bases are shut-down. This is why the U.S. Conference of Mayors has urged the U.S. government to cleanup contaminated military bases. For more information, visit www.usmayors.org/uscm/resolutions/68th_conference/expeditious_urb.html.

[495] "Groups Criticize Homeland Security Plans To Relax Radiation Cleanup Standards For A "Dirty Bomb" Or Terrorist Nuclear Explosive," Committee To Bridge The Gap and the Nuclear Informa-

tion & Resource Service, 2 December 2004. More than 50 public policy organizations called on the Department of Homeland Security to halt plans to dramatically weaken requirements for cleaning up radioactive contamination from a terrorist radiological or nuclear explosive. The weakened requirements would allow for doses equivalent to tens of thousands of chest x-rays with an officially estimated to cause cancer in up to a quarter of those exposed.

[496] "Civilians reported killed by military intervention in Iraq," The Iraq Body Count Project, as of December 2004. The latest count of civilian deaths is available at www.iraqbodycount.net/.

[497] David Espar, War in the Nuclear Age: Part IV, Europe Goes Nuclear, 1988. Internet address is http://alsos.wlu.edu/information.asp?id2=863. Nuclear weapons deployment information is highly classified. Turkey, Germany, England, Belgium, Italy and the Netherlands are widely believed by research experts like the Natural Resources Defense Council to be current launching points for U.S. nuclear weapons. Declassified information confirms the United States began deploying nuclear weapons in Europe in the 1950s.

[498] Physicians for Social Responsibility call for this exact measure in the Sensible Multilateral American Response to Terrorism or SMART initiative. Additional SMART recommendations are available at www.psr.org/documents/psr_doc_0/program_4/SMARTSecurityBrochure_Final_10_6.pdf.

[499] Ibid.

[500] Chris Floyd, "Dark Matter," Space.com, 9 April 2004. The "Near Field Infrared Experiment" or NFIRE will be the first time in history that any nation has put a weapons platform in space.

Jeffrey Lewis, "Programs to Watch: Near-Field Infrared Experiment (NFIRE)," Arms Control Today, November 2004, 12. The NFIRE launch date is scheduled for late 2006.

INDEX

DEDICATION

AMERICAN HIROSHIMA IS DEDICATED TO people who defend the defenseless, work to serve the poor, and open their hearts to see that all life is equally precious. This book is specifically dedicated to a living saint and an amazing defender of the defenseless. Her name is Sister Mary Sponsa Beltran. She has dedicated her life to the poorest of the poor in Africa.

In November 2004, she demonstrated tremendous courage and in the process prevented the slaughter of the disabled Muslim children living at the Our Lady of Fatima Rehabilitation Center just outside Monrovia, Liberia.

Mosques and churches were being burned by angry mobs and the tension between various tribes and faiths escalated out of control. As the attack on the compound for 300 disabled children was about to begin, the Christian children separated from the Muslim children. Sr. Beltran immediately went to the Christian children and said, "What have I taught you? How can you leave your brothers and sisters in their hour of need. Did I not accept all of you on this compound as children of God?"

This amazing woman then went immediately to the attacking force at the compound gate and began to pray for peace. The attackers began to leave and Sr. Beltran's cell phone rang. A former disabled Muslim student, now living in another part of Liberia, called to ask her what she had just done for he felt God's presence in a powerful way and he knew that she had done something. She responded "I prayed and experienced a miracle."

ISBN 1-41204421-9

9 781412 044219